Global Corpse Politics

Taboos have long been considered key examples of norms in global politics, with important strategic effects. Auchter focuses on how obscenity functions as a regulatory norm by focusing on dead body images. Obscenity matters precisely because it is applied inconsistently across multiple cases. Examining empirical cases including ISIS beheadings, the death of Muammar Qaddafi, Syrian torture victims, and the fake death images of Osama bin Laden, this book offers a rich theoretical explanation of the process by which the taboo surrounding dead body images is transgressed and upheld, through mechanisms including trigger warnings and media framings. This corpse politics sheds light on political communities and the structures in place that preserve them, including the taboos that regulate purported obscene images. Auchter questions the notion that the key debate at play in visual politics related to the dead body image is whether to display or not to display, and instead narrates various degrees of visibility, invisibility, and hyper-visibility.

Jessica Auchter's research focuses on visual politics and culture. She is author of *The Politics of Haunting and Memory in International Relations* (2014), and dozens of academic articles and edited volume chapters. She is the winner of the Fred Hartmann paper award from the International Studies Association.

Global Corpse Politics

Cambridge Studies in International Relations is a joint initiative of
Cambridge University Press and the British International Studies
Association (BISA). The series aims to publish the best new
scholarship in international studies, irrespective of subject matter,
methodological approach or theoretical perspective. The series seeks
to bring the latest theoretical work in International Relations to bear on
the most important problems and issues in global politics.

Series list continues after index

Global Corpse Politics

The Obscenity Taboo

JESSICA AUCHTER
University of Tennessee, Chattanooga

CAMBRIDGE
UNIVERSITY PRESS

Shaftesbury Road, Cambridge CB2 8EA, United Kingdom

One Liberty Plaza, 20th Floor, New York, NY 10006, USA

477 Williamstown Road, Port Melbourne, VIC 3207, Australia

314–321, 3rd Floor, Plot 3, Splendor Forum, Jasola District Centre, New Delhi – 110025, India

103 Penang Road, #05–06/07, Visioncrest Commercial, Singapore 238467

Cambridge University Press is part of Cambridge University Press & Assessment, a department of the University of Cambridge.

We share the University's mission to contribute to society through the pursuit of education, learning and research at the highest international levels of excellence.

www.cambridge.org
Information on this title: www.cambridge.org/9781009054386

DOI: 10.1017/9781009053471

First published 2021
First paperback edition 2023

A catalogue record for this publication is available from the British Library

ISBN 978-1-316-51165-7 Hardback
ISBN 978-1-009-05438-6 Paperback

Contents

v

Acknowledgments

My editor at Cambridge University Press, John Haslam, has been excellent to work with. I thank him for believing in the value of my work and shepherding it through to completion. Thanks to Tobias Ginsberg at Cambridge for his assistance throughout the process. I also thank the series editors, Evelyn Goh, Christian Reus-Smit, and Nicholas J. Wheeler, for their support of the project throughout the process, and the anonymous reviewers, whose feedback was excellent and instrumental in making this book what it is today. Though there are many to thank here, any errors and mistakes of course remain my own.

Numerous friends and colleagues participated in some way in offering feedback on pieces of this book, which has been several years in the making, including: Anna Agathangelou, Caroline Alphin, Fernanda Alves, Alex Barder, Tarak Barkawi, Dovile Budryte, David Campbell, Roxanne Doty, Stefanie Fishel, Rob Flahive, Anna Geis, Emily Gilbert, Tom Gregory, Jairus Grove, Charlotte Heath-Kelly, Christina Hellmich, Chris Hendershot, Ali Howell, Erick Langer, Daniel Levine, Renee Marlin-Bennett, Ben Meiches, Dan Oberg, Kandida Purnell, Lisa Victoria Purse, Erica Resende, Andrew Ross, Tim Ruback, Mark Salter, Gabi Schlag, Nisha Shah, Rose Shinko, Brent Steele, Finn Stepputat, Eric Van Rythoven, Matt Weinert, Lauren Wilcox, and Andreja Zevnik.

Particular thanks are due to Daniel Monk, who pushed me to consider the dynamics of doxology and the taboo, and whose influence can be seen throughout the book, but particularly in Chapter 3. Also, Francois Debrix's work has been a tremendous intellectual influence, but beyond this he consistently asks questions that push my work further, something which is rarer than one might wish in the academic world. I have been lucky to have him as a discussant at several conferences where I have presented pieces of this work, and this book is the better for it.

Early on in my academic career, Rick Ashley pushed me to be a better scholar and thinker. He was never afraid to ask the difficult questions;

he pushed me to take risks intellectually, and he also inspired me to understand how important teaching is to my identity as a scholar. He passed away in 2020, as I was finalizing this project. I hope this book honors the memory of his mentorship.

The University of Tennessee Chattanooga has been a supportive place to work on this project. Several internal grants, and a supportive department head in Dr. Michelle Deardorff, provided me time to work on these ideas, and for that I am grateful. At various times I had the assistance of undergraduate research assistants to work on these ideas. The work of Rachel Emond was particularly helpful, and I thank her.

Special thanks to Tom for unwavering support and for acknowledging that, for me, this research is also a personal ethical commitment as much as it is a scholarly endeavor. I like to think I can see the influence of your compassion in my approach to this work.

Chapter 3 draws on "Imag(in)ing The Severed Head: ISIS Beheadings and the Absent Spectacle," *Critical Studies on Security*, 6, 1, 2018, 66–84. I thank Taylor & Francis for permission to reprint. Some of my initial thoughts on humanization and dehumanization of the dead, which this book draws upon, were originally published as "On Viewing: The Politics of Looking at the Corpse," *Global Discourse: An Interdisciplinary Journal of Current Affairs*, 7, 2–3, July 2017, 223–238 (16). Re-published with permission of Bristol University Press, UK. Some thoughts that appear in Chapter 4 also appear in "Visible Dead Bodies and the Technologies of Erasure in the War-on-Terror," in Lisa Victoria Purse and Christina Hellmich, eds, *Disappearing War: Interdisciplinary Perspectives on Cinema and Erasure in the Post-9/11 World*, Edinburgh: University of Edinburgh Press, 2017.

I also thank *Der Spiegel* and Getty Images for image permissions related to the figures included in this book.

Ultimately, I acknowledge that the dead bodies I discuss in this book are individuals with loved ones. They lived complex lives and, in many cases, experienced complex deaths. My own ethical commitment to better understanding the complexities of political violence has driven this analysis, but I have sought to do so in such a way as to acknowledge that the dead bodies depicted in these images are not simply brute data.

1 | *Visualizing Corpse Politics*

Several years ago, when the images of Syrian torture victims' dead bodies were released by a photographer who had worked for the Syrian security forces and defected, I printed them out on a communal office printer, since my individual office printer did not print in color. I wanted to have them as a reference to go back to and, given the uncertainty of internet links, I didn't want to rely on being able to access them again online. In fact, having followed the publication of dead body images as an area of academic study for quite some time, I was also concerned that over the following days, the pictures would be removed from public access due to their graphic nature, the same way beheading images had been removed from online platforms and rescinded by media publications. The 9/11 falling body images had steadily been removed over time as they became considered too obscene to be seen (Auchter 2014), and some news outlets determined after the fact that, in the name of propriety, they should not have published the image of dead Syrian toddler Aylan Kurdi (Papailias 2019, 1054). In working on this project, I wanted a printed record of these images coming out of Syria to refer back to later, to examine for the evidence they provided of the atrocities carried out by the Syrian government. The communal printer was located in the office area of our administrative assistant. I began printing the images, then I realized that anyone could access them before I had a chance to get to the printer, so I ran down the hall and yelled out, don't look at the stuff I'm printing! I then realized how strange that request was, and said, I am printing something graphic and obscene, so I didn't want you to be startled unnecessarily (my form of a trigger warning to our administrative assistant, I suppose). This then led to an awkward conversation where I had to explain that indeed I was not printing pornography, and I was not violating any university regulations by viewing pornography on my university-owned computer. Indeed, I was looking at a different type of obscene images altogether: those of tortured and dead bodies, images

1

that bore the photographic evidence of state violence against civilians, and some that depicted violence done to young children. After explaining the context, I began thinking about my reaction to the photos, and this led me to several thoughts.

First, the idea of obscenity itself seems to be clear-cut initially, but there is a whole set of responses that blur these lines. If I had been printing out graphic sex, that would have been inappropriate, but printing out graphic violence was acceptable, yet still only within the confines of my research. In other words, obscenity was rendered acceptable for that particular purpose, along with the assumption that I was doing something important with it. I have often asked the students in the Genocide class I teach to reflect on similar dynamics: To what extent is it acceptable to break the taboo governing viewing dead bodies if it serves an educational purpose, such as teaching students about the Holocaust or the Rwandan genocide? Museum curators struggle with these same questions, in terms of how to drive home the reality of what occurred, given cultural norms governing human dignity, balanced with the need for viewers to have emotional responses to atrocity. In this sense, obscenity is not an objective reality, but a construct that takes different forms in different instances.

Second, there is a protective impulse at play with regard to viewing obscene things. My first inclination was to prevent others from having to see the things that I was seeing and that I had to look at as part of my research. This can be seen in the media's injunctions to not view obscene images, where the media acts as an intermediary, viewing obscene images so that the public doesn't have to, but still premised on the notion that someone needs to be the one looking at these, primarily for information-gathering purposes. But in the humanitarian context, we often see the exact opposite: the injunction for everyone to look by invoking an ethical imperative. Indeed, these same images, that I was so careful to protect anyone else in my office from accidentally seeing in the communal printer, were later displayed at the United Nations building in New York as evidence of the atrocities committed by the Syrian regime, purposefully placed on display as a mechanism of raising awareness about the issue. Yet I have also had to struggle with the notion of myself as a necessary viewer of these images for the purpose of this project and consider the ethics of how to engage with images of violence and death, and have made some deliberate choices about the images I show in this book and those I do not.

Third, my main reason for printing the images was to act as evidence, which I would use later on to make specific arguments in a research project such as this one, similar to the way in which the pictures themselves were circulated by organizations such as Human Rights Watch as primary source evidence of a crime against humanity, the main reason for their display. Such images, then, are both objective evidence and deeply emotional. In this vein, viewing the dead can be human-making and humanizing – by spurring an affective and emotional response to the dead – and can also be destructive of the human, human dignity, and human empathy – by rendering the dead an inert commodity for our visual consumption. In other words, viewing the dead involves taking account of an inherent tension at play with regard to the display of the dead. Additionally, it is only acceptable to display some dead bodies and only in some contexts, and displaying some dead impacts how others are hidden, while hiding some impacts how others are viewed (Sentilles 2018).

This book begins from this premise and asks about the visual politics of dead body images. Specifically, it examines the taboo that governs the viewing of the dead and the politics of its construction, reinforcement, violation, and instantiation. Under what circumstances is it deemed appropriate, and perhaps even necessary, to publish and look at images of dead bodies? Under what other circumstances is viewing such obscene images taboo, and what can this differentiation tell us about international politics?

In other words, this project begins with the taboo that governs viewing the dead. I ask after the circumstances in which the taboo, which I characterize as the "obscenity norm," is transgressed and others in which it is upheld via a complex mechanism of fear and trigger warnings, to illustrate the complex visual politics of the global dead. I argue that choices about what images to show and whether to put them behind a trigger warning are not simply choices made by individual media outlets (though I do examine the rules governing such publication), but rather indicative of larger political discourses that determine what counts as obscene and thus which bodies are sufficiently human to be entitled to the dignity that is culturally and politically associated with the dead. That is, there seems to be a difference between images we are "supposed" to engage with and those we are not. This difference can tell us something about contemporary global politics.

Specifically, the key argument of this book is that the taboo governing dead body images is applied inconsistently across cases, and this can
demonstrate how political communities muster the obscenity norm in
service of a story of who belongs. The taboo on viewing the dead is in
fact violated frequently in ways that cannot simply be understood
through the politics of self/other and require very specific discursive
justifications. These narratives of exceptionality make possible particular politics.

The book takes obscenity as a framing concept and illustrates the
politics of obscenity by looking at several cases: where images of the
dead are so obscene that they must be seen to spur humanitarian action
(such as the display of photographs of torture victims in Syria); where
images of the dead are so obscene that they are circulated to project
a narrative that the persons depicted are subhuman and easily defeated
(such as images of a dead Qaddafi in Western media outlets); where
images of the dead are too obscene to be shown (as in beheading videos
or the images of American soldiers dead in the war-on-terror); and
where images achieve a complex visual status because they are deemed
threatening in themselves (such as the unseen images of a dead Osama
bin Laden). At times, such as during humanitarian disasters, we are told
that there is a moral imperative associated with looking that can spur
empathy and international action. At other times, we are told that
looking is disgusting and treasonous, as with Islamic State (ISIS)
beheadings or the images of 9/11's falling bodies. This inconsistency
in application of the obscenity norm, or what counts as *too obscene* to
be viewed, can shed light on the political functioning of obscenity as
a mechanism of image regulation.

This argument speaks to recent work on visual politics in the field of
international relations (IR) that examines how war in particular is
mediated through visual images (Guittet and Zevnik 2014). I follow
David Shim's notion that images have a "visual grammar" that can tell
us how objects and subjects are positioned relative to one another and
to the viewer (Shim 2014, 34). Indeed, it is important to examine the
visual politics of dead body images precisely because people are often
characterized as ethical subjects by virtue of their ability to see, defined
as "agents of sight (regardless of their biological capacity to see) and as
the objects of certain discourse of visuality" (Mirzoeff 2005, 3). In
other words, seeing is often equated with political subjectivity, and
being seen is often considered to be a prerequisite for political change.

Methodologically, then, this book follows a critical visual methodology in which the focus is on "the visual in terms of the cultural significance, social practices and power relations in which it is embedded; and that means thinking about the power relations that produce, are articulated through, and can be challenged by, ways of seeing and imaging" (Rose 2001, 3). It is about the images themselves, their wider context, but also about us as viewers, including who we are, what we see, and how and why we see.

While several scholars have noted the emergence of new visual regimes wherein war is rendered hyper-visible, at the same time these visualities are managed via a technology of erasure that blurs parts of images and removes others from our line of sight, so as to manage the context under which the visual encounter occurs. Such regulation matters partly because of the presumed taboo that exists governing viewing the dead. This taboo tells us that dead bodies are something private and should be managed by the funerary industry, yet instances of political violence and even natural disasters thrust such bodies into the public realm and raise questions for statecraft. That is, what happens to dead bodies is more than ever a key question given the nature of political violence, the fact that it is often materially enacted on bodies, and the forms of new media that allow images of such violence to proliferate. Despite the emergence of new genres of visual politics and new materialisms within the IR literature, there still haven't been sustained examinations of the dead body as a key nexus in the intersection of these genres. Part of this is likely due to the way in which dead bodies are both literally and figuratively buried after atrocities, and the norm that persists across most cultures that the dead body is not routinely intended to be viewed outside of the funerary industry, and is largely consigned to the private realm, even if the circumstances of death were deeply political in nature. Yet debates about release of dead body images and indeed media regulations governing their publication indicate that there is something about the presence of particular dead bodies that can be disturbing.

The dead body, then, is a key site where international politics is taking place in numerous ways. Each visual engagement with the dead body, particularly when enmeshed in larger discourses of grief, triumph, pity, vengeance, threat, nationalism, and others, may tell us something about the political communities we form and the deaths and lives invoked to construct, structure, and preserve them. Indeed, "how the dead ... are depicted expresses the aesthetic, epistemological, and political preoccupations of a particular cultural moment" (Tait 2006).[1] Obscenity is circulated and recirculated through photography and the new forms of media that so much of the world now has access to. The obscene corpse is very much a political figure, despite narratives that often try to consign the dead body to the private realm as a family matter. As a result, it bears examining those circumstances when dead bodies proliferate, when they are viewed and why, and what this can tell us about how we form political communities and consider politically qualified life and death.

To address the politics of viewing the global dead, I explore a fundamental paradox, which emerges because we assume that dead bodies are possessed of human dignity, yet the two main types of viewing of the dead I discuss throughout the book speak very differently to this notion. In the case of humanitarian awareness, dead body images are displayed to give these deaths the dignity of global attention. Yet in the case of dead enemy bodies, dead body images are displayed to strip the bodies of their dignity as a means to dehumanize the enemy. How can dead body images both rehumanize and dehumanize? A key aim of the chapters that follow is to reckon with this paradox, and to begin to clarify not only the nature of these images, but the political work they do, which is key to understanding how these very different narratives emerge. That is, each visual engagement with the dead body, particularly when enmeshed in larger discourses, may shed light on the deaths and lives invoked to construct, structure, and preserve the political communities we invoke as the subjects of security.

As these images circulate, there is a "we" invoked in the framing. That is, images intended to rehumanize the dead focus on doing so to a specific audience, while images that dehumanize invoke the boundaries of particular political communities to speak to an audience who "gets the joke," so to speak. To be clear, the book is focused on the role of dead bodies in Western modernity, and thus focuses on Western media outlets and sensibilities, which is the "we" and "our" invoked throughout. It specifically focuses on two main empirical contexts: the "global war-on-terror," which, despite its name, is primarily a Western

---

[1] I should note here that Tait's point is mainly about how such bodies are depicted in popular culture, and she views popular culture as the scene to examine the expressions of culture. My milieu of examination is a less conventionally accepted cultural site to examine similar functioning.

narrative, and the use of images in humanitarian awareness, whose narratives tend to primarily begin in the West and be driven by Western assumptions (Durand 2012). Though this focus is limited and does not allow for generalization across cultural context either with regard to media framings or norms governing the dead, it allows me to pinpoint the functioning of two particular and paradoxical narratives of the global dead in Western discourse, one cut at thinking about the politics of viewing the dead. Though I do make some assumptions about the "West" for the purposes of this project, I also problematize the idea of this "we" further in Chapter 2, where I note that this narrative is itself embedded in exclusionary politics from within as well as related to outside others. The role of the remainder of this introductory chapter is to contextualize my initial arguments within work on visual politics.

Representing the Dead in Global Politics

The main focus of this book is not on images in and of themselves, but on images of a very particular subject matter: dead bodies. Life and death are increasingly coming to the fore of investigations in global politics, following Achille Mbembe's notion of necropolitics (2003). Similarly, bodies have recently emerged as a key subject matter of IR scholarship (Agathangelou 2011; Marlin-Bennett and Walton 2010; Shinko 2010; Steele 2013; Wilcox 2014). While death and killing as a mechanism of sovereign governance have been explored by those adopting Mbembe's framing, and embodiment is being theorized heartily, dead bodies as material artifacts have been under-addressed. Dead bodies and death are out of place in most approaches to global politics (Dixit 2015), and "even when the dead and injured do make an appearance, they tend only to appear in the most narrow and one-dimensional form" (Gregory 2016, 949). Himadeep Muppidi has noted that "International Relations is a field littered with dead and dying bodies. But the dead never seem to rot or stink ... International Relations overflows with corpses" (2012, 3). His point is that while IR tends to focus on conflict, global political economy, or international law, these subjects often remain separate from the material aftereffects and impacts of these on human bodies.

Due to the assumption long held in many cultural traditions that dead bodies are a matter for the private realm, they have not frequently been considered to be the subject of investigations of global politics, with few exceptions, focusing primarily on the dead body as forensic evidence of atrocity or issues of dead body management (Verdery 1999). Similarly, IR's association with global or state levels of analysis has consigned dead bodies to the private realm. This book should be seen as a response to Muppidi's call to engage the sensory evidence of the stench of dead bodies in the way we theorize global politics and as an effort to begin to situate the global dead within existing visual politics approaches to global politics, adopting a needed micropolitical approach to global corpse politics.

When they have been examined, scholars focusing on dead bodies in global politics have emphasized the dimensions of dead body management, particularly sovereignty (Stepputat 2014). Such work examines tensions between states and non-state actors related to how corpses are managed, including the key site of mass graves, which have been theorized as transnational spaces (Robben and Ferrandiz 2015). Gravesites in particular have been discussed as significant sites of contestation within ethnic conflict or as forensic evidence of mass atrocity (Rosenblatt 2015). Yet this focus on graves only addresses dead bodies tangentially, as symbols of larger forms of identity conflict or as hallmarks of state mismanagement or crises of sovereignty. Still, it nicely highlights the larger politics of emotion at play with regard to corpse politics, including grieving, mourning, and remembering the dead. During ethnic or identity conflict, tensions often rise surrounding sites of past conflict, symbolized by exhumation of the dead (Ross 2013). Bereavement itself has been considered a political form (Weisband 2009), key to understanding the role of memory in international politics.

Within historical approaches to conflict, scholars have examined dead bodies and the larger politics of burial and repatriation (Hawley 2005; Sledge 2007). This work catalogues the history of soldier remains, including the priority given to military fallen in strategic development and in conflict resolution. In the wider context of military effectiveness, body recovery in wartime is a key soldier morale issue (Sledge 2007, 16). Specifically, in the US context, during and after the Vietnam War, the issue of the missing and the larger dilemma of effective repatriation highlight the way in which corpses often enter into more traditional security and conflict policy discussions (Hawley 2005). This also raises larger questions about the legal personhood of the dead (Cantor 2010).

While these texts are significant, they tell us several things about the limitations in how the dead are addressed. First, studies that examine the dead body in global politics tend to focus on management. While many of these studies are comprehensive in scope, they tell us more about the state or international organizations than about death or the dead, with Heath-Kelly (2016) as perhaps a key exception.² In much of the work addressing the global dead, corpses become the empirical context to explore larger questions about sovereignty (Stepputat 2014), statecraft (Verdery 1999), globalization (Casper and Moore 2009), ethnic tensions (Rosenblatt 2015), or body counts (Fazal 2014; Spagat et al. 2009).

Second, some scholars are already talking about the dead and the impact dead bodies may have on how we think about global politics, but dead bodies remain only implicit referents, as I have noted elsewhere (Auchter 2016b). Particularly within security studies, the dead are often treated as material objects to be counted and managed, where large numbers of dead can be evidence of military success or of humanitarian crisis. In this way they are seen in the public realm as forensic objects and in the private realm as immensely human loved ones still. This binary treatment makes it difficult to conceive of the myriad ways the dead are lively political actors. How and when they are rendered visible and narrativized in global politics can tell us a lot about the political communities we form and the structures, practices, and identities that sustain them. Indeed, as Giroux (2006, 174) notes: "[C]adavers have a way of insinuating themselves on consciousness, demanding answers to questions that aren't often asked."

There has not been a large-scale study that examines the visual politics of the global dead, which this book purports to do. Why does this matter? Seeing the dead body is not simply material fact, but enmeshed in larger discourses of how we see, especially given the role of mediators in the context of images and their circulation, dissemination, and curation. Beyond this, constructivists have emphasized the importance of norms and their regulatory effects in global politics, and there has even been work on the taboo itself as a mechanism through

---

² In her *Death and Security: Memory and Mortality at the Bombsite*, she focuses on how the state performs sovereignty by managing mortality. While her theorization of how the state performs sovereignty by managing mortality is excellent, her focus is more on death itself and less on the politics of corpses, as I address here. Still, I draw on her work theorizing mortality in my examination of the larger security dilemmas at play here.

which social construction impacts policymaking (Dolan 2013; Tannenwald 1999). The main goal of such work is to describe the strategic impact of a norm, the nuclear taboo for example, on behavior. The nuclear case offers some interesting parallels, as scholars in this area have focused on the emotional underpinning of norms, as in examinations of atomic anxiety (Sauer 2015). My focus draws on a social constructionist approach to describe the parameters of what could be termed the obscenity norm, discussed more thoroughly in Chapter 2, yet the main focus is not on the strategic effects of this norm, but rather on the assumptions and understandings it relies on, which can speak to the recent turn to examining emotion in social constructivist work, following scholars such as Solomon (2015), and the wider focus on how emotions are learned and reinforced through social interactions (Crawford 2000, 128). In this sense, I focus on the emotional response of the viewer to particular images, and how that response is curated, constructed, and reinforced via the mechanism of the obscenity taboo.

Beyond this, my focus is on questions of security, and the extent to which things that are obscene function within a discourse of security questions. As Charlotte Heath-Kelly has noted, "death is ontologically coupled with state security practice" (2016, 1). Her work offers an excellent examination of mortality and the performance of sovereignty in mortality management at memorial sites. My book should be seen as a complement to her argument, particularly her encouragement that we move beyond a focus on killing, as it puts mortality in the control of the state (Heath-Kelly 2016, 3). I would argue that a focus on killing has removed our ability to engage with the material and visual aftereffects of such violence: dead bodies themselves. In this sense, while she moves beyond killing by focusing on mortality, I take the dead body image as the empirical focus to ask what work it does to sustain particular forms of security practice via the construction and transgression of the obscenity norm. In this vein, I follow the call for more substantive work on the role that emotions play in the relationship between visuality and security (Bleiker 2018b, 194).

Rehumanization and Dehumanization: Viewing the Global Dead

To highlight what is at stake in a text about corpse politics, the rest of this chapter primarily functions to introduce the two main stories that will frame the empirical cases in the rest of the book. One examines how the disturbance associated with dead bodies thrust into the public sphere is used toward humanitarian ends: images of the dead are key ways in which awareness of atrocity circulates. The graphic nature of these images is precisely what provides the grounds for their power to effect change; that is, the social and cultural taboo against viewing dead bodies means that when we are invited to view them, it must be under extraordinary circumstances, and our viewing is itself posited as a political act. Yet this may not match the way these bodies are actually consumed by the viewer, and some spectators may look at these images in a voyeuristic manner, referred to as "pain porn," or may refuse to look altogether.

The second story at play here is the display of dead enemy bodies, as a means to dehumanize them by breaking the taboo governing sacralization of the corpse. The display of images of this nature can exacerbate the distance between subject and viewer, rather than cultivating the empathy often associated with the wider humanitarian narrative of their display. Indeed, images of dead enemies are often viewed in a context that perpetuates a distancing between the viewer and the subject of the image. While we may normally feel empathy when viewing the dead, they are (or seem) so different than us, if even by virtue of the fact that they are displayable, that it simply reinforces the distance. *Our* dead are not visible; if *their* dead are, then perhaps they are very different than us, and not worthy of the same type of action as those within our own political community. This is further exacerbated when the image is displayed in a context that instructs us to celebrate the death, as is often the case with dead enemy bodies. Thus, when we see images of our dead enemies, they are in a context designed to cultivate affective responses of retribution, hatred, and satisfied revenge, rather than empathy.

I briefly compare and contrast the depiction of the dead in humanitarian awareness and dead enemy bodies to begin to outline this, a framing that continues through the rest of the book in the empirical cases I describe in Chapters 3, 4, and 5. I detail how bodies become hyper-visible in both instances, yet the narratives these images are situated in, and the political work they do, are very different. The history of images of suffering invokes the notion that caring about the pain of another is a thoroughly modern sensibility (Halttunen 1995). The notion that considering the suffering of others is modern persists in the notion invoked by humanitarians that only the barbarian would not care about atrocities, and in a bizarre way by the display of dead enemy bodies, invoking the notion that we do not need to be civilized or humane with regard to those who are themselves less-than-human. I trace both of these instances in more depth in this section. These two stories also lay the groundwork for how looking or not looking is often situated as a moral question and exemplify the functioning of the dead body taboo, which I take up theoretically in Chapter 2.

I introduce these two stories precisely because the binary between bodies we display and bodies we don't display needs to be examined and problematized. In the literature, it is often treated as though there is an equation governing the viewing of dead or injured bodies: viewing the dead body of the other is acceptable while viewing "our" dead bodies is not. While this may be the case at times, I argue that the visual politics of viewing the dead is actually quite a bit more complex. Additionally, it is less about which dead bodies are viewable than about what this can tell us. Sometimes dead bodies that "look like us" are rendered viewable to highlight a politics of exceptionality that depicts particular violence as particularly horrendous: so much so that it breaks the taboo governing images of the dead. And sometimes dead bodies of "others" are not viewed, because their extreme otherness renders them a threat to security, as in the Osama bin Laden case I describe in Chapter 4. In other words, my key argument is that graphicness and obscenity are political concepts, not objective ones, and they serve particular political ends. Studying the processes of how something becomes determined to be obscene and when and how particular dead bodies are rendered viewable or hidden from view can shed light on the complex visual politics of the dead. Thus, while I trace these two stories: of the humanization and dehumanization of the dead, this serves as an introduction to a picture of corpse politics that will become progressively more complex as the book evolves. It begins to illustrate what is at stake in the context of the politics of emotion at play as well, in the sense that emotions are constructed and shaped through binaries of self and other, though, in the end, these distinctions are always tentative and hard to secure.

Story One: The Moral Imperative to Look

Dead body images in the context of humanitarian awareness campaigns are often displayed to draw attention to a human rights violation as a means to drive some sort of global response and are seen to materially hold a particular power to convey a message. This is premised on the assumption that photography gives us access to a frozen moment in time, and on the notion emerging from memory studies scholars that trauma defies representation. In this sense, the image can reveal a stark reality that "transcends its historical and political causes by revealing the utter senselessness of traumatic violence" (Baer 2005, 179). This emphasizes the way in which visualizing atrocities is seen to provide us a sense of transparency with regard to a particular event (Kozol 2014, 1). Visual encounters that stage a confrontation with moral failure can foster the ethics of the recognition of the humanness of others while contending with the spectator's own gaze (Kozol 2014, 19).

In this sense, this first story is about how viewing dead bodies can be ethically humanizing, because we are forced to reckon with the extreme violation of that humanity in visual form in front of us. In this sense, the photograph mirrors the lacuna that exists in the real world: we know of human rights because we live in a world where they do not exist. Because you cannot image human rights, what photographs of suffering can do for humanitarianism is show us what the absence of rights does to a person, and how those without rights look (Linfield 2010, 34–39). Linfield vigorously argues against the notion that images of suffering are akin to pornography. Yes, these images expose suffering, a part of human life as personal as sexuality. But, while pornography depicts something that strangers should not see, images of suffering instead "are the revelation of something that ought not to exist" (Linfield 2010, 41) and indeed, we should look at them as a result. She goes on to argue that suffering is not personal and private, but that the forms of misery depicted in these images are a shared, social, condition. At the very least, while we may experience compassion fatigue, photography of suffering means we can no longer claim ignorance, and this itself is important for humanitarian awareness (Linfield 2010, 46). The assumption then is that such photographs can rehumanize and can spur additional support for humanitarian efforts, becoming key to shifts in public opinion and the development of political responses to conflicts or famines (Fahey 2015). In this sense, the emotive power of images, particularly of suffering or death, is seen to form the basis of their exceptionality.

Within studies of visuality, debates rage over the role of photographs. Many critics, including Susan Sontag, argue that viewing images of suffering places the viewer both morally and physically in the position of the original photographer, which is the position of a killer, and that looking is a form of re-victimization. Others, such as Linfield (2010), argue that images can show us how people were destroyed, and that, just as you can read *Mein Kampf* and be repelled, you can see photographs of atrocity and be repelled by those. There is no automatic way to react to a photograph. Indeed, as Linfield points out, the Holocaust was designed to be an event without witnesses, so there is something ethical to witnessing it visually (2010, 97). Thus there remains debate about the precise circumstances in which atrocity images should be shown, and a recognition that the tentativeness of this imperative to look belies an ethical dilemma at the heart of the dead body image.

To briefly illustrate this notion, the work of international humanitarian organizations is premised on the idea that drawing attention to suffering forces the viewer to become a witness, to feel their responsibility to do something about it. Sontag (2002) has said that the only viewers who should view these sorts of images are those in a position to do something about the suffering depicted therein. Though she means this as a critique of images of this sort, her point remains salient: that viewing these images is seen to inculcate a specific relationship with these images. The viewer of these images is *supposed* to assume responsibility to do something by viewing, even if they may not be able to do so. Indeed, in 2014, a *Time* magazine article titled "Why Violent News Images Matter" sought to explore precisely this argument: that we should look upon war and suffering and death, quoting photographer Christoph Bangert, who asks, "how can we refuse to acknowledge a mere representation – a picture – of a horrific event, while other people are forced to live through the horrific event itself?" (as quoted in Ritchin 2014). It is thus perhaps considered our ethical penance, even if we cannot do something, to live with the gruesome images even in their horror, because someone else has to live with the reality.

Because the viewer is seen to have an ethical obligation to view the image and account for the suffering depicted therein, the photographer is also seen to have a responsibility to share the image, else they are not keeping the promise they have made in the compact of taking the photo itself.

Photographers have maintained that they feel it necessary to witness and represent the deaths, calamitous injuries and grief that they discover in conflict situations, and in many cases have been asked to do so by those who are its victims. Once those pictures are made, however, the implicit contract is that they be transmitted and seen by others, especially by those who have even a small chance of preventing such tragedies from continuing or from multiplying. If these pictures remain unpublished there may be a guilty sense that a promise, a redemptive one, has not been kept. (Ritchin 2014)

That is, invading the privacy of another in their moment of absolute vulnerability is only worth it if that vulnerability becomes the site of humanitarian action, if the viewer is made to be witness, and thus vicariously take on responsibility to prevent the tragedy.

This language has persisted with regard to the ongoing conflict in Syria, and particularly with the publication of the image of dead toddler Aylan Kurdi, a Syrian child who died making the perilous crossing to seek refuge in Europe. The image became an iconic representation of the refugee crisis, spurring a global conversation about responsibility: indeed, it was the top trending picture on Twitter within hours (Smith 2015). The image did not depict a gruesome death, but it did depict a dead body. Though much of the discussion about the image centered on responsibility related to the migrant crisis, a substantial amount of the discussion instead focused on the responsibility of the photographers, media, and viewers in terms of viewing an image of the dead. Two different versions of the image ended up being published in media outlets: one, which was considered more gruesome, was a close-up image of the child dead on the beach where his body washed up. The other, considered a less disturbing version, depicted a Turkish police officer carrying the dead body off of the beach, where the body was visible, but the child's face was obscured. The latter was published by *The New York Times*, *The Wall Street Journal*, and *The Baltimore Sun,* while the more gruesome version was published by *The Los Angeles Times*, *The Washington Post*, and Canadian newspaper *The Globe and Mail* (Mackey 2015).

Media outlets immediately felt the need to justify why they had published the image in the face of the public outcry. *The New York Times* executive editor Dean Baquet noted, "[W]e debated it, but ultimately we chose to run a powerful version of this photo because it brings home the enormity of this tragedy" (Mackey 2015). The image was equated with showing the "reality" of the crisis, playing on the notion discussed earlier that we view photographs as giving us access to some unfettered truth, as can be seen in the words of Nicolas Jimenez, photography director at *Le Monde*, who noted that "I'm convinced that until you've shown this photograph, you haven't shown the reality of this crisis" (Laurent 2015).

Jamie Fahey at *The Guardian* notes that they received emails from readers criticizing the decision to publish the disturbing pictures unpixellated and without a warning that needed to be clicked through to see the image. Fahey's article details the process of the decision they made to publish the image, their way of addressing these criticisms by offering an explanation to counter them. He describes:

Shortly after the pictures dropped on the news wires at 11.30am, discussions between the editor in chief, Katharine Viner, the deputy editor, Paul Johnson, and the web editors began. The stark human tragedy, pathos and sense of heartbreak were weighed up against potential privacy issues and the risk of repelling the reader with indecent bluntness. The Guardian's editorial code is clear in such cases involving photographs and children that a "strong public interest justification" is necessary. (Fahey 2015)

Ultimately, Paul Johnson's argument that they could be the images providing a "tipping point" (Fahey 2015) held sway in the decision to publish. The point here is that the images of the dead, while disturbing, were exceptional enough to be released despite social norms and media guidelines that would normally dictate otherwise. Indeed, Hugh Pinney, Vice President of Getty Images, noted precisely this: "[T]he reason we're talking about it after it's been published is because it breaks a social taboo that has been in place in the press for decades: a picture of a dead child is one of the golden rules of what you never published" (Laurent 2015).

The public interest justification needed to break such a taboo is detailed by Peter Bouckaert, of Human Rights Watch, who noted that "I think that when we have this discussion time and time again, it always comes down to: 'This is an image people have to see. This is an image that can galvanize attention around a crisis that has been ignored for too long'" (Laurent 2015). Bouckaert's tweets harshly censured the international community for not doing more, as a justification for why the image should be viewed. One noted, "What is offensive is dead kids

washing up on our beaches when deaths could have been prevented by
EU action, not the pictures themselves," while another argued that
"People should be offended by their politicians lack of action in face
of such suffering and death, not by the pics showing results of failure"
(Mackey 2015). Leslie Plommer of *The Guardian* similarly drew on the
historical discourse of human rights crisis to argue that seeing the image
was necessary because of the impact it could have, invoking the iconic
image of Kim Phuc running from a napalm attack in Vietnam: "Given
the heightened concerns of today about photographs of children, particularly unclothed children, could we publish such a photo today? Yet
that picture brought home in a massive way to the US domestic audience the human effects of the Vietnam War" (Fahey 2015). Thus, the
connection is made to a wider historical story of human rights violations and atrocities.

Similarly, *The New York Times* hammers home the idea that showing these images of the dead Syrian toddler can have political power,
noting that those who posted and shared the photos felt that "the
distressing images needed to be seen and could act as a catalyst for
the international community to finally halt the war in Syria" (Mackey
2015). The article goes on to depict tweets invoking the image as a sign
of "collective failure" and as potentially able to "spark the world into
action" (Mackey 2015). *The Los Angeles Times* assistant managing
editor Kim Murphy noted about their decision to publish that "the
image is not offensive, it is not gory, it is not tasteless – it is merely
heartbreaking, and stark testimony of an unfolding human tragedy that
is playing out in Syria, Turkey and Europe, often unwitnessed"
(Mackey 2015).

Still, there remains a tension within humanitarian images of the
dead: viewing them is considered to bring us in touch with our shared
humanity through our empathy, yet news outlets who do not show
these images claim to do so because they are trying to keep coverage
"humane and decent" (Ritchin 2014). Indeed, some news outlets chose
not to publish the Aylan Kurdi photo for this reason: Vox Media
editorial director Max Fisher expressed concerns about how the
photo had gone "viral," and that it had become for some "less about
compassion than about voyeurism," continuing to say that "I decided
against running it because the child in that photo can't consent to
becoming a symbol" (Mackey 2015).

There is also a dilemma when it comes to images of trauma: "trauma is supposed to be unrepresentable" (Mitchell 2011, 60), and thus even a photograph cannot transmit trauma directly via the mechanism of representation. This is what Max Fisher of *Vox* is expressing when he examines the symbolic role of iconic photographs: if the image has become an icon, it is no longer tied to the banality of this suffering for those involved in it, and as a symbol, it may not communicate the unrepresentability of trauma any longer; instead, the image can become commodified. Indeed, the image did become the background for various online memes both related and unrelated (Mackey 2015). To some extent, the category of visual witness is more complex than Linfield (2010) acknowledges, when she argues we should become witnesses of events like the Holocaust by viewing images of the sort under discussion here. Becoming a Holocaust witness is not simply viewing, because this does not overcome the chasm of representation inaugurated by a trauma of this sort, an issue that I take up further in Chapter 2.

The other issue with the framing of images of the dead in a humanitarian context is often a focus on death rather than life, which can create a distancing between human beings who look at images and those who are the subjects of them, which, in the context of mass violence such as genocide, leads the viewer to believe that only the "other" can be the subject of such violence, and that it could never happen here. Similarly, images of deaths due to hunger seem alien to the Western viewer who may not have ever experienced material deprivation, or certainly not to this extent. The same is true of travel images: while *National Geographic* can publish images of "natives," they are always natives of other places, and we do not consider ourselves to be natives, and the other is exotic in their foreignness. Ulrich Baer (2005, 128) details the same issue in Holocaust memorialization. As she says, if we remember only the killings, this aligns with the Nazi perspective of viewing Jewish life as extraneous. In the same context, dead body images cultivate such an extraordinary spectacle to generate humanitarian response that it can have the opposite effect: to draw attention away from the humanity of these lives and deaths, to render them simply a product for our consumption rather than worthy of our empathy and action.

To sum up, one of the main stories often told about images of the dead contextualizes them as depicting a suffering which we have an ethical responsibility to encounter. I have outlined the way in which such viewing draws on the logic of exceptionality as a justification for breaking the dead body taboo, which highlights one way in which the taboo is in fact reinforced through its rupture. The way in which media outlets themselves contextualize their decision to publish is premised on the emotive impact such images can have. The second story, about dead enemy bodies, relies on emotions of revenge and hatred and triumph, not empathy, yet it still highlights the ways in which the dead body taboo can be ruptured for a political end.

Story Two: Taking Pleasure in the Death of the Enemy

In the context of dead enemy bodies, it is precisely the raw humanity of these deaths that becomes a product for consumption, quite purposefully, invoking narratives of triumphalism. As John Taylor (1998, 29) has noted, images of pain can be delightful to us because it is the death of the other that we are confronted with, not the death of ourselves or those with whom we may share immediate forms of identity or community. While some of us may find the celebration of pain abhorrent regardless of whose pain is in question, the cases of dead dictators and dead terrorists indicate otherwise, as I will discuss further in Chapter 4. Indeed, after 9/11 there was the desire to identify and distinguish not only the remains of the victims from the rubble of the towers but also the remains of the attackers so that they could be kept separately. John Cartier, whose brother died in the World Trade Center, said, "OK, you found these bastards, now take them out from the same place where our loved ones are." When asked what should be done with the remains, he suggested "stomping on them." New York Governor David Paterson suggested in 2009 to "finish burning them" (Conant 2009). Instead, they were kept in an FBI vault, separate from the remains of victims.

This story, of the desire to degrade the remains of the enemy, is at odds with the sacralization of human remains in public discourse, and with the notion that dead bodies are entitled to dignity and protection in both a cultural and legal sense, as I have traced elsewhere (Auchter 2016b). Cultural norms often dictate that dead bodies should not be viewable outside of the funerary industry, especially when they are graphic by virtue of a bloody and violent death. These cultural taboos tell us that dead bodies do not belong in the public sphere, and something extraordinary must be the case for them to be on display and rendered visible.

Indeed, much of war photography centers on displaying images of suffering, at times obscene, as a means of showing the horrors of war so as to avoid them. Yet the viewing of dead enemy bodies is not intended to support a narrative about the horrors of war. They rather tell us that obscenity can be part of the triumphs and successes of war. If, as Susan Sontag (2003: 21) notes, "something becomes real by being photographed," then the way these obscene images circulate may tell us something significant about how we are not horrified by the effects of some kinds of violence. Beyond this, though, the examples discussed later in the book examine the functioning of obscenity in the technologies of erasure. It examines the uses of obscenity framing to legitimize viewing, as in the case of the dead body of Qaddafi, to decide on which parts of images to blur, as in the case of US soldiers posing with dead bodies mentioned earlier, and to legitimize the disappearance of particular images in the service of security narratives, as in the case of the dead body of Osama bin Laden. As Elizabeth Dauphinee (2007: 140) has noted, the "drive to make *visible* the body in pain often evokes a particular kind of seeing, which ultimately works to further the Cartesian rupture between self and other." If this occurs even when the aim of the circulation of the image is to cultivate empathy, we can imagine how this takes effect and is exacerbated when the image is circulated for the purpose of disseminating a dehumanizing narrative that instructs the viewer to engage with the photograph, and the body depicted therein, not as a suffering, vulnerable human, but as a "body part" worthy of serving as a trophy or souvenir.

That is, most work on the body in pain looks at the ethical gap in our ability to receive and witness the suffering of others (Dauphinee 2007). But what if we are directed, by the context and content of the image, to engage with it, or perhaps to consume it for a particular political agenda? It is important here to move beyond the oft-privileged notion that witnessing pain automatically translates into (at least the struggle involved in) representing suffering, and ask questions about celebrating death rather than mourning it, especially in the context of visual interactions and the visuality of obscenity. As Susan Sontag (2003: 72) notes, "the other, even when not an enemy, is regarded only as someone to be seen, not someone (like us) who also sees." Elizabeth Dauphinee (2007: 144–145) has spoken of this in the context of the Abu Ghraib images: "[T]he gaze enabled by the photograph also works as a sort of 'hooding' of the subject, maintaining the inherently violent fantasy that we can see without being seen."

In this sense, the instrumentalization of the dead body depicted in the image can work to dehumanize and de-subjectify the subject of the image. As Daryl Morini (2011) notes, "dehumanising dictators may be a natural enough reaction," noting that the dilemma with his natural reaction is the devaluing of human life more generally. The same is perhaps true of the treatment of the dead bodies of enemy militants in the war-on-terror. Several analysts have made the argument that dehumanizing the enemy is central to military strategy, and to make killing easier. Rick Moran, in a conservative online website devoted to American foreign policy, argues that "dehumanizing the enemy in war, then, is unavoidable if we wish our warriors to survive and achieve success" (Moran 2012). This same logic recurs in the display of the dead in ways designed to generate a spectacle that is dehumanizing, to instrumentalize the dead. Thus, unlike humanitarian narratives which seek to redeem the dead bodies they depict, images of enemy dead instruct us not to empathize, to go against our human instincts to care about the suffering of the other, and instead to view the other as an object rather than as the material remains of a subject possessed of dignity.

The hyper-visibility of enemy dead can be directly correlated with a long history of maltreatment of enemy dead (Sledge 2005). Treatment of enemy dead reflects the attitudes toward the enemy's social and cultural system. There is a long history of abuse of enemy corpses, focusing on those cases committed by Americans, including decapitations of Japanese and Vietnamese soldiers during World War II and the Vietnam War, carving bones into letter openers, and other such abuses (Sledge 2005). One might add other cases of abuses of dead bodies that establish a broader context, such as the way the skin of concentration camp victims was turned into lampshades in Nazi Germany, or recent cases of urinating on Afghan corpses by coalition soldiers there.

Thus, while simply showing the dead body raises questions of dignity in a humanitarian context, images of enemy dead are unlikely to raise such questions. Ewen MacAskill, for example, in *The Guardian*, said of images of a British RAF soldier giving a thumbs up next to the dead body of a Taliban militant after a battle:

The emergence of the pictures is unlikely to have any serious consequences. There is no suggestion of any abuse or violation of the corpse or the kind of humiliation associated with the treatment of prisoners at Abu Ghraib in Iraq, which led to fresh violence against US troops and their allies. . . . The incident is a breach of the law of armed conflict, but the military hopes it will be seen in context, a young man doing something foolish in the post-battle adrenaline rush. Protests could be expected if there were pictures of desecration of the Koran, but Taliban fighters are viewed as hardened enough to be relatively unmoved by a member of the British forces demonstrating victory or a sense of relief at the end of battle. (MacAskill 2014)

That is, he leaves the viewer of the image to conclude that despite the prohibition against this act, it is not abuse of a corpse. The discussion focuses not on the issues of dignity associated with posing with the dead, but rather on reassuring a British audience that no harm is likely to come to British soldiers as a result of this man's foolishness. A sigh of relief, and we can all stop worrying. Desecration of a book is posited as worse than treating a dead body in an undignified manner, because the concern is not with dignity or desecration, but with the potential insult the enemy may feel at the act and how they might respond, a question of military effectiveness and strategy. There is also something interesting in that Taliban fighters are depicted as battle-hardened enough to not be bothered by maltreatment of a corpse that was, after all, all in good fun (i.e. the Taliban are depicted as less-than-human because they do not care about human dignity in the same way *we* do).

This section has demonstrated the paradox inherent in viewing the global dead, in that certain images seek to redeem the humans depicted therein as vibrant subjects lost to tragic circumstances that the viewer can and should do something about, placing the agency on the viewer-as-witness. Contrary to this, images of enemy dead often depict vibrant agents who are typically members of our own political communities, posing with corpses that we are designed to interpret as less-than-human, thus setting aside any questions of dignity associated with their viewing. As noted earlier, it is less about what is depicted in these images than what they are used for, what Gabi Schlag (2016) has called the performance of images, or how a specific reality is constructed visually. Both of these stories have emphasized the justification of media outlets showing dead body images, which helps establish the groundwork for the very existence of the dead body taboo and a brief sketch of what it looks like. I explore the taboo more substantively in Chapter 2.

Outline of the Book

As this introduction has noted, the main purpose of this book is to ask what claims to obscenity can tell us about international politics by examining cases where dead bodies are rendered visible or partially visible: instances of humanitarian awareness and those of dead enemy bodies. If certain deaths are rendered acceptable for viewing for particular political ends, then what do these decisions tell us about the value accorded to particular lives and deaths? Claims that images are obscene tell us that particular humans are accorded dignity, while others are not. Images are labeled too obscene, not obscene, or obscene-but-not-obscene-enough-to-not-be-shown. I broadly frame the chapters to come in the context of these two stories: of how dead body images are aggregated into categories that instruct the viewer how to engage with them and what political work they can do. The following chapters draw on these initial questions and themes, and proceed as follows.

Chapter 2 describes my theoretical approach to the concept of obscenity by examining what counts as "horrifically graphic." Drawing on a variety of theorists, it uses the framing of the taboo to articulate the idea of an obscenity norm that functions toward a particular politics. I situate the contributions of this work more substantively in terms of how it speaks to constructivist work on norms, the growing literature on emotions in global politics, and the visual politics literature. Specifically, in this chapter, I theorize three main ideas related to the obscenity norm and its functioning: (1) the existence of the taboo itself as something that plays with our perception of whether images depict the *Real,* (2) the functioning of regulations on images such as trigger warnings or image bans, and (3) the relationship between the obscenity norm and the larger dynamics of security and securitization. Each empirical chapter to follow then primarily takes up one of these three components.

Chapter 3 takes up the case of ISIS beheadings to examine the regulatory mechanism of obscenity further via the image ban. It examines a double paradox with regard to ISIS and fear: first, that ISIS beheadings are a spectacle, while at the same time, there exists an image ban on viewing these images, and second, that ISIS is both inherently known to us as a threat, yet also fundamentally unknowable. I use the framing of the *Bilderverbot,* the secularized image ban of biblical origin, to examine how beheadings are represented as unrepresentable, and how this paradox enters into normalcy. This discussion of the image ban draws on Freudian theory related to the taboo and castration, and following from this, Slavoj Zizek's theorizations of desire in such an encounter. Zizek has traced the paradoxical sentiment of being ashamed when one desires something considered unworthy of one's desire, and this chapter seeks to get at the play of desire and disgust related to how ISIS beheadings are framed, capturing this contradictory simultaneity.

The chapter demonstrates the relation between the image ban and the naturalization of an embodied fear by telling the story of two beheadings: one of an Iraqi head and one of a Western one. The first is shown but not seen, and the latter is seen but not shown. A micro-level examination of the severed head image allows these stories to emerge. The first account, concerning the severed head of an Iraqi man working as an informant for American soldiers, allows for an examination of how beheadings are often depicted in the language of horror, or as an example of "body horror." In this story, the audience never learns the name of the man who was beheaded, and whose severed head is rendered background to a story of the excesses of war. The second story, the story of ISIS beheadings, is a different story: one in which the severed head has become a fact of international politics, something doxic in which fear of ISIS beheadings is taken for granted. In this story, numerous names of those beheaded could be said that have been discussed in Western media accounts, but I explore the general notion of the Western severed head rather than one specific image. That is, the story isn't the story of *a* Western beheading, but of *the* Western beheading, as a category. It is the story of the absent spectacle generated around this severed head.

Telling these two stories together is important because the story of the severed head is always instead a set of stories about how the unrepresentability of the severed head is represented. It is also the case that most examinations of taboo focus on those instances when the image is shown, such as pornography, but there is more to the visual politics of images than simply whether so-called obscene images are shown or not. That is, rather than focus on the transgression of the taboo, I seek to explore the repression of the image that constitutes the taboo, which is a way of representing the image by way of its denial.

Chapter 4 further draws out the way obscenity is used as a regulatory mechanism by focusing on dead enemy bodies in the war-on-terror: dead terrorists and dead dictators, to examine the larger question of security at play. It uses the cases of Muammar Qaddafi and Osama bin Laden to explore the purposes for which particular dead bodies are rendered (in)visible, and further, the visual politics of the encounter with the bloody body in a political context where bodies are often key sites inscribed with and resistant to power. To do so, I argue that obscenity is mustered as a visual and political tool, to both place a taboo on the viewing of certain dead bodies, and invite the viewing of others. Obscenity here provides the framing concept for visual engagement, precisely because what constitutes or is suggested to constitute the obscene is a political decision, one which generates particular erasures and legitimates particular narratives. I explore how the dead body is enabled for the viewer, and we, as the viewers, are intended to appropriate the obscenity as a mechanism of our own visual and political agency. Thus the way this visual asymmetry is replicated and recirculated through the visual asymmetry of the photographic context forms a particularly interesting case.

Images of violently dead bodies have been circulated and mobilized in the service of the war-on-terror. Some bodies are rendered hyper-visible, such as that of Qaddafi, so as to enable a story about the triumph of democracy over dictatorship, and the madness of a dictator that continues beyond his death. Other bodies are displayed in a complex schema of visuality, as in the command to look at Syrian victims, or to look at pieces of blurred images of atrocities committed by soldiers. Still others are deemed too volatile to be displayed, as in the case of the corpse of Osama bin Laden. The images are part of a wider discourse, used strategically and to specific effect. Circulating images of Qaddafi reinforced the notion of the inevitable failure of dictatorship, supporting a policy of democratization. The body of Osama bin Laden, on the other hand, represented a success of the war-on-terror, but its visibility was considered a security risk that could further heighten tensions and provoke retaliatory attacks by Al-Qaeda.

The privileged act of seeing at a distance is often equated with witnessing, yet it also inculcates a model wherein we experience modern war by proxy, and this framing shapes understandings of what war is via which images of war are deemed legitimate grounds for visual consumption. Obscenity provides a means of generating a spectacle out of dead enemy bodies, both in their display and in the way they are visually erased. It does so through technology: the editing of images, the pixellation of parts of obscene images as a means to blur and remove certain images, thereby visually managing them and their meanings. That is, in thinking about the technologies of erasure in the war-on-terror, what matters may be questions surrounding who is *seen* and how, but also who is *seeing* and how.

Chapter 5 takes on the display of bodies for evidentiary purposes to further interrogate the politics of displaying dead bodies and the question of the *real* and *unreal* in obscene images. It explores two main cases to examine when and how dead bodies are obscene, and the tensions between obscenity, dignity, and evidentiary value, particularly in the context of contemporary humanitarianism and humanitarian intervention. First, it explores images of torture victims in Syria from 2013 to the present, which provided evidence in two ways: they were initially taken by an Assad regime photographer to act as proof that these individuals had actually been killed, and then, when the photographer defected, they acted as evidence on a global scale of the atrocities of the Assad regime. These images, which I have already briefly introduced, illustrate the ways in which obscene photographs must justify themselves as sufficiently obscene to be seen, reinforcing the taboo in its rupture, as a means to spur humanitarian awareness about an atrocity. I contextualize this in the wider context of atrocity images, and take up the published photographs of Aylan Kurdi as a shadow case to tease out the dynamics of the functioning of the obscenity norm.

Second, the chapter explores the cases of Kayla Mueller and Giulio Regeni. Mueller was an American aid worker working in besieged Syria held captive by ISIS, who was ultimately killed in an American airstrike. Her family refused to believe she had been killed, and ISIS sent them a photo of Mueller's dead body to act as evidence, as "proof of death." Similarly, Giulio Regeni was an Italian student working in Egypt who was arrested and killed by the Egyptian police, and his body dumped on a street. When the Egyptian government refused to acknowledge their role in his death, his family threatened to send them a photo, to act as proof of the truth surrounding his death. The chapter examines the various ways death images and dead bodies themselves act as evidence, raising questions about how and when the dead are too obscene to be viewed, and when they are situated within a logic about what must be viewed.

The conclusion ties together the framing of obscenity in how we evaluate corpse politics. It focuses on how viewing inculcates a power relationship by defining what can be visually consumed despite a taboo, what we can be visually rather than simply discursively horrified by, what is just obscene enough and what is too obscene. Put differently, I highlight in the conclusion the arguments in the book about obscenity as a serviceable convention that is dependent on who is invoking it and toward what political end. The project as a whole seeks to complicate the notion that the key debate at play in visual politics related to the dead body image is to see or not to see, to display or not to display. I seek to move beyond this binary to instead draw out conclusions about the functioning of the obscenity norm not only to regulate what we see but how we see it, and to narrate various degrees of visibility, invisibility, hyper-visibility, and particular framings of images.

2 HORRIFICALLY GRAPHIC
The Obscene Corpse

In 2015, a Jordanian pilot who had been captured by ISIS, Moaz al-Kasasbeh, was murdered by the group. Specifically, he was burned alive in a cage and then the cage was run over by a large vehicle. The video footage was then released by ISIS. "The brutal video is both one of its most violent and most slickly produced ... filled with wire-frame drawings and digitized cuts that dissolve its subjects in a flicker of pixels" (Groll 2015). Nesrene Malik (2015) notes that a friend described the film to her as "Bond villain-like," noting that "ISIS, it seems, has created a whole new kind of murderous cinematic experience." The burning of al-Kasasbeh is near the end of the more-than-20-minute video. It begins with a faux-news program with al-Kasasbeh discussing the Jordanian involvement in airstrikes in Iraq and Syria, as well as the specific involvement of other states in the region, such as Morocco, Saudi Arabia, and UAE, including specific kinds of aircraft used, and the involvement of the United States and France, culminating in his death and the listing of bounties on other Jordanian pilots involved in the airstrike campaign.

This particular video was deemed to be a key moment in the evolution of ISIS's brand of brutality, with some referring to it as a stylistic evolution from beheading videos, and as illuminating the use of the spectacle of death as a form of psychological warfare or even terrorism itself (Tomlinson 2015). This focus on the aesthetic dimensions of the video gestures at some of the larger issues at play in examining images and films that depict death and violence. Philip Gourevitch, for example, writing on his visits to sites of mass atrocity and genocide memorials in Rwanda, refers to the skeletons at the Nyarabuye genocide memorial as "beautiful," noting "the randomness of their fallen forms, the strange tranquility of their rude exposure, the skull here, the arm bent in some uninterpretable gesture there" (Gourevitch 2001, 66). This follows with some working on visual politics who have noted that representations of horror cannot be separated from aesthetic pleasure or even beauty, and that there can be something artistic about the human body, even in death (Taylor 1998, 8), implicitly invoking the notion of the sublime. Thus, what is being produced in the video described earlier is not simply the depiction of the death, but a system of representation that invokes particular audiences and references particular aesthetic cues.

Immediately, media groups began to report on the video, to release parts or the entirety of the video, and to raise a discussion about the purpose of showing it. One of the most significant controversies surrounding the video was the choice made by American news organization Fox News to link to the full video on their website. Additionally, on February 3, Bret Baier, Fox News anchor, showed graphic images from the video on his television news show, stating, "[W]e feel you need to see it." On their website, the video was accompanied by a warning: "WARNING, EXTREMELY GRAPHIC VIDEO: ISIS burns hostage alive." John Moody, executive editor of Fox News, explained why they chose to post the full video:

After careful consideration, we decided that giving readers of FoxNews.com the option to see for themselves the barbarity of ISIS outweighed legitimate concerns about the graphic nature of the video … Online users can choose to view or not view this disturbing content. (McKelvey 2015)

Nearly all other news outlets chose not to show the video. Even tabloid papers such as the United Kingdom's *Daily Mail* noted that they would only show the images leading up to the burning. Though they described the burning itself, they noted "the images are far too distressing to publish" (Tomlinson 2015).

I watched part of the video online on the website of the *Moroccan Times*, which offered up the following warning.

WARNING: The Content is Very Disturbing. We Urge You Not To Watch The Video. If you decide to watch the video despite our aforementioned disclaimer, The Moroccan Times Does NOT BEAR ANY RESPONSIBILITY FOR TROUBLES of all sort that You May Suffer From as a result. This content is Strictly Forbidden for people less than 18 years old. ("Video Included" 2015)

The warnings surrounding the video are particularly interesting giving the stylistics discussed earlier. That is, in the part of the video prior to the burning itself, when Moaz al-Kasasbeh walks across the landscape, the video pans to faces of Islamic State fighters half-covered, and the production and editing work make it look like a movie, playing with the viewer's perception of reality via Hollywood techniques. That is, the video itself doesn't look *real* because of the artistic techniques its visual practice is situated within. Despite the warning, the website of the *Moroccan Times* does not show the full video but ends with al-Kasasbeh in a cage, thereby not showing the most graphic portions of the video, the same choice made by most other news organizations, making the extensiveness of its trigger warning seem out of place. The website also does not show the portion of the video that claims to depict the damage done by Jordanian forces, such as the demolished buildings or crying children (Groll 2015). It may be the case that the *Moroccan Times* has chosen not to show its viewers this portion of the film so as to avoid critique of the Moroccan involvement in the campaign against ISIS. Yet this regulation of viewing generates the notion that there is something to see, even if we shouldn't see it, and that something-to-see plays on our ingrained taboos about viewing death and dead bodies. Indeed, the extensive trigger warning primes the viewer to respond in a particular way to the very idea of the video and images, even without seeing them.

The story of this video, and the debates surrounding its release, offers an introductory cut into the key theoretical questions that motivate this book, outlined here in this chapter. Specifically, it raises many of the key tensions and concepts that will color the analysis of obscenity. First, it demonstrates the taboo that governs images of death in the contemporary era. Indeed, there is a larger politics of the image at play here in terms of what constitutes the *Real* in international politics. Second, it offers initial insights into the forms of production at play beyond videomaking: the trigger warning present on the website of the *Moroccan Times*, for example, produces a spectacle through the very regulation, and perhaps absence of, the images. That is, the viewer does not even have to view the video to know how to respond to it, something constructed both by trigger warnings and by the narration of the footage by media outlets. The revulsion at the act is present even without viewing, but this is precisely because the potential viewer is made to participate in the spectacle even without seeing anything at all, or at least not yet. Third, this spectacle is one of securitization, one that tells us that some images are themselves security threats, and that some visible dead bodies need to be governed, regulated, and secured. In reference to this particular video, the very image of dying was considered a threat, both by ISIS, who intended to send a strong message, and by Western audiences, for whom bodily disintegration violates modern notions of human material integrity. This chapter lays out the theoretical arguments of this book, articulating each of these ideas in turn.

The purpose is to lay out the larger argument: examining the functioning of the obscenity norm to regulate dead body images can shed light on the political communities we form and the structures in place that preserve them, such as taboos that regulate purported obscene images in specific ways. In other words, obscenity matters precisely because it is applied inconsistently across multiple cases. What counts as "horrifically graphic" is a political decision, and what we choose to be horrified by can form the basis of policy decisions regarding humanitarian intervention or counter-terrorism, as illustrated by the two main empirical contexts this book takes up.

In this vein, I follow in an established tradition of visual politics that I will detail further in the various sections of this chapter, but which roughly follows the approach to images concisely laid out by Gillian Rose (2001, 10):

An image may have its own visual effects (so it is important to look very carefully at images); these effects, through the ways of seeing mobilized by the image, are crucial in the production and reproduction of visions of social difference; but these effects always intersect with the social context of its viewing and the visualities its spectators bring to their viewing.

She encourages a focus on images without reducing them solely to their contexts or effects, and in considering not only images but also a wider politics of viewing that involves considering the situatedness of the viewer. This also follows with WJT Mitchell's (2005) assertion that there is no such thing as wholly visual media, but rather all media are sensory multiplicities. This frames the theoretical conceptualization of obscenity that I lay out in the remainder of this chapter. As I noted in the stories told in the beginning of this chapter and Chapter 1, there is something singular about the viewing of death, precisely because it disrupts a taboo that is constructed, reinforced, and yet also shattered by image depictions in the media. Thus, we must begin with this taboo, as it offers insights into the regulation of the dead body image.

The Obscenity Norm

This section highlights the way in which the taboo governing viewing the dead, which I refer to as the "obscenity norm," functions to shape the way we think about political community. Taboos are "the intrinsic 'don'ts' of society," largely considered to be related to proscriptions that govern particular behavior (Bentley 2016b, 14). In international politics, prominent examples include the chemical weapons taboo (Bentley 2016b; Price 1995), the nuclear weapons taboo (Tannenwald 1999), the land mine taboo (Price 1998), the taboo against killing of civilians (Sluka 2008), and the torture taboo (Frankenberg 2008). Michelle Bentley, for example, focuses on the purported taboo against the use of chemical weapons, arguing that it is the claim that chemical weapons are so *excessively* offensive that renders their use illegitimate and focusing on the way in which policy governing chemical weapons reflects a normative expectation that is premised on the taboo (2016b, 1, emphasis mine). In other words, the taboo does things, discursively and materially, primarily through invoking an exception to our shared understandings, through the notion of excess, typically excessive violence or brutality. This is because of the way discourse constructs a "field of conceptual possibilities that defines what is normal and natural, and what is unthinkable and reprehensible" (Price 1995, 87). The emphasis on what is normal and what diverges from the norm is key to the functioning of a taboo, and this explains why much of the work cited here focuses on prescriptive behavior associated with the taboo: that is, enforcement.

Scholars have typically classified taboos as a type of norm because of "the socially integrated nature and taken-for-grantedness" (Bentley 2016b, 14). Still, much of the previous work on taboos focuses on how the prohibitions associated with them become codified as rules in international politics, including in institutional forms, that is, on compliance (Price 1998; Stein 2003) or on stigma and shaming (Adler-Nissen 2014). My focus is instead on the functioning of a norm that governs behavior in the context of identity rather than in the context of institutions. In other words, this is not an argument explicitly about foreign policy or enforcement of state behavior, but about the assumptions at play that enable particular claims about political community and its qualified members, and thus that enable particular kinds of politics. Specifically, constructivists have for some time argued that norms are productive "in that they constitute identities and impose meanings of what is to count as legitimate reality" (Price 1995, 87). It is this process of identity construction that concerns me here, in analyzing what gets taken for granted when an image gets labeled obscene, and what political work the claim that an image is obscene performs. In other words, invoking the obscenity norm also invokes the moral dimension associated with this norm, which carries along with it a set of assumptions about how one should respond to the image.

It bears focusing on the way in which the idea of obscenity I lay out in this chapter can be characterized as a norm. Michelle Jurkovich (2020) has recently argued for conceptual clarity in the use of "norm," and it is her criteria I follow here. She elevates early definitions of norms, particularly Finnemore and Sikkink's definition: "a standard of appropriate behavior for actors within a given identity" (Finnemore and Sikkink 1998, 891). Jurkovich delineates three criteria for something to be a norm. First, it is associated with a moral sense of oughtness. In this context, the obscenity norm is that the viewer ought to be horrified by the dead body image. Second, norms involve a defined actor with a given identity. The obscenity norm as I discuss it here invokes a viewer who is part of a particular moral or political community with associated notions of identity and self/other. Third, norms imply a specific behavior or action expected by that actor. In this context, when one encounters a particular dead body image, it is accompanied by expectations of how we should react, often outlined in a trigger warning such as the one that started this chapter from *The Moroccan Times*. Trigger warnings structure our engagement. Even referring to these images as pain porn emphasizes that they are socially unacceptable, using language that references other salacious and taboo behaviors, such as voyeurism related to sex.

The idea of community associated with the taboo's construction and reinforcement is a key feature, particularly to my analysis, as my focus is on what obscenity norms can tell us about the construction of particular political communities. The notion of expected behavior associated with Jurkovich's (2020) explanation of norms is significant because it assumes a defined community, and the members of that social group are expected to engage in particular behavior. For my purposes, this is a particular reaction to an image labeled obscene. Yet it is precisely the membership in that group that implies the specific reaction. A member of ISIS, for example, will not be horrified by a beheading video the way an American civilian would be, and as I discussed in Chapter 1, particular dead bodies are dehumanized and not granted the dignity typically accorded to corpses, largely because they are not members of, or even directly threaten, a particular social or political community. In other words, the regulation of dead body images via the obscenity norm sets expectations according to particular bodies and what they look like, something that has important implications for racialized bodies in the West, who do not conform to these expectations. Several scholars have noted the ease with which black and brown bodies are depicted in Western media in ways white bodies would not be or are not (Agathangelou 2011; Zelizer 2010).

Beyond this, norms about which bodies are visible are directly related to visual representations of who is deemed to be a member of the political community. Benjamin Schrader, following Charles Mills, has noted the ways in which the Social Contract is racialized. As he describes related to his work on veteran activism:

Looking at the US military historically, we see that it [Social Contract] has not only been used to "protect" the nation from foreign invaders, but that it has primarily been used to maintain the Social Contract internally–from employing the military to put down slave revolts to the use of the National Guard to stop black children from entering white schools in the 1950s. (Schrader 2019, 11)

He notes that we should ask ourselves who are the beneficiaries of the Social Contract and suggests a complex relationship between the Social Contract and the Soldier's Contract, and soldiers as enforcers of the Social Contract. For my purposes here, though I tend to focus on the West's "enemies" in the context of the war-on-terror in the empirical cases in the rest of the book, it also bears mentioning that these same mechanisms apply when it comes to black and brown bodies within the West, for which obscenity norms may be less likely to apply than for white bodies, and whose dead bodies may be rendered more visible without the same ethical dilemmas resulting on a wide scale.

In this sense, community functions both to differentiate and exclude those without, but also to differentiate and exclude particular bodies within. In other words, the norm associated with the obscenity taboo constructs the "us" but this has both external and internal features, and takes shape against racialized internal others, evident in the way the US military has been used to control Native American, Native Hawaiian, and black bodies within the United States (Schrader 2019, 11–13). Indeed, it is no coincidence that much of the literature on visual politics in IR related to bodies begins with lynching photographs. Brent Steele, for example, addresses how the display of the body of Emmett Till, a teenage lynching victim, functioned as a form of accountability and justice, after his mother decided to display his body as evidence of what happened, given the failure of words to describe the atrocities committed on his body (Steele 2013, 103–107; see also Shinko 2010). Lynching photographs, and the circulation of these postcards among white communities, were rendered to make those depicted, black Americans, seem less human (Ramirez 2020). Emmett Till's mother repurposed the way in which black bodies were rendered disposable and a spectacle for white viewing by displaying the brutalized body of her dead son. Some suggest that the photograph of Emmett Till's body catalyzed the civil rights movement in the United States (Ramirez 2020).

Indeed, recent global protests against police brutality have re-raised the issue of the inequality of the visual image with regard to particular bodies. Specifically, the ease with which images and videos of black victims of police violence in the United States circulate on social media has placed the visibility of their gruesome deaths in question. Their very circulation may reinforce the devaluing of black existence, even as they provide important evidence of the event itself and the injustice associated with it, as some commentators have remarked (Ramirez 2020; Williams 2016), acknowledging the complexity of these images and the ethics and politics of their circulation, to the point that some have suggested that they should be not be casually circulated, but rather as sacred items to be viewed solemnly and with careful circulation, the same way lynching photographs are in the modern era (Richardson 2020). This example raises not only the complexity of how images are made, circulated, and used, but also complicates the picture of the political communities that the obscenity norm relies upon. These communities are often themselves political myths that rely on a series of external and internal exclusions. Thus, each time in the following chapters when I examine the application of obscenity as an idea that sheds light on a political community, that community is itself a precarious one, constantly being constructed, re-visioned, and reimagined through a variety of discursive constructions, of which the obscenity norm is only one.

In sum, the obscenity norm invokes a moral sense that depicts particular deaths as injustices and others as justified, particular bodies as grievable and others as not, and reifies the borders of political communities, excluding "others" both within and without. It functions to construct a near-mythological notion of a community that upholds this norm. Yet this narrative can be most fully examined in the moments of its rupture. The following sections examine the practical politics of which images come to light and which dead bodies are rendered visible via the mechanism of the obscenity norm.

The Image Ban

The obscenity norm functions as such because of the taboo governing the dead, but also because of the dilemma of representation that emerges related to images in particular. The *Bilderverbot,* or image ban, has its roots in a biblical commandment found in Exodus 20: 4–5, which forbids the making of a likeness of anything in heaven. As Elizabeth Pritchard details: "These activities are forbidden, so the text reads, because YHWH is a jealous god … the divine is utterly transcendent or ineffable, i.e., beyond the confines of discursive reason" (Pritchard 2002, 291). Thus, the image ban begins in the context of religious understandings of the transcendent and the inadequacy of its representation. Yet even as there is to be no worshipping of images, the religious framings of this also get at the dual nature of the image ban: we cannot make an image of a God we must nevertheless represent as unrepresentable or invoke by inadequate means. This juxtaposition is at the heart of the *Bilderverbot.* I should also note here that many of the cases I take up in later chapters, particularly the severed head, draw on this religious iconography. God is not visible, yet man is made in God's image, so the destruction of man is not only inhumane, but ungodly, and generates a problem of the representation of the death of God.

The *Bilderverbot* has entered into secular politics, chiefly in discussions surrounding representations of the Holocaust. Dominick LaCapra notes that, in Claude Lanzmann's film *Shoah*, for example, "trauma becomes a universal hole in Being or an unnamable Thing" (LaCapra 1997, 246). The film *Shoah* often plays a role in these discussions about representation related to the Holocaust, given its aesthetic form and its disruption of traditional forms of representation. Holocaust representation seeks to gain access to a loss that itself corrupts the means of representing it (Baer 2005, 20), and the Holocaust itself remains inassimilable to historicist or contextual readings (Baer 2005, 66–67). What was generated by the acts themselves was a certain type of trauma that then became an unnamable thing, "unimaginable" and "inexplicable." And yet, as is true of other traumas, there remains a paradox inherent: that which is unspeakable must also be referred to as such.

In other words, even as such violences are posited as horrific, they also generate a certain fascination qua horrific positings. In a larger context, this fascination has driven a veritable industry of trauma porn or torture porn (Hallam 2010; Jones 2010). Even as the fascination is attested to in trauma porn, beheading porn, the larger fascination is exhibited in the discussions about not watching (Kayyem 2015; Larson 2015a; Schwartz 2014; Snyder 2015). Even British Prince Charles chimed in in 2014 to suggest that the general public should not watch ISIS beheading videos, for example (Mitchell 2014). In other words, questions of trauma and representation also come to the fore in any discussion of corpse politics, particularly the display of the dead body image that I am concerned with here.

The *Bilderverbot* is often situated as not simply that which is unrepresentable, but a refusal to represent, an injunction against mimesis. Lanzmann's *Shoah* has been described as avoiding the "delusions of presence" and thus his refusal to represent – that is, his adherence to the *Bilderverbot* – becomes the grounds for its very claim to authenticity in Holocaust memory (Huyssen 2001, 30). That is, the *Bilderverbot* is not simply a description of the unsayable and unrepresentable, it is an ethical injunction against speaking or showing when representation is inadequate. The case of the Holocaust *Bilderverbot* serves as a useful lesson in understanding secularization of the *Bilderverbot* in the context of dead body images. An injunction against representation occurs in the framing of ISIS's acts as obscene, for example, or in the functioning of trigger warnings, or the media debates about what images should be published (Cole 2015). If this refusal functions in particular ways to frame policy, and frames a discrete political ends, the *Bilderverbot* is much more than this, insofar as it is "no longer at issue since it has itself become part of official strategies" (Huyssen 2001, 39). As with Huyssen's claims about the representation of the Holocaust, here the injunction against mimesis comes to constitute its own unacknowledged political end. In this sense, the image ban functions to construct the obscene through the mechanism of its regulation.

I have noted the religious origins of the *Bilderverbot*, and it is worthwhile calling attention to the dual dimensions of this, and how that plays out in a secular context. While the image ban focuses on that which is not representable due to its sacralization: the divine, it also invokes the extreme opposite of this: the demonic, which both "inhabit the extreme zones of the human imagination of which we cannot or should not speak, and which we certainly should not depict in visual images" (Mitchell 2011, 63). In this sense, extreme circumstances of death, particularly mass atrocity, are often characterized using language that invokes the image ban.

Dominick LaCapra identifies three components to the *Bilderverbot*: religious, epistemological, and psychological:

It would apply most clearly to representations of divinity or of objects construed as immanently sacred or as incarnations of divinity. On an epistemological level, there is positivism in the idea that an objectifying notational system can ideally represent, transparently render, or capture the essence of an object. On a psychological level, there is what might be seen as the reversal of positivism in the reliving or reincarnation of a past that is experienced as fully present. (LaCapra 1997, 239)

In the context of the commonplace taboo against showing images of the dead, all three of these components come into play in slightly different ways. The religious mechanism plays on our assumptions of the human body as sacred, one way in which the taboo functions in the context of ISIS beheadings to naturalize fear, as I will discuss further in Chapter 3. On the epistemological level, rhetoric that depicts spectacular violence against humans as fundamentally unexplainable or inexplicable invokes an assumed fear surrounding things that cannot be "transparently rendered," in LaCapra's terminology, as I will discuss further in Chapters 3 and 5. On the psychological level, there is also the blurring of linear time in ISIS-related rhetoric, in the invocations of ISIS as "medieval," "barbaric," and trying to "turn the clock back to the 7th century" (Vick 2015). This may also manifest as the notion that ISIS constitutes a media politics of the future (Rogers 2016), an idea that Western media focused on in the context of the slick production of the Moaz al-Kasasbeh video described at the beginning of this chapter.

The tension surrounding the inability to represent often results in the application of the obscenity taboo to that which is deemed unrepresentable, or to atrocities whose representation is ethically tangled. As Francois Debrix has argued, this is because "horror is what 'our' politics of security cannot confront and must representationally cast away" (Debrix 2017, 63). Such notions of the inability to represent are constituted by a complex web of ethical, visual, and political invocations regarding what is or should be rendered visible.

"What's Real? What's Not Real?"

The previous section articulated the problem of representation of trauma, but one key component of this is the dimension of the *Real* associated with the obscene images I address in this book. The idea is that certain dead bodies are shown to draw attention to the reality of a crisis and cultivate empathy, while others are too obscene to be shown because getting too close to the *Real* makes us realize that images may tell only partial stories, for example, of how someone died rather than how they lived, as Ranciere (2011) reminds us in the context of images taken after the liberation of Auschwitz. Indeed, he uses the language of lying to describe the images, noting that the photos did not represent the reality of the Shoah because they did not show extermination of the Jews in the gas chambers. To return to the framing of the *Bilderverbot,* any image of the Shoah was bound to "lie," in Ranciere's words, because "reality is never entirely soluble in the visible" (2011, 89), and because the Shoah is fundamentally unrepresentable. That which can be adequately represented by a photograph must necessarily be banal.

What makes an image obscene is not simply whether it depicts atrocity, injury, or death: indeed, these terms are subject to interpretation, and different cultures may differently posit restrictions on what should be rendered visible. Death, for example, is typically confined to the funerary industry and managed behind closed doors in much of the United States and Europe (Doughty 2015; Mitford 1998), whereas, in India, it may be common to see cremation pyres on the banks of the Ganges River in full public view. It is not the content but the problem of representability that articulates the framing of obscenity. Obscene images depict the unrepresentable, and specifically the unrepresentability of body horror, which plays with our conception of what is real and what is not, of what can "structurally be fixed in an image" (Ranciere 2011, 89), and what exceeds representation. Death itself is often articulated in these latter terms, as something that cannot be represented, precisely because it is non-presence or absence, one of the key reasons why this book takes up dead body images. In this vein, the analysis I take up is very much in line with recent work done on scopic regimes, which argues that the effective point of analysis is not achieving visual verity, but understanding "how particular fields of vision are constructed such that their representational properties are perceived as truthful ... if they are generally understood as capturing the 'real'" (Grayson and Mawdsley 2019, 433).

But beyond this, the problem of representation is articulated in what Jacques Ranciere has defined as intolerability. This stems not from what is depicted in the image but from the shift from the unbearable reality depicted by the image to the recognition that it is an image rather than the *Real*: "what it shows is deemed too real, too intolerably real to be offered in the form of an image" (Ranciere 2011, 83). In other words, it is the play with what is real that makes an image obscene. Representing itself becomes intolerable because of the dilemma of the *Real*. The visual politics literature has acknowledged this dimension associated with photographs, which "provide us with the seductive belief that what we see in a photograph is an authentic representation of the world" (Bleiker 2018, 12). The language of seduction is perhaps appropriate here, given my focus on the taboo, which has the twin element of desire and disgust I will examine more later in this chapter. Indeed, while the viewer may want to see the photograph as giving us access to a truth about the world, the dynamics of image production and circulation, combined with the cultural impact of films and their style of production being increasingly adopted by organizations such as ISIS, the rote equation of a photographic image with reality is no longer taken for granted. Liam Kennedy, for example, has characterized the post-9/11 American worldview as being the "suspension of belief," noting that perpetual war blurs the previously held notion that the workings of power are subject to the media's evidentiary claims through photojournalism (Kennedy 2016, 133).

In examining what I call the *Real*, my focus here is on the obscene photo's play with this dilemma of photography's claims to authenticity: the obscene photo is too real, so as to be unbelievable, and in its framing as a spectacle, it joins together the real and the fantastic

(Taylor 1998, 8). It pushes the boundaries of our connection between photography and the real it purports to represent.[1]

Modern technology has enhanced and manipulated this. Images such as those from Abu Ghraib have blurred the boundaries between documentation of events and entertainment, with "the 'real' . . . increasingly mediated by spectacle" (Lyford and Payne 2005, 125). Teju Cole has illustrated this in his piece *Death in the Browser Tab*, in which he explores how you no longer need to be present physically to witness someone's death. The internet's ability to circulate images and video often plays into the metaphor of the Hollywood film in terms of the inability to distinguish the real from the staged, given that both are now produced for audiences. For example, an American ISIS recruit who traveled to Syria to join the terrorist organization said, when asked about it in early 2019, "I'm not interested in bloodshed and I didn't know what to believe. These are videos on YouTube. What's real? What's not real?" (Callimachi and Porter 2019). While this recruit speaks of the dilemma of creative editing of film and image, in fact, this gets at a deeper issue: she did not know if the images were real precisely because they seemed *too real*. How could it be that the images of ISIS beheadings were actually real rather than cinema, in her mind? Two responses to media coverage of suffering are worth highlighting here: Kay Hammer, who notes that "you can see real true-to-life pictures, but your mind reacts to it almost as if it's just a movie," and Roux Harding, who notes that "it's too surreal when you're watching television" (as quoted in Moeller 1999, 36). Indeed, it isn't because of a failure of *reliability* of a documentary image that we are having this

---

[1] I should also note that scholars such as Mirzoeff have drawn attention to the confirmatory bias inherent in images. He notes that "in war, the image takes on a new guise. People do not suspend their disbelief in the truth of what they are being shown so much as subordinate it to the geo-political agenda of the nation state. It no longer matters whether the image is accurate, only whether it expresses a sense of the nation" (Mirzoeff 2005, 76). While this capacity in images is important, my purpose here is not to examine the gaps between what is depicted and reality, or even the process by which we confirm accuracy, but rather how images are used and the degree to which they are seen to give us access to the *Real*, which is less about verifiable fact than an understanding seen to be hidden in the content and context of the image, as this section details. Indeed, Gillian Rose describes Baudrillard's notion of the simulacra as being a hallmark of the postmodern world we live in, where it is "no longer possible to make a distinction between the real and the unreal; images had become detached from any certain relation to a real world" (Rose 2001, 8).

discussion in the postmodern world, but because of the failure of *reality*, whether we are referring to ISIS beheading videos or the depiction of large-scale human rights violations.

As *too real* or *surreal*, such obscene images become what Zizek (2008, xlix) has referred to as the sublime, described as "an object which starts to function as the empirical stand-in for the impossible-noumenal Thing." I detail this more with regards to ISIS beheadings in Chapter 3, but it is worth connecting this notion to the obscene here further. Zizek's point is that the failure of representation that I illustrated earlier with regard to the *Bilderverbot* is itself related to the sublime object. "The sublime object evokes pleasure in a negative way: the place of the Thing is indicated through the very failure of its representation" (Zizek 1989, 204). In other words, we know something is *real* because it cannot be represented, the paradox inherent in the dead body image, particularly as it relates to the evidentiary value of the photograph, which I take up in more detail in Chapter 5.

It is precisely the role of the atrocity image to act as the stand-in for the impossible *Real*, which is posited as too horrible to contemplate: both *too real* and *unreal* at the same time, thus shattering the very idea of reality. Our desire for an encounter with the *Real* also constitutes our disgust at getting too close to it, as Zizek details, and this desire–disgust nexus forms the basis of the taboo governing obscenity in global politics. Indeed, he identifies this as the "surplus of the Real over every symbolization that functions as the object–cause of desire" (Zizek 1989, 3). In other words, it is precisely the reality of the image that seems *unreal* to us, and the gap between the representation and the *Real*, that renders an image obscene. When we watch a film where someone is killed, and blood spurts out, we know with certainty that it is not real, and therefore the image is not obscene. Yet when the cinematic form depicts the real death, such as that of al-Kasasbeh, it is the reality of it that renders it obscene: it is *too real* and therefore *unreal*. Sue Tait notes that "explicit media make a particular claim to the 'real' yet simultaneously evacuate the subjectivity of the suffering subject" in her examination of Ogrish, a website devoted to body horror, including accidents, suicides, crime scenes, and later the beheading videos of Daniel Pearl and Nick Berg in 2002 and 2004 (Tait 2008, 94). In other words, the more graphic an image, the more *real* it is said to be, as if the *Real* is a deep understanding that can only be accessed by setting aside our own subjectivities. This presumes that the *Real* speaks for itself because the obscene grants access to something hidden from daily life, now rendered visible in the graphic image of death.

Ranciere examines this problem that he refers to as the paradox of the spectator, where "the spectator is held before an appearance in a state of ignorance about the process of production of this appearance and about the reality it conceals" (Ranciere 2011, 2). The paradox is that the spectator is rendered a witness to something that she can neither know nor act on, primarily because of the difficulty in determining the *Real*. This also gets at the issues of technology in the display of images, since they complicate our ability to determine what constitutes the *Real*. The way images are disseminated is part of the process of generating not only what matters in global politics, but what is or seems to be *real*. Our carefully curated reactions can then tell us something about how we are not horrified by the effects of some kinds of violence. It is worth emphasizing here that "the closer we supposedly approach the real or the truth, the further we draw away from them both, since neither one nor the other exists" (Baudrillard 1995, 49). Ulrich Baer has similarly referred to trauma as the perplexing condition of a missing original (2005, 73).

The dilemma of the *Real* can be amplified by the multilayered nature of images. Ranciere traces this in the art of Martha Rosler on the Vietnam War. Rosler's work places images of death and atrocity from the Vietnam War alongside backdrops of American domestic interior scenes. Ranciere uses Rosler's art to examine the emancipation of the spectator, yet in doing so he offers insights on the complexity of the relationship between image and reality. As he notes, the image said:

Here is the hidden reality that you do not know how to see; you must become acquainted with it and act in accordance with that knowledge ... here is the obvious reality that you do not want to see, because you know that you are responsible for it. (Ranciere 2011, 27)

Yet the spectator must already be emancipated in order to see that in the image (Ranciere 2011, 85). Rosler's image does not depict reality, in the sense that the scenes layered on top of one another are very clearly disjunctures, yet in depicting the *not real*, she also depicts the *all-too-real*: the problematic nature of US intervention and the narratives that sustained and legitimized it.

This investigation into the *Real* occupies an interstitial space in global politics, because it calls into question the idea of objective truths, of pure being/presence or pure absence. I have written previously of this idea under the framing of hauntology, drawn from Jacques Derrida: the idea that the ghost is prior to ontology (Auchter 2014). In other words, there has not been sufficient attention paid to the paradox of the *Real*, partly because it has not been considered a legitimate arena of scholarship. In the words of Jacques Derrida:

A traditional scholar does not believe in ghosts – nor in all that could be called the virtual space of spectrality. There has never been a scholar who, as such, does not believe in the sharp distinction between the real and the unreal, the actual and the inactual, the living and the non-living, being and non-being. (1994, 12)

In this sense, it is our frameworks that have been limiting in our ability as scholars to encounter and understand the paradoxes that structure the functioning of the taboo governing dead body images in global politics.

The Voyeurism of Looking

In new forms of media, dead body images are more accessible than they have ever been, but they often still remain taboo. For my recent book, I engaged in Internet searches for the falling body photos of 9/11, and repeatedly came across websites with comments arguing that anyone seeking out these photos must be perverse. Indeed, volunteers who flocked to Ground Zero after 9/11 in an attempt to help were accused of voyeurism and told that their desire to help was a morbid fascination with death and destruction (Edkins 2011, 107). The same is true of ISIS beheading videos or the streamed video of the New Zealand mosque shootings in 2019, the viewing and circulation of which was outlawed in the United Kingdom and New Zealand, respectively. The notion that one would want to view these images is depicted as abhorrent and disgusting, and this contestation over viewing these images is the main reason why more traditional news outlets have largely chosen not to show them, and why they often only emerge in tabloid outlets. The presence in tabloids implies a voyeurism associated with such viewing, which invokes the potential pleasure that viewers could derive from looking at others in pain (Taylor 1998, 5).[2]

There is also the fact that showing these images is all about the cultivation of the spectacle, whereas death is usually private and intimate, so much of the taboo may be about merging separate and distinct realms of relating to one's own body and the bodies of others. The notion that such viewing may be voyeuristic emphasizes not only the taboo surrounding viewing particular images, but that the taboo is derived from the pleasure associated with such viewing, death pornography, so to speak, inculcating the same shame as consumption of sexual images. But this shame is not necessarily the case – that is, the visual taboo surrounding viewing the dead body may persist, but in many instances, it is not accompanied with the correlative shame. Taylor (1998, 13) notes that in photographs, destroyed human flesh becomes "treasure recovered from the wreck, remnants of exotic endings unveiled before survivors' eyes."

This notion of destroyed human flesh as "treasure recovered from the wreck" gestures to the twin notions of disgust and desire inherent in the taboo. That is, there is a fascination with violence and its instantiation on bodies that has an aesthetic dimension, an aesthetic view of death "in which it is permissible, sometimes even desirable, to publicly display death" (Azoulay 2001, 4). An entire category of war photography has emerged related to this genre, including the work of photographer James Nachtwey, known for graphic images of violence that are often referred to as war porn. When viewers view these images, "we are simultaneously fascinated and repulsed, we cannot bear to look and we cannot stop looking" (Bernstein 2004, 11). The spectacle of body display and its regulation via the obscenity norm then can only be understood in the context of the taboo that has this twin function of desire and disgust. The effect of such disgust includes the rendering of particular bodies invisible from the public eye, such as the Dover Ban in the United States, which attempted to remove death as an effect of war from the visible sphere (Purnell 2018). This may be because of the social and political status accorded to the cadaver (Auchter 2016b;

---

[2] Indeed, Foucault in *Society Must Be Defended* refers to the gradual disqualification of death associated with biopolitics, particularly the way death, rather than sex, has become the object of the taboo (Foucault 1997, 247).

Cantor 2010). In other words, it is precisely because things should not *normally* be displayed that they become spectacular in their display.

When I visited genocide memorials in Rwanda several years ago, I traveled to multiple memorial sites where bones and bodies were on display. When you see these bodies and bones, you don't know if you should look. You are there to look, indeed these sites are designed to be visually and physically engaged with, as you traverse rooms full of mummified corpses. But somehow it seems shameful to just look. John Taylor (1998, 13) refers to this as the idea that it is "morbid or unhealthy" for "unembarrassed witnesses" to feast their eyes on the misery of others. In this sense it is the ultimate paradox: the visual witness is called to look at precisely that which no one is supposed to look at. This is true both in the triumphalist displays of dead dictators, but also with humanitarian rhetoric and the consumption via mass media of images of body bags or corpses. In short, the taboo is not simply a matter of a complete denial of viewing but rather a complex set of expectations and exceptions that construct the taboo in its very breaking. In other words, despite the existence of the taboo, images of the dead are shown. These images and the way they are narrated can not only tell us how the obscenity norm is constituted but also how this norm governs behavior.

Take, for example, ISIS beheading videos, where media guidelines censor traumatic and obscene images on the viewer's behalf. However, this is usually done by viewing them and then telling their audience about what is contained within them. That is, certain media figures acted as visual intermediaries, as visual witnesses, so that the wider public would not have to, and could instead only listen to their testimony, implying that there was something to be gained in terms of testimony from viewing the video to the extent that the news anchor needed to watch it despite his revulsion, to then act as witness to the visual disturbance to those who needed the information and testimony, but without the visual revulsion. There is a specific politics to the choice not to show, to partially show, or to display.

What Counts as Horrifically Graphic?

The taboo involves the twin impulses of revulsion and of desire. This manifests physically as well, as in the idea of rubbernecking at a car accident site, a salaciousness surrounding looking at the crash, a literal, physical phenomenon where one turns one's head so far it can be analogized to rubber. Yet how this manifests can tell us about claims to being horrified. The horror of the "other" is viewable, rendered for consumption, in the way our own is not. As David Campbell has traced (2004, 64), the media is more likely to show the dead bodies of foreigners when they do show dead body images. "And more often than not, images of dead foreigners are little more than a vehicle for the inscription of domestic spaces as superior, thereby furthering the 'cultural anaesthesia' produced through media representations of the other." Sontag has similarly described the visual asymmetry of body display: "[T]he other, even when not an enemy, is regarded only as someone to be seen, not someone (like us) who also sees" (2003: 72).

This visual asymmetry is reinforced by the taboo that reinforces the notion that dead bodies are not to be viewed, yet there are specific circumstances under which this taboo can be broken. Elizabeth Dauphinee (2007: 144–5) has spoken of this in the context of the Abu Ghraib images: "[T]he gaze enabled by the photograph also works as a sort of 'hooding' of the subject, maintaining the inherently violent fantasy that we can see without being seen." These extraordinary circumstances invoke these violent fantasies governing the other, enabling consumption of dead body images for particular purposes. Viewing thus inculcates a power relationship by defining what can be visually consumed despite a taboo, what we can be visually rather than simply discursively horrified by, what is just obscene enough and what is too obscene: the horrifically graphic.

This phrase, "HORRIFICALLY GRAPHIC" that appears in the title of this chapter is taken from news coverage of an incident that happened in Fallujah, Iraq, in 2004. In early 2014, the entertainment and news website TMZ published photographs of this incident that depicted American Marines pouring gasoline on human remains and lighting them on fire. It chose to only publish eight out of forty-one images, noting that the rest were too gruesome to show. As the *New York Times* describes the images:

Two of the photos posted on Wednesday show a man in a Marine's uniform pouring liquid from a gasoline can on two decaying bodies. Two other photos show the bodies on fire, and two more show the charred remains. In one photo a man poses on one knee with his rifle pointed towards a human skeleton. In another, a man is running his hands through the pants pockets of one of the bodies. (Southall 2014)

This dispassionate, descriptive delineation of the images aims at neutrality, at lack of ethical judgment about the photographs. Even the specification that it is a "man in a Marine's uniform" is intended to avoid concluding too much about the individuals involved.

TMZ was much more inflammatory in its descriptions. The eight photographs on its website were placed behind a warning banner to avoid inadvertently clicking on them, thus those who viewed them did so intentionally. The banner announced: "WARNING: THESE PICTURES ARE HORRIFICALLY GRAPHIC DEPICTING DEAD BODIES VIEWER DISCRETION ADVISED" ("Pics of Marines" 2014). The images were not published in *The New York Times* or any other news source that wrote about the story. The language of horror is an interesting one: these images are not simply graphic but HORRIFICALLY GRAPHIC. This is particularly significant given that the images that were not shown are labeled as even more grue-some. What is worse than HORRIFICALLY GRAPHIC, and why are we allowed to see HORRIFICALLY GRAPHIC photos online on TMZ, but not in the *New York Times*? Like the warnings on the Moaz al-Kasasbeh video, what norms of obscenity as a visual concept are inaugurated by the notion that images can be described but not shown?

One of the photographs shows an American soldier kneeling on the ground, with his gun barrel pointed at a charred skull. The skull's mouth is open as if in a scream at the foreground of the photograph, and the char marks are evidence that the skull was burned in a fire. The soldier appears to be sharing a joke with the photographer, as if the display and the staging of the photograph is itself funny. TMZ has chosen to blur the face of the soldier, and the fuzziness of this individu-alizing feature, the face, is in stark contrast with the hollowed eyes of the skull that stare at the viewer as evidence of what seems to have been a horrific death. The photograph is not gory in any way; there is no blood, no torn limbs or flesh or wounds. But the way the skull is charred, the way it looks, disembodied, detached from its material context, yet replicating the fear and agony an individual might feel when subject to the threat of a gun aimed at him or her, as the soldier is doing in the photo, the terror, the horror, the casual way in which the soldier interacts with the skull, is disturbing.

As TMZ puts it, the photograph "shows a Marine crouched down next to a dead body and mugging for the camera." Yet there is an important distinction here between a body and bones that is elided by the rhetoric. TMZ deemed it appropriate to show the less obscene of the photographs: those with bones clearly visible and not blurred, or distant views of bodies on fire. These have been evaluated as somehow less obscene than the other photographs, which depict fleshy bodies rather than bones, and are thereby viewable, though with "appropriate" disclaimers and protections from unexpected encounters with these images. We are told that the images not shown are "just too gruesome," depicting "well over a dozen bodies" and "some covered with flies and one is being eaten by a dog" ("Pics of Marines" 2014).

A choice has been made then about what images and what parts of the images are obscene. Another case is illustrative: when photographs of US soldiers urinating on Afghan corpses were published, the faces of the soldiers were blurred, as were their potentially exposed genitals, but the faces of the corpses were not blurred out (Auchter 2013). In other words, the genitals were considered the obscene part of the image, not the dead bodies themselves. A commenter on the TMZ story incisively critiques the use of pixellation in the context of the Marines burning bodies in Iraq: "I'd rather see the grahic [*sic*] human remains blurred out and the jerk wads who are commiting [*sic*] these crimes revealed. It looks like some of them are proud of their work – let them have their moment of fame TMZ!" ("Pics of Marines" 2014).

That is, when the face of a soldier burning bodies is considered the unviewable portion of the photograph, perhaps it is time to think about the political work obscenity is doing in legitimizing these disjunctures. When a man urinating is considered the obscene part of a photograph of that man urinating on corpses, it says something about obscenity and the human body: that sexualized body parts are obscene, and identifying information can be rendered unviewable in the service of a narrative about safety and threat, but there are no such prescriptions governing specific dead bodies. That is, while we normally consider the dead body unviewable as a matter of dignity, specific stories are enabled by the enabling of viewing of non-normalized, obscene dead bodies and body parts.

Trauma studies has focused on the immediate present display of the bloody body, a horror that is considered disruptive of subjectivity. Cole (2015) notes that what is disturbing about the death image is precisely the viewer's "engagement with that mysterious instant in which a self is deprived of itself." In contrast, my focus is largely the circulation and display of images of dead bodies as replications of these immediate traumas, which raises the question of how the visual engagement with bloody bodies is managed. The display of a body involves active decision-making, but there are more decisions involved in the circulation of and encounter with images of the body. There is a transgression of a norm when a dead body is made visible outside of display in a funerary rite, thereby offering an indicator of how identities and communities form through the display of corpses deemed to be non-normative. Beyond this, the role of the cinematic in the way bodies are depicted both in images and in popular culture, such as film, offers ways of thinking about the disappearance, reappearance, visibility, and invisibility of dead bodies in war.

In this context, these decisions surrounding which dead bodies are rendered visible are political ones that reference moral priors: that is, we are told that viewing images of the dead is necessary for humanitarian purposes in some instances, and that viewing images of the dead is a threat to our security (and at times, sanity) in other instances. Trigger warnings are an example of this. Indeed, *Slate* magazine declared 2013 the year of the trigger warning, emphasizing their emergence as a new phenomenon (Bentley 2016a). Trigger warnings of obscene images such as the ones I have already begun to discuss and the one from which I draw this chapter title frame the encounter with the image in such a way as to produce preemptive trauma that would perhaps not otherwise be there, drawing on an ideological fantasy of security (Danil 2016). That is, the context doesn't prepare one for the psychological encounter with the image, but rather for the political work of the image. A trigger warning in place for an ISIS beheading video that in fact does not show an actual beheading then is not in place to stave off the inevitable mental trauma, but rather to cultivate an aura of trauma surrounding the video. The traumatized viewer then becomes a privileged witness to a visual atrocity that is narrativized via the warning.

The framing of the trigger warning, the claim that one is about to view graphic images, not only generates an expectation of what one will see but also means that we enter into the visual relationship already ready to respond to it in a specific manner. It is similar to the somber tone one adopts before visiting a memorial site: we already know how we will feel before we even get there. The same is true for the image: the horror, and the shame of viewing something taboo, cultivates a sense of outrage at the image itself, and the sense that the viewer is a necessary witness, hence the breaking of the taboo established by the very presence of the warning in the first place. The warning thus creates, reinforces, and also breaks the taboo of viewing the dead. In Zizek's words, the desire is constituted by its very repression (Zizek 1989, 13).

But what political work does this do? By privatizing the spectacle of the global dead via the warning, the dead body itself remains in the private realm, outside of the realm of consideration for global security. While the number of the dead is seen to matter, the individual dead body is instrumentalized as another piece of evidence of brutality, another legitimating factor in continuing the fight. Our encounters with the global dead via trigger warnings then reference moral priors that underpin the political work of these images. A dead and bloody Qaddafi is rendered hyper-visible without the warnings, instructing the viewer to celebrate the death of a dictator, as I describe in Chapter 4. There is no moral repugnance at the idea of the dead body in this instance in the media forms in which it circulated, thus there was no need for a trigger warning. On the other hand, the images of Syrian torture victims mentioned in Chapter 1 were designed to develop moral repugnance and trauma in the viewer.

In the context of the trigger warnings on these images, what is interesting is that we seem to not necessarily be offended or disturbed by the depiction of dead bodies, as evident in the comments sections of the stories about the burning bodies described earlier: while some commenters remain concerned about the act, most situate it within a larger logic of us/them that values certain lives above others, that grieves American soldiers but not burned Iraqis, regardless of their identities. John Taylor (1998) posits a consensus in the West that the decay and dismemberment of the body is revolting. But, he argues that non-normative bodies are routinely displayed and that there is the least restraint in the media in depicting the dead bodies of Africans, Arabs, and Asians.

Even those who critique the act depicted often also critique the display of the photographs, noting that it is more important to maintain the community of soldiers and their safety, the sense of "us," than to threaten their mission by depicting these acts. This schema is maintained by the notion that websites and newspapers are allowed to publish them, with the caveat that there is yet something else out there that does qualify as too gruesome to show. This distinction legitimizes the viewing of the photographs they do decide to show, even as they are also obscene. Yet these narratives of what is rendered visible and what remains invisible reinforces these images as more normalized. It has the effect of reinforcing distances between the viewer and the body depicted by virtue of its depiction and the story of legitimate viewing that contextualizes it. As Elizabeth Dauphinee (2007, 148) notes about a similar example,

the photograph of the tortured body at Abu Ghraib already confirms the disjuncture between our worlds and theirs, and this, in turn, becomes the baseline through which we (ultimately fail to) interact. The suffering of the other is emptied of its immanence, and reread back both to and by us in ways that work either to condemn or excuse – and in any event explain – the violent politics that caused the pain.

David Campbell (2007: 369) has noted that the news media is reluctant to portray "unvarnished horror." He describes the way it has become conventional wisdom to argue that media depictions of the obscene are commonplace, but in actuality displays of death are not very common (Campbell 2004). The dominant view of desensitization to images of suffering is not accurate: rather, the media selects and curates images for us, and "we see a lot more faces of experts telling us how to make sense of the images than the images themselves" (Ranciere 2011, 95). Thus, decisions around what is shown, what is considered too obscene or acceptably so, and what we view are significant beyond just journalistic conventions, which themselves reflect larger social norms. Graphicness is a "moveable, serviceable, and debatable convention, dependent on those who invoke it and for which aim," in which it is deemed acceptable to show Rwandan skulls but not the victims of American airstrikes in Iraq, for example (Zelizer 2010, 22). In other words, it is not the graphicness itself that is at issue, but the circumstances under which graphicness is deployed.

The Image: Where Have All the Corpses Gone?

What happens to dead bodies is more than ever a key question given the nature of political violence, and the fact that it is often materially enacted on bodies. Despite the emergence of new genres of visual politics and new materialisms within the international relations literature, there still haven't been sustained examinations of the dead body as a key nexus in the intersection of these genres. Part of this is likely due to the way in which dead bodies are both literally and figuratively buried after atrocities. Even disaster management handbooks focus on how to properly identify dead bodies for the precise purpose of properly burying them. Aside from the rather infamous cases of dead body display of Lenin and Ho Chi Minh, dead bodies are not routinely displayed. Even in these two cases, the bodies are not presented as evidence of atrocity, and it should be noted that their display remains a strange and puzzling spectacle to most Westerners that seems like an ideological vestige of the hero worship of communism. Adding this to the way in which, even with the proliferation of television shows in the United States such as *Crime Scene Investigation*, *NCIS*, and others which do depict forensic examinations of dead bodies that are simply props, true crime television shows blur the dead body as a matter of dignity.

All of these features contribute to an assessment that the dead body is not routinely intended for viewing. Similarly, debates about where to bury the bodies of Boston Bomber Tamerlan Tsarnaev and Charlie Hebdo attackers Said and Cherif Kouachi ("Paris Attacks" 2015), and even the controversy over news footage of dead bodies in the water after a recent plane crash in Indonesia, indicate that there is something about the presence of particular dead bodies that can be disturbing. This section focuses on the political power of images, together with the regulatory taboos that govern viewing the dead, as a means to introduce the visual politics of the corpse. In other words, my inquiry is located within and seeks to contribute to the burgeoning literature on visual culture and world politics.

The Image

Images themselves often have tremendous political power: "[P]hotography is often understood as a device that mechanically freeze-frames virtual chunks of time" (Baer 2005, 4). This is particularly true in the context of Western modernity that is the focus of this book: indeed, Gillian Rose has noted that one of the hallmarks of the shift from the premodern to the modern is the evolution of the equation of seeing with knowledge as an epistemological shift (2001, 7). Knowledge about the world is mediated through images. Visual images have long been part of world politics, as evident in the genres of photojournalism and documentary photography, shaping global events and how we understand them (Bleiker 2018, 1). Yet photographic images are not themselves brute material representations of reality, and photographs are not simply visual artifacts. They are "both verbal and visual entities, both metaphors and graphic symbols. They are, at one and the same time, concepts, objects, pictures, and symbolic forms" (Mitchell 2011, xvii).

Images become dispersed through the schemas of viewing associated with cinema and other mechanisms of display, which often act as a filter for what can or should be viewed. From Facebook to Twitter, contemporary technology has shifted the frame, wherein war is rendered hyper-visible; at the same time these visualities are managed via a technology of erasure that blurs parts of images, and removes others from our line of sight, so as to manage the context under which the visual encounter occurs. Discussions of photography frequently focus on understanding how images are made and the narratives of what is left out in the decisions surrounding what is visually depicted (Sliwinski 2011; Sontag 2001). As Griselda Pollock has noted, "what is at stake in representation is not so much a matter of what is shown as it is of who is authorized to look at whom with what effects" (Pollock 1994, 15).

There has also been recent scholarly attention to images in international politics, perhaps first emerging with what has been referred to as the aesthetic turn (Bleiker 2001). In that vein, this book contributes to the field of recent work in IR loosely termed "visual politics." The work done in this area tends to focus on specific issue areas: aesthetic theory (Bleiker 2009; Pusca 2009), art (Danchev 2009; Luke 2002; Martin 2014), scopic regimes (Mirzoeff 2016; Shim 2014), war and visuality (Virilio 1989), targeting and militarized regimes of hypervisibility (Arnold 2017; Bousquet 2018; Cronin 2018; Gregory 2011, 2017; Mieszkowski 2012), the positioning of the viewer as political agent or witness (Berger 1977; Moller 2013), the taker of the image, as in the politics of photojournalism (Azoulay 2008; Hariman and Lucaites 2007; Kennedy 2016; Kennedy and Patrick 2014; Sliwinski 2011), film (Shapiro 2008; Weber 2005), or the political impact of one or more specific images (Hansen 2011).

Within these focal points, we tend to see three main approaches to images. First, images are articulated as evidence of atrocity and suffering that will make humanitarian efforts more likely by cultivating empathy (Chouliaraki 2006; Linfield 2010; Moeller 1999). Susan Sontag, for example, argues that the only people with a right to look at horror are those who could do something to alleviate the suffering depicted (Sontag 2003, 42), and this is invoked by various human rights organizations, as I take up further in Chapter 5.

Second, images are articulated as part of securitizing narratives that justify specific policies (Heck and Schlag 2013; Williams 2003). Liam Kennedy has demonstrated the relationship between photojournalism and American power enacted as foreign policy, for example (2016), and Cronin (2018) uses the visual language of the bugsplat to analyze the functioning of US drone warfare and civilian casualties.

Third, images are characterized as resistant to specific securitizing narratives (Hansen 2011). Much of this work has emerged to address and explain the post-9/11 security theater, from an examination of the role of images of planes crashing into towers (Moller 2007) to a study of the importance of icons via the example of Abu Ghraib (Hansen 2015) to an exploration of editorial cartoons or the larger politics of visuality related to the war-on-terror (Amoore 2007; Dodds 2007) to work on art photography (Danchev 2011) to the visual politics of beheading videos (Friis 2015). Claudia Aradau and Andrew's Hill's work (2013) is also a political sociological approach to understanding how images and their circulation generate particular forms of politics and claims to truth. The book follows these insights and relies on a conceptualization of images best articulated by Gabi Schlag: "[P]ictures are not reflecting reality but are constitutive of what can (not) be seen and (not) be shown" (Schlag 2019, 3). In that sense, the image of the dead body is not only about what is depicted, but about the politics of production, viewing, and consumption of the global dead.

This wide-ranging visual politics literature seeks to question the often taken-for-granted status of images by highlighting the ways in which they are political. As the literature discussed in the previous paragraph all notes, the image and its construction, reproduction, and dissemination all shed light on how we understand questions of agency in world politics. As Roland Bleiker notes, "making something visible is not necessarily positive. Visibility can also entrench existing political patterns" (2018, 22). Complicating the issue of visual images is part of my task in this book, then. In this vein, this book methodologically follows Gabi Schlag's approach to reading images, informed by a combination of iconology and visual discourse analysis, focused on how images are "sites of analysis for understanding how subjectivities and realities are visually constituted" (Schlag 2019, 8). It also follows on Mitchell's injunction that we need a "method that recognizes and embraces both the unreality of images and their operational reality" (Mitchell 2011, xviii), something which I explicate further in this chapter.

The Corpse

Craig Young and Duncan Light refer to the corpse as the complex and neglected form of the body (2012, 145). Thus, despite the recent turn to bodies in IR (Agathangelou 2011; Epstein 2007; Shinko 2010; Wilcox 2014), much less has been said about the corpse. One key exception within the field of IR is Thomas Gregory's work on dead bodies, particularly his focus on the performative dimension of contemporary violent practices via an examination of the Maywand District Murders, and his call to focus not on the legal structures governing the dead but on the destruction of the victims as humans (Gregory 2016).

Outside of the field of IR, there has been some coverage of depictions of the dead in popular culture and popular media. In 2008, a special issue of the journal *Mortality* was devoted to the corpse in contemporary culture, and focused on popular forensic television shows, necrophilia laws, the "living dead," and human remains in museum collections (Bogard 2008; Foltyn 2008). Other approaches have focused on media depictions of death, as in David Campbell's 2004 article "Horrific Blindness," on the disappearance of images of the dead in contemporary media, and how to ethically engage with images of the dead in the face of atrocity. Similarly, his 2007 article "Geopolitics and Visuality: Sighting the Darfur Conflict" focuses on disaster iconography in Africa in the context of genocidal violence and war crimes.

However, on the whole, dead body images remain the exception, invoking extraordinary circumstances and exceptional status. David Campbell (2007) has identified a lack of photographs of dead bodies in coverage of Darfur. He traced media coverage of Darfur in the *Guardian/Observer* news photographs; out of forty-eight photographs published across two years, only one depicted a dead body; this, despite the fact that the very problem being addressed in this time frame was the deaths of thousands of people. That is, death was the matter of the story, yet it was deemed unfit for photographic depiction. Indeed, many news agencies subscribe to ethical codes governing the publication of graphic images. Yet, as this book addresses, the judgment of what counts as too graphic tends to be subjective, as images of the dead are in fact published *in some contexts*. Similarly, when images of the dead are not published, death is still described via words, implying that images can evoke a more affective response than words can, the very reason death images are not shown: yet, paradoxically, the affective response is also the reason that they are shown in the context of some humanitarian crises. Beyond this, as Gabi Schlag (2019, 15) has traced, photographs associated with the death of Osama bin Laden, such as the image of the moment in the Situation Room where the news of his death was shared with those present, can stand in for the documentary evidence that the death photo itself would have otherwise provided to the general public. Thus, there is more to images of the dead than simply those images; they are part of a larger story about what is shown and what is not shown.

Because corpses are not imbued with the vitality we associate with being a qualified member of a political community, they are often considered to be inert subjects. Though this logic is flawed, the corpse does not look back at the viewer, the way other objects of humanitarian images do, such as the starving child or the refugee. This asymmetry disrupts the idea that our vision can be pure and untainted, because that which we look at does not look back, even as our visual cues indicate it is or once was human. There is also an added quality to the photographic image which may imbue the viewing with a particular distancing associated with the medium: even while photographs bring a particular reality to us, they also, by their very medium, imply something that is not immediate to us. In the image, some things are blurred by the intermediaries: the media. Yet the photograph, especially in the context of humanitarian awareness, is designed to be consumed by the audience.

In short, various dead bodies are represented in different ways for a myriad of cultural, social, economic, and political reasons. While the deaths of soldiers are mourned, obsessively counted, they are not seen, except via their national representation: the casket covered by the flag. However, they appear as visualizations via war memorials and monuments, represented by heroic figural statues or monumental representations of loss, such as the Vietnam Veterans Memorial in Washington, DC. The bodies of dead US soldiers have been placed at the very limits of the public's frame of vision, rendered a spectacle precisely because of the rules governing viewing them (Purnell 2018). The deaths of militants, on the other hand, are seen, circulated, and exhibited as evidence of military success. That is, there is a visual politics invoked along with the material human body. The body itself matters in a very material sense, but the ways in which it is visually marked and consumed by the viewer posit the body as such. Seeing the dead body is not simply material fact, but enmeshed in larger stories about how that body is positioned relative to the space around it, how we learn to see bodies in specific ways. As Nisha Shah notes in her materialist approach to weapons, "objects and the people who use and are affected by them emerge as products of an ontology and ethics that makes these objects (and not) others intelligible" (Shah 2017, 83). In this sense, the corpse is not simply a material object, though it is that, but is also enmeshed in a network that narrativizes its existence and how we should interact with it, a framing that is similar for the corpse image as well.

Images of the present dead body, present in a way it should not be, inculcate a visual norm of engagement based on the particular stories told by or alongside the image, especially because dead bodies are not traditionally viewed. Even in a new media culture where images are consumed more than ever, most news outlets do not show photographs of the dead body. They are much more likely to show a variety of about-to-die photos, including ones that presume the deaths of the individual depicted or show them as they are dying (Zelizer 2010). Though debated, these images are considered appropriate for depicting horrific events and atrocities, as anyone who has watched or even heard the debate around the Zapruder film that depicts the JFK assassination can attest.

But photos of dead bodies seem to violate an unsaid norm about our schemas of viewing, and can only be published in very specific instances toward very particular ends. According to the BBC Editorial Guidelines, "images portraying dead and dying humans" are in a category of exceptional images that "should be selected with special care and with editorial justification" ("Stills Photographs and Images" 2016). The practical effect of this is that images of the dead are rarely shown, despite their evidentiary value to testify to an event (a killing) that is itself typically also not shown. The problem with this, of course, is that in the context of war photography, it can make war seem acceptable, "where victims expired gracefully out of sight rather than bled to death" (Taylor 1998, 75). Dead body images have been widely published toward the end of human rights campaigns to counter this, as in the contexts of the Dachau liberation photographs and images taken during the Rwandan genocide (Sliwinski 2011). John Taylor has argued that the "media widely publicize certain experiences as both 'universally' horrible and newsworthy: gruesome, sudden death in accidents, disasters, massacres, murders, disease and war" (Taylor 1998, 2).

Such questions matter because of the larger politics of death in global politics. Indeed, in the al-Kasasbeh case, one of the key points of debate was whether showing the video was providing free advertising for ISIS. As Nesrene Malik (2015) argued, watching the video made the viewer complicit in ISIS terrorism. She writes, "viewing it writes us into the killers' script," emphasizing the production involved in the creation and indeed viewing of the video. Viewing the video then becomes rendered morally equivalent to creating it and to the act depicted within, raising the issue of how deaths are coopted into particular political narratives, in this case of ISIS terrorism, of the legitimacy of airstrikes against ISIS, and so on.

Charlotte Heath-Kelly has examined the anxiety associated with dead body management, in the sense that emergency management becomes a technique of mortality effacement (Heath-Kelly 2016, 36). In this sense, the debate over whether to show the video or whether to watch became itself a performance of anxiety over the presence of death in the public sphere, and the perceived lack of ability of the state to properly manage it. In other words, the corpse, and death more broadly, becomes that which it is difficult for states to account for. As a result, examining the image itself and its regulation and narration can shed light on the political functioning of this anxiety and its larger connections to security.

Conclusions

This chapter has illustrated a theory of obscenity that involves tensions and paradoxes over the *Real*, the taboo, and the politics of visuality. First, I laid out the taboo governing the images of death and dead bodies in contemporary Western politics, noting that graphicness serves a particular political aim, and thus it is worthwhile to examine the circumstances where it is invoked to regulate the viewing or dissemination of dead body images. I will take up examination of this process in the next three chapters.

I also discussed the tensions at play in the role of images, in this case photographs, to show us the *Real,* drawing on Zizek's theorization of the sublime to connect the play of the *Real* and *unreal* to the taboo's invocation of the twin emotions of desire and disgust, Freud's idea of the taboo as both the unclean and the sacred. I noted that the very idea of the sacred, drawing on the *Bilderverbot,* invokes something which cannot be represented, and indeed an ethical notion that it should not be represented. This disjuncture in representation becomes paradoxical when we are told that images can give us access to a reality depicted therein. In other words, what counts as obscene may be that which is *too real*, and thus unrepresentable, making certain images themselves disruptive. Thus, the framing of the obscene becomes a way to encounter our fears through their regulation, a process I trace more closely in Chapter 3 with regard to ISIS beheadings and the management of the taboo governing bodily integrity.

This chapter also examined the idea of regulation more closely using the example of the trigger warning, which functions to regulate images by invoking their absence, something which we see in the al-Kasasbeh story I started the chapter with, and in the discussion of TMZ's release of images of burning bodies in Fallujah. Such framing invokes the idea of obscenity to tell the viewer he or she does not even need to see certain things to understand them: invoking a particular politics of the absent spectacle. As I have illustrated here, graphicness serves a particular political aim. Invoking the idea of obscenity draws on a series of assumptions about an audience both constructed and reinforced by the invocation of the term. This serves the function of securitization, which can tell a story of which bodies need to be governed, managed, and secured.

Throughout this chapter, which sought to excavate the complex functioning of an obscenity norm, I relied on a particular understanding of Western identity, a thread which carries on throughout the rest of the book. Examining obscenity allows us to focus in on the relationship between norms and taboos and the identities needed to sustain particular conceptions of the "we" that is at stake in such viewing. The remainder of the book lays out what this regulation of obscenity looks like in specific cases to ask what we choose to be horrified by, and how this constructs and sustains particular political communities. Each of the next three chapters takes up one main component of what I have discussed here in this chapter: the image ban (Chapter 3), the securitization of images (Chapter 4), and the *Real* (Chapter 5). While these facets are inherently connected, focusing on one component helps demonstrate how the obscenity norm is applied inconsistently across cases and allows me to focus on the way in which this norm is invoked via the framing of images.

3 | The Visual Politics of ISIS Beheadings

Beheadings have reached the level of visual icon in the modern era, synonymous with terrorism as a result of ISIS propaganda films. Yet there is also a larger visual politics of such beheadings. This chapter examines a double paradox with regard to ISIS and fear: first, that ISIS beheadings are a spectacle, while at the same time, there exists an image ban on viewing these images, and second, that ISIS is both inherently known to us as a threat, yet also fundamentally unknowable. I use the framing of the *Bilderverbot*, the secularized image ban of biblical origin that I introduced in Chapter 2, to examine how beheadings are represented as unrepresentable, and how this paradox enters into normalcy. This discussion of the image ban draws on Freudian theory related to the taboo and castration, and following from this, Slavoj Zizek's theorizations of desire in such an encounter. Zizek has traced the paradoxical sentiment of being ashamed when one desires something considered unworthy of one's desire, and this chapter seeks to get at the play of desire and disgust related to how ISIS beheadings are framed, capturing this contradictory simultaneity.

In other words, while this chapter is framed on the larger politics of fear related to ISIS beheadings, it is in fact not really about ISIS beheadings at all, but rather about the visual regulation of the obscene beheading image. In the previous chapter, I traced three main components of the concept of obscenity that frames this book: the question of what counts as *real* in the context of images that depict horrific violence, the functioning of regulation of images via the image ban or trigger warnings, and the way in which images of the dead become a matter of security. This chapter focuses specifically on the image ban, and how it is invoked in the discourse surrounding beheading images.

The media, and particularly cable news, commonly instructs observers how to approach and respond to images and videos of ISIS beheadings and killings, telling them to be disturbed and afraid and to take on a particular emotional orientation to the acts depicted. Media outlets tell viewers that they must rely on privileged witnesses to interpret these visuals, to avoid the emotional disturbance of actually viewing them themselves (Auchter 2016a): see, for example, Fox News anchor Shepard Smith on the video of the death of Jordanian pilot Moaz al-Kasasbeh:

I'm going to tell you about it, all of it, every bit of it . . . I watched it over the last hour, not because I wanted to. I absolutely did not. I watched it because I felt like those of you who want to know what's on it, but don't want to watch it or be subjected to some sort of gruesome descriptive adjectives, can get the information. (Hollander 2015)

The media's self-imposed image ban, and its instructions to the public to do the same, draws on the notion that dead body display is taboo. As John Taylor (1998, 2) has noted, "there is a consensus on horror in the West concerning the decay and dismemberment of the body." He traces the way this manifests in the field of photojournalism in the injunction against depicting photographs of corpses, one instantiation of the regulatory mechanism of the taboo.

As exhibited in media injunctions against watching ISIS beheading videos, fear is taken for granted precisely because we are told that we don't even have to see these images in order for them to have a particular political function. Though I suspect that the reader is likely familiar with the larger sense of the taboo nature of these images, I offer here a few exemplary statements to illustrate this idea of the image ban as norm, and the corresponding "we watch it so you don't have to" statements: Andrew O'Hehir (2014), writing in *Salon:* "I have watched one of these videos (the Sotloff one) all the way through. I'm not proud of it and do not recommend the experience"; Ian Tuttle (2014), writing for the *National Review:* "beheading has assumed a much-deserved taboo. Call it moral progress if you like: In the West, we no longer accept as permissible rending a human being in twain"; and James Ball (2014), explaining why *The Guardian* chose not to show the beheading video of James Foley, wrote: "Social networks are banning users who share the footage. Newspapers are facing opprobrium for the choices they make in showing stills or parts of the video." There is something interesting in this language about Western sensibilities related to beheading videos, as well.

Discussions of beheading images and their wider impact aren't based on "what we actually see, but in large part on what we are told by leaders and experts that we are shown" (Friis 2015, 741). The avoidance of disturbance is carefully cultivated within a discourse of what we should fear, or rather, what we already do fear, invoking the natural dimension of a fear associated with viewing. We are instructed to fear the spectacle of the beheading precisely because it is visually regulated, invoking fears of the unknown and unknowable, and the inhumane. But who are the agents of this disciplinary move? A facile answer might be the media, and they do play a significant role in framing these images. As one example, *Wired* magazine has traced the very real work carried out by workers handling "content moderation," specifically the removal of obscene images from social media, apps, and cloud storage: more than 100,000 people, which is more than the total headcount of Google and Facebook combined (Chen 2014). Media outlets every day make decisions about what images to publish and the stories that accompany them. Yet this would be missing the more complex dynamics of the ocular and spectacular politics of beheading images, which come into being with regard to a particular viewer and audience. In this politics of viewing, there is an interrelationship between the media and the viewer that reinforces the image ban: the media both shapes and reflects the public. As one example, in polls at the height of the release of ISIS beheading videos, a majority of Americans did not think people should watch them (Schwartz 2014). The "we" I refer to then is the imputed Western audience: those for whom fear of ISIS has become naturalized through the singular iconography of beheadings.

Beheading videos are not themselves anything new, yet with regard to discussions of ISIS, these acts are presumed to exceed the given excesses of war, in the sense that that they cannot be fundamentally understood or even visualized. As CNN national security analyst Juliette Kayyem (2015) suggests of airing killings on television, "I have never watched an ISIS beheading film. I know what they are. And so do viewers. We may not be able to stop violence in our nation or the world, but we can at least refuse to play in these murder games": Statements like this demonstrate that images and videos of beheadings and related ISIS acts are taboo for viewing, even as they are rendered a spectacle for our consumption.

What comes to be assumed in this juxtaposition of visualities is the fear of ISIS: it is unknowable, uncivilized, yet we *know* we should be afraid, as invoked in the CNN analyst's quotation. The aim, here, is not to explore what the effects of such fears might be, but rather to ask what is at stake in posing the fear question in relation to an injunction against watching in the first place. More specifically, what are the politics that emerges in *claims* regarding the self-evident effects of the fears engendered by representations of dismemberment that are not to be viewed? As Ulrich Baer (2005, 87) has described, the photograph can "make the viewer aware of a dimension of reality that is at once indisputably 'there' yet cannot be perceived." For Baer, whose focus is on trauma and witnessing, this exhumes the problem of witnessing itself, which seeks to reconcile knowing and seeing. For Baer, such a reconciliation is impossible in a context like that of the Holocaust, where the victims are themselves radically alienated from their own experiences (Baer 2005, 89). Similar questions arise in the present context, in the sense that ISIS beheading videos are presumed to present us with the fear of something, even when (and precisely because) no one should see or know it. What is the politics of this fear? What must be assumed prima facie so as to fear an unseen image, even as we envision ourselves as witnesses of the atrocities supposed to be depicted therein? In what way have we been made to be radically alienated from our own experiences, our own histories, in the context of such a doxology of fear?

Beheadings and the Visual Taboo

The Real/the Fake

While the main focus of this chapter is the image ban, the visual regulation of beheading images, it bears contextualizing the beheading image as a wider cultural icon more substantively first. Despite the positing of ISIS's beheading tactic as unique, posing with decapitated heads is not new. There is a long history of beheading as a cultural practice (Janes 2005), and it was a popular practice among Aztec warriors to decapitate conquered enemies (Baquedano and Graulich 1993). The French guillotine was one among many cases of executions carried out by beheading, and Saudi Arabia still uses this tactic, with a long, curved sword in a public square. This also fits with a larger history of dismemberment and the body part as souvenir, including the way American soldiers in the Vietnam War took enemy heads and body parts home as souvenirs (Sledge 2005). A famous photo from *LIFE* magazine from World War II depicts a Japanese head impaled on the end of an American tank (Cosgrove 2014). More recently, beheading has become a tactic of Mexican cartels, with more than a hundred beheadings annually, and specific targeting of police (Bunker, Campbell, and Bunker 2010).

During the early days of the war in Iraq, the videos of journalist Daniel Pearl, beheaded in Pakistan by an Al-Qaeda-affiliated group, and Nicholas Berg's decapitation by Al-Qaeda, said to have been carried out personally by Abu Musab Al-Zarqawi, sparked debate about the gruesome nature of not only this tactic, but of the videotape itself that depicted it, and connected beheading to terrorism in an iconic and decisive manner (Zech and Kelly 2015). James Wright-Foley's beheading was the first video released that brought ISIS to global attention. The United Kingdom's Metropolitan Police quickly declared it a crime to view or circulate the James-Wright Foley beheading video (Halliday 2014). That is, the images themselves were (literally) policed, and the very act of looking was criminalized. The vulnerability of the body was itself considered too obscene to be viewed, the liminal space between life and death was made hypervisible by the video footage, and the law was an attempt to re-secure the human body from these disturbing visuals. Not only is viewing prohibited, but rather one is seen as participating in the act of the death if one recirculates the image, rather than raising awareness of the act itself, a departure from many of the understandings of why images of atrocity are circulated and viewed. Ultimately, as Adam Taylor (2014) notes in describing how beheading has changed since Daniel Pearl in that we are no longer surprised: "[G]iven the ethos of the Islamic State and the scores of journalists who had gone missing in Syria, something like this always seemed possible." That is, ISIS becomes naturalized as a group that carries out unspeakable violence, that has always had the potential to do so even before it did. After the initial ISIS beheading videos were released in 2014, political officials immediately began to comment on this type of violence. They used phrases such as "barbaric," "repulsive," and "uniquely evil" (Friis 2015, 735). This terminology is linked to the tactics they use, not their political goals or even their religious radicalism.

The head bears symbolic value in the context of being the location of the brain and the capacity for thought which characterizes most anthropocentrism. The head was long revered for being the "seat of wisdom and consciousness" and many cultures believed "it must be connected to the body for the soul to pass into the next life … the head is also the only body part which, when removed, can be easily identified as belonging to that person" (Jones 2005, 2). Indeed, dissection was for a long time considered forbidden because of the notion that the soul would later join the body, and if it was incomplete or disaggregated, it would disrupt this, still a lingering belief in some religious traditions that prohibit autopsy. "Criminals were sometimes sentenced to dissection as an extra layer of punishment after their execution, thus condemning them in both life and afterlife" (Lovejoy 2013b). Taking it apart and rendering that disaggregation hyper-visible through the taking and circulation of photographs is an effort to strip the body of its symbolic potential to be resurrected in any sense, spiritual or otherwise, which is why we often see dismemberment of enemy bodies in war. That is, beheading invokes dismemberment more broadly as well, which brings up narratives of forensics, of body parts as evidence, that testifies to a particular story by physically piecing together the material body, and as an act drawing attention to the fragility of the body itself, wherein the dismembered body is considered obscene in its incompleteness: the anti-body that is disturbing to our own perceptions of the inviolability of our own bodies, our own material frameworks.

Additionally, beheading disrupts the visual notion of personhood typically associated with the face. As Andreja Zevnik has noted:

In a world driven by representation and modes of visibility, the face is commonly an image assigned to a subject. It is the material side of subjectivity, a medium through which the subject is read and inscribed into a larger social field. Face is also a surface upon which practice of knowing aligns with the practice of seeing. These two governing practices, when placed together, produce evidence for the existence of worldly phenomena. (Zevnik 2016, 122)

She goes on to note that the face follows a form of production that "turns a person into a visible political subject" (Zevnik 2016, 123). The face then is not only the locus for identity and recognition, but this identity and recognition is how we assume our place in the world. This function acts to delimit membership in political communities to that which is visible in particular ways. As a result of this, the face is often what makes severed heads so captivating: Frances Larson (2014, 8) describes the dead human face as a "siren: dangerous but irresistible."

If this is the case, recognition of the face on the severed head, or even of the face as a human face with human features, coupled with the anonymity of the body, is symbolic of the human fear of material existence without reference to a particular community.

As David Brooks (2014: A27) details, the "monstrous" way the killing of Foley and Sotloff took place arouses a "strong visceral response." He asks, "Why does separating a head with a knife feel different from a shooting, or a bombing?" and provides several answers to the question. First, beheading allows ISIS to "deny the slightest acknowledgement of our common humanity" and allows them to terrorize and bully. This is ironic in some sense, because beheadings tear us down to our common material frameworks and invoke our common human vulnerabilities, meaning our common humanity is precisely why beheadings are so disturbing to us. Second, the desire to look and the taboo against looking makes us confront this disturbing desire within ourselves to watch something gruesome. But it is his third reason that is the most salient here, perhaps. Describing it as a "moral revulsion," he examines how beheading is more than a regular crime of injury and is a physical indignity more like "rape, castration or cannibalism." As he notes, "it is a defacement of something sacred that should be inviolable."

This follows with the most common theme in scholarly analysis of beheading: that it is a tactic used precisely because of the disturbance it cultivates, yet decapitation is also invoked as a metaphor cleansed of this disturbance in scholarship in IR. Discussions of drone strikes against terrorist leaders often refer to these tactics as "decapitation strikes," for example (Brooks 2016). Several scholars have explored whether decapitation strikes work, both invoking the symbolism of beheadings, while positing the tactic as simply an ethically neutral military strategy (Jordan 2009; Johnston 2012; Price 2012). Indeed, in Patrick Johnston's aptly named "Does Decapitation Work," he never explores or explains the phrase decapitation, but rather invokes it as if we are already a knowing audience who gets the metaphor. He never once mentions taking out terrorist leaders as cutting off the head of the organization – indeed, a search for the word "head" in the article yields only footnotes to other articles with that word in the title.

While there exists what might be referred to as a "beheading discourse," the positing of a novelty and uniqueness associated with ISIS's brand of such discourse often emphasizes the use of sophisticated technology. Beheading videos seemed to discursively construct the difference between ISIS as the "j.v. team" and ISIS as significant national security threat (Sinha 2015). Indeed, there is a marked shift between the rhetoric before and after the beheadings. Before, ISIS was depicted as a humanitarian issue, and after, as a threat to national security, despite the fact that its characteristics had not changed much (Friis 2015, 734). ISIS beheading videos have drawn on slick Hollywood-style production as they seek to circulate their films to the masses, yet as I noted in Chapter 2, such technological production of images can blur the lines of whether an image is real. Indeed, a 2014 ISIS propaganda film in which twenty-two Syrian soldiers were beheaded took numerous takes across four to six hours, evident by changes in light and shadows across time, and used film equipment estimated to cost more than $200,000 USD. Researchers who have analyzed the film suggested that it likely involved a producer, director, and editor, and the type of story boards used in traditional filmmaking (Bajekal 2014). In short, the technological and mediated dimension of images has put into question the reliability of photographic images as evidence or providing access to a particular truth.

Nowhere is this more salient than in the circulation of fake beheading images, which have recurred across numerous cases, from the attempted coup in Turkey (Osborne 2016) to the image of a drug cartel beheading in Mexico being circulated as proof of Assad's brutality in Syria (Shelton 2012). These fake images are often used to add emotional impact to larger discussions about threat and security. In 2004, a beheading video was broadcast that showed a close-up of a man being beheaded under the title "Abu Musab al-Zarqawi Slaughters an American." The video, showing Benjamin Vanderford as the beheading victim making a statement about the need for the United States to leave Iraq, with images of disfigured people in Iraq in the background and a soundtrack of Koranic music, was a fake. Vanderford created it as stunt to draw attention to his campaign for a local city election. When the fake nature of the video was revealed, he noted that he also created it to draw attention to the ease of faking videos in the technological age ("American Admits" 2004).

In 2019, as another example, amid debates about the return of Shamima Begum, a UK citizen who had left to join ISIS in Syria as a teenager, a photo was circulated on social media that purported to show Begum beheading an ISIS captive in 2015 (Shaw 2019). While this photo was debunked, as the timing did not line up and the image in fact depicted a young boy carrying out the beheading, the fake beheading image formed part of the discourse of threat associated with the return of radicalized British citizens from Syria and Iraq, drawing on the deep emotion associated with the iconography of beheadings, and the way this emotion is linked to government counter-terrorism policy.

The spectacle of the fake beheading image, disseminated as a fake image, has also been used to make political statements. In 2017, a photograph of American comedian Kathy Griffin holding a fake severed head of Donald Trump was posted to the entertainment website TMZ ("Kathy Griffin Beheads" 2017). The fake head was dripping with blood and was labeled as "gory," "edgy," and "shock-cking" (Puente 2017). Much of the response emulated this same discourse, with *Variety* magazine proclaiming the image too obscene to show (Rubin et al. 2017), and many news programs blurred the Trump mask when showing the image (Ali 2017).[1] However, Lauren Duca (2017) refers to this response as "performative outrage," noting that while Griffin's apology acknowledged that she had crossed the line, it was unclear in the contemporary political context just where the line actually was. In other words, such a politics emulates a politics of shock, when it may in fact be a politics of horror. It also raises the question I examined in the previous chapter about the existence of the *Real* and its connection to the obscenity norm. Still, news organizations struggled with how to report on the story and whether to show the image in much the same way they would have for an authentic beheading image that actually depicted someone's death and someone's dead body. In this sense, there was disagreement over whether merely invoking the iconography of beheading was sufficient to render the image obscene, as opposed to its *real* depiction of a dead body, since the Kathy Griffin images depicted the former but not the latter.

Other fake beheading images emerged as well in the context of the figure of Trump, including the cover of *Der Spiegel* showing Donald

[1] One of the interesting things about the *Variety* story is that it puts Trump's name in quotation marks, to denote that it was not the *real* Trump, but it does not put beheading in quotation marks to denote that it was not actually a beheading either. In other stories, it is beheading placed in quotation marks (Puente 2017). There was clearly a bit of a struggle as to how to define this case by various reporters relative to its nature as a fake image.

Figure 3.1 Cover of *Der Spiegel* magazine, April 2017, depicting US President Donald Trump beheading the Statue of Liberty, © DER SPIEGEL 6/2017

Trump beheading the Statue of Liberty (Figure 3.1), and websites such as Zazzle selling t-shirts showing Donald Trump as Perseus holding the severed head of Hillary Clinton as Medusa. These images draw on the deep iconography associated with beheadings, playing with the dynamics of the taboo. The *Der Spiegel* cover generated a lot of controversy when it was published, precisely because it called forth a comparison between Trump and ISIS, which is a good indication of how inextricably linked ISIS and beheadings have become. The artist of the image, Edel Rodriguez, an American political refugee from Cuba, noted that he purposefully made the comparison between Trump and ISIS because both are extremists (Borchers 2017). The *New York Daily News* had also published a cartoon showing Trump beheading the Statue of Liberty, though less gory, in 2015, after Trump's initial comments about the so-called "Muslim Ban" (Borchers 2017). While these beheading images are all fake, they all operate on the enactment and reinforcement of the beheading taboo, while also emphasizing the significance of the performance of shock, which plays a role in the dynamics of ISIS beheadings as well.

The Image Ban

This section uses the framing of the *Bilderverbot,* the secularized image ban of biblical origin, to examine how beheadings are represented as unrepresentable, and how this paradox enters into normalcy. This discussion of the image ban draws on Freudian theory related to the taboo and castration, and following from this, Slavoj Zizek's theorizations of desire in such an encounter. Zizek, for example, has argued that desire is constituted by its very repression (1989, 13). There is a question of desire then related to the creation of the spectacle around a double absence: the absence of the head (the act of beheading itself) and the absence of its image (related to the *Bilderverbot*). Zizek has traced the paradoxical sentiment of being ashamed when one desires something considered unworthy of one's desire, and this chapter seeks to get at the play of desire and disgust related to how ISIS beheadings are framed, capturing this contradictory simultaneity.

Fear of ISIS comes to be taken for granted in the way beheading images are depicted as an un-shown and un-showable spectacle. The appropriate focus then is not on the history of beheadings or even the act of beheading(s), but rather on the imagined/invoked image of the severed head, as a way to examine the work that the image ban does to generate and maintain the naturalness of an embodied fear. It demonstrates the relation between the image ban and the naturalization of an embodied fear by telling the story of two beheadings: one of an Iraqi head and one of a Western one. The first is shown but not seen, and the latter is seen but not shown. A micro-level examination of the severed head image allows these stories to emerge. The first account, concerning the severed head of an Iraqi man working as an informant for American soldiers, allows for an examination of how beheadings are often depicted in the language of horror, or as an example of "body horror." In this story, the audience never learns the name of the man who was beheaded, and whose severed head is rendered background to a story of the excesses of war. The second story, the story of ISIS beheadings, is a different story: one in which the severed head has become a fact of international politics, something doxic in which fear of ISIS beheadings is taken for granted. In this story, numerous names of those beheaded could be said that have been discussed in Western media accounts, but I explore the general notion of the Western severed head rather than one specific image. That is, the story isn't the story of *a* Western beheading, but of *the* Western beheading, as a category. It is the story of the absent spectacle generated around this severed head.

Telling these two stories together is important because the story of the severed head is always instead a set of stories about how the unrepresentability of the severed head is represented. It is also the case that most examinations of taboo focus on those instances when the image is shown, such as pornography, but there is more to the visual politics of images than simply whether so-called obscene images are shown or not. That is, rather than focus on the transgression of the taboo, I seek to explore the repression of the image that constitutes the taboo, which is a way of representing the image by way of its denial.

Images are regulated by the mechanism of the taboo, and more specifically, the *Bilderverbot*, the image ban. In what way is the argument for the *Bilderverbot*, the image ban, the notion that "we must represent this for you because it cannot be represented," in *itself* represented as something self-evident? To what degree does this self-evidence tell us something about the naturalization of fear as the horizon against which we should study ISIS? As noted in the previous chapter, the image ban functions to invoke the very idea of representation of the unrepresentable. While there are various mechanisms through which this occurs, such as the framing of trigger warnings, the focus is on the need to tell an important story through images, yet this is juxtaposed with the inadequacy of the representation due to the sacred identity of the transcendent.

Questions of trauma and representation come to the fore in any discussion of ISIS beheadings. What was generated by the acts themselves was a certain type of trauma that then became an unnamable thing, "unimaginable" and "inexplicable." And yet, as is true of other traumas, there remains a paradox inherent: that which is unspeakable must also be referred to as such. In this specific instance, it is the reason why beheadings stipulated as unwatchable continue to be situated as spectacular (because the spectacle is itself constructed via both our horror and our fascination, simultaneously). That is, even as we are fascinated, such violence is posited as uniquely unique as a means to reinforce the taboo of viewing. For example, there were wide discussions about not watching ISIS beheading videos (Schwartz 2014; Kayyem 2015; Larson 2015a; Snyder 2015), and even British Prince Charles chimed in in 2014 to suggest that the general public should not watch ISIS beheading videos (Mitchell 2014).

Relatedly, ISIS beheadings more broadly have been described by media outlets, policymakers, and even a UN Security Council resolution as being uniquely unique. See, for example, Douglas Ollivant's (2014) argument that "the Islamic State poses a unique threat" and that it is "in a category all their own," John Kerry's (2014) description of ISIS as "a profound and unique threat to the entire world," and the text of UN Security Council Resolution 2249, which refers to ISIS as "an unprecedented threat to international peace and security." Similarly, Zech and Kelly (2015) say that beheading has "served to distinguish its 'brand' of violence from others in the global jihadi struggle for hearts and minds." The distinction here is the fact that the beheadings become spectacles. This suggests that the media's *posited* genealogy of beheadings is more important than the actual history of the phenomenon. What identifies ISIS with horror is a staging of the same horror, in both a dramaturgical sense and, because it is filmic, as a spectacle. Indeed, as David Campbell has noted, we end up producing the imagery of ISIS, because the (beheading) images that become iconic have been cut from an original video with the larger ISIS-produced narrative and context removed: we ourselves have a performative part in constructing the threat of the visual icon (Campbell 2016). As Simone Moline Friis (2015, 741) notes, it isn't even necessary to view the images, because our perception of them is colored by what we are told by experts that we should see in them. In other words, because there can be no image of the unimaginable, fear of ISIS is taken as a given in the *Bilderverbot*; that is, in the act of un-imaging the images ISIS releases.

All of these features of the *Bilderverbot* gesture to its status as a visual taboo. As Freud details, the taboo has two correlative meanings: first, it is the sacred, and second, it is the "uncanny, dangerous, forbidden, unclean" (Freud 1919, 30). I have spoken here of beheading, and more specifically, of the severed head, as taboo. It is taboo precisely because the human body is a sacred object (by virtue of being a subject), and because the severed head represents the uncanniness of an encounter with not only one's own mortality but also the physical lack. Horror is not just about death, but about dismemberment and disfigurement, which takes its historical form in the severed head of Medusa and continues in the contemporary form in the suicide bomber. The decapitated head offends the "ontological dignity of the singular body" (Cavarero 2009, 8), and as a result, implies a specific relationship between materiality and visuality. This is also the notion of the void: what the *Bilderverbot* invokes is a lack, something missing, which is precisely why the image would be horrifying to us. That is, the beheading image is considered obscene because it is the icon of the disruption of bodily integrity,[2] yet there is both a material and a visual component here. Freud has referred to beheading as "a symbolic substitute for castrating" (1918, 207), and in his essay *Medusa's Head* also equates decapitation with castration, arguing that "the terror of Medusa is thus a terror of castration that is linked to the sight of something" (Freud 1997, 264). At the same time, Freud elaborates that turning stiff with terror – the castration moment associated with dismemberment – also constitutes what he refers to as the "stiffening reassurance of possession." Thus, there is a dialectic in the moment of terror, which is simultaneously terrifying and compensatory (the reassurance that one has not been castrated). Similarly, Neil Hertz (1983), reading Victor Hugo through Freud, examines the epistemological anxiety associated with the disbelief of the figure of Medusa, and by extension, of the decapitated head. He traces how, via the decapitated head, a political threat and loss comes to be experienced as a *sexual* one.

Freud (1919, 61) has argued that "the taboo upon the dead arises, like the others, from the contrast between conscious pain and

---

[2] The focus on decapitation also privileges the equation of the head with the seat of rationality and the locus of visual recognition, focused on the face (Edkins 2013). As Andreja Zevnik has noted, "in a world driven by representation and modes of visibility, the face is commonly an image assigned to a subject. It is the material side of subjectivity, a medium through which the subject is read and inscribed into a larger social field. Face is also a surface upon which practice of knowing aligns with the practice of seeing" (Zevnik 2016, 122). The head also bears symbolic value in the context of being the location of the brain and the capacity for thought which characterizes most anthropocentrism.

unconscious satisfaction over the death that has occurred." He goes on to note that taboos arise from "fear of temptation." The prohibition against touching or viewing, which he sees as the expression of the taboo, is related to the double meaning of the taboo: as both unclean and sacred (Freud 1919, 66–7). The dangerous nature of images of beheadings, as noted in the media example earlier, is exemplary of what Freud (1999, 72) calls the "contagious" character of the taboo: if the desire is gratified, it will ignite the same desire in others, so stopping it is the regulatory mechanism of the taboo. Following Fredric Jameson's arguments about the visual, John Taylor (1998, 17) similarly notes that: "the visual is essentially pornographic, which is to say that it has its end in rapt, mindless fascination." The *Bilderverbot*, the idea that certain images should not be viewed, generates a taboo image that we desire to see, precisely because it cannot be represented. If we are fascinated by ISIS, it is because of what has come to be taken for granted as given in the way that a specific "we" should and do relate to its actions. Such taken-for-grantedness relies on a specific visual asymmetry that invokes both danger and desire as a way to regulate the beheading images. The following two sections tell the story of two different positings of danger and desire, of two different regulations of beheading images.

How War Can Make Horror Seem Normal: The Story of an Iraqi Severed Head

In 2008, two American soldiers posed for a photograph with a decapitated head. The head belonged to an Iraqi man who had given information to the Americans, and who was killed by militants in retaliation for this collaboration. When American soldiers found the head, left as a message to potential collaborators, they brought it back to their base and posed for photographs with it. The image, taken by photographer Danfung Dennis, actually depicts the moment when the two American soldiers are posing for a photograph that is being taken by someone else, presumably another soldier, and for personal rather than documentary purposes. It is a photograph of the moment of yet another separate photograph of posing with a severed head. Dennis describes the circumstances surrounding the photograph:

I was embedded with a U.S. Army unit north of Baghdad in 2008 at the height of the violence. During a patrol, the unit came across a decapitated head sitting on a market stall with a note on the forehead that read: "This is what happens if you work with the Americans". The young soldiers playfully packed up the head, took it back to base, and then took pictures with it – holding it up and grinning with their war trophy. (Siegel 2012)

Since the troops were taking pictures, no one thought it was unusual that Dennis was also taking photographs.

One soldier has a big grin on his face as he holds the severed head upright in the photograph. He looks directly at the other photographer, so he does not meet the gaze of the viewer of this photograph. The severed head is gory. The eyes are closed, but the face is bloodied. At first, it is not distinguishable as a disembodied head because of the way it is placed, but as one looks further, the realization is made that this is simply a head without a body attached. The second soldier in the photograph smiles and looks at the head, as if excited about the actions of his fellow soldier. Presumably this man, the man who was beheaded, knew the risk he was taking in collaborating with Americans. But he likely could not predict the way his decapitated head would be visually consumed as a trophy of the conflict.

Dennis, the photographer, sought to publish the image in a variety of outlets, but by some it was deemed too obscene to print. As he details, "I sent those pictures back to *Newsweek*, but at the time they decided not to publish them because they felt they were too incendiary. So, these types of acts are more commonplace than we think" (Siegel 2012). Ultimately, the image was published with a story in *Rolling Stone* magazine, precisely in the framework of it not being obscene. It is not systematically analyzed as part of the story in the magazine, nor is it presented as something entirely out of the norm of the other photographs of soldiers that are part of the same story. In the *Rolling Stone* story very little is said about the circumstances surrounding the generation of the image. It simply appears under the sub-headline "the cost of collaboration," and the only mention of the head is the following description:

Violence in Iraq is on the rise again – and much of it is aimed at the Awakening, Sunni fighters who have abandoned Al Qaeda and sided with the Americans. At night, two US soldiers pose with the severed head of an Awakening member – a US ally – who was decapitated by Al Qaeda. (The soldiers were later reprimanded for their behavior.) The killing was intended to send a clear warning: Those who aid the Americans are marked for death.

Nothing is said about Al Qaeda's choice to behead the collaborator. It is simply described as a "killing," and there is no reference to dismemberment. The beheading becomes an act that is normalized in the wider context of the violence. The act of posing with the head, of constructing the image of two US soldiers posing with a decapitated head, is normalized in the context of the larger story itself: of the difficulty of the fight in Iraq when the US military arms groups who have previously fought with the militants. It is a warning story about arming former insurgents.

This severed head image, then, was published as background to a larger story concerning the psychological excesses of war and its effects on the American soldier. The headline of one of the news stories about this image, which contains an interview with Danfung Dennis, is: "How War Can Make Dehumanizing and Horrific Events Seem Normal." This headline places the photograph within a narrative about the psychological effects of war on soldiers, but it also says something about the visual consumption of such images by everyone else. As Francois Debrix has argued, the fragmented bodies of others have "become normal, almost expected, and possible ordinary realities" in the war-on-terror (Debrix 2017, 2). This is particularly the case when it comes to fragmented Iraqi bodies. Indeed, there has been very little reporting in the West about ISIS beheadings of Iraqis, which seem to number in the hundreds if not thousands (see Tomson 2017 for one exemplary case).

This particular Iraqi severed head becomes an image in the background, a taken-for-granted part of the "normal" yet "extraordinary" excesses associated with war. This is a story of twin productions: of the production of the head itself (the beheading), and of the visual production of images of this head that reached the American viewer when the head was taken to an American military encampment, photographed, and then circulated in Western media. This beheading, however, was one whose image was published as just obscene enough to describe the psychological effects of war on the American soldier, but not obscene enough to occasion the ensuing taboo.

As I have noted, the photo remained largely invisible at first because it was deemed too obscene, and later because it was considered not obscene enough to merit substantive attention. This paradox of first being treated as too horrific and then normalized as unworthy of horror is linked to the paradoxical construction of the taboo itself. The taboo is both sacred and profane, a paradox that Agamben has referred to as the "ambivalence of the sacred" (Agamben 1998, 75). Indeed, the entire point of Agamben's *homo sacer* is the idea that *sacer* is both sacred and damned, which he associates with the idea of the taboo (Agamben 1998). In other words, the contradictory construct is already built into each register. It is through this paradox that the image is transformed from taboo to "merely" body horror. Precisely because the image is not the story after all, at least not in the way the story is told, the image loses its sacred/profane (taboo) quality.

The story then is one where war becomes simply a theater of encounters with beheadings, one which fundamentally changes soldiers through these visual encounters, and one which is fundamentally unknowable to the rest of us. Even Danfung Dennis, the photographer, situates the image within this narrative, in the earlier quotation where he refers to this as "commonplace" and in the following:

I think it's hard for most people to comprehend the complete absurdity and the horrific nature of war. It's hard to imagine just how absurd these events are, and when they do happen, there are no rules on how one acts. Moral codes break down in these horrific situations. (Siegel 2012)

The image of this head then is just obscene enough to give the Western viewer a window into a world where this image is construed as less-than-obscene. This is the politics of transformative identification of the Iraqi severed head from taboo into the realm of "mere" body horror. The following section traces the visual and rhetorical move from the severed head as body horror to the severed head as fact of international politics.

Watching the Absent Spectacle: The Story of ISIS and Severed Heads

The second account of decapitation to be covered here concerns moments when ISIS beheaded Western captives, and these beheadings enter into the realm of spectacle by way of their absence from vision. This story is about the absent spectacle generated by the image ban and how it relates to a fear of ISIS. Rather than focus on one particular individual victim, I focus on the common story told of the "Western victim of ISIS," whose severed head is too obscene to be viewed. This is because, as a genre, the reported cases of ISIS beheadings actually

introduce a simultaneous mobilization and mitigation of affect in relation to an image that, simultaneously, inaugurate both spectacle and its
contrary: an image ban. ISIS is often characterized as a unique producer
of the beheading spectacle: John Kerry noted that images of the ISIS
beheadings are the "most disturbing, stomach-churning, grotesque
photos ever displayed" ("Kerry Condemns" 2014). As J.M Berger
describes, snuff films have existed, but it took the Internet to widely
distribute them; similarly, Al-Qaeda conducted beheadings and video-
taped them, but it took ISIS to turn them into a spectacle for entertainment. He argues that this is largely on technological grounds, and as
a result of the high-definition format in which the videos were made:
"they didn't just portray a terrorist act; they told a story and reveled in
its brutality" (Berger 2016). This section asks after the politics of this
obscenity, wherein ISIS beheadings are turned into a spectacle which
draws on the desire of the viewer, but the material and visual representations of these acts are so real as to evoke disgust.

The spectacle is an inherent part of the logic of the taboo. Guy
Debord's notion of the spectacle emphasizes that the spectacle escapes
the dialogue of men and is not simply mere gazing. ISIS beheading
images then are not a spectacle because they make beheadings visible
via the production of images, but rather because the beheading is
socially mediated (Debrix 2017) and presents itself as indisputable
and inaccessible (Debord 1983): the ISIS beheading has become simply
a fact of the international. That is, despite the differences in accounts of
the phenomenon of the spectacle as elaborated by various theorists,
common to these are two key features of spectacular politics.

First, the spectacle is not about viewing per se, but is a socially
mediated constitutive process, which in the case of beheadings is
approached through the collective engagement with its taboo character. This follows on the insights of Steve Jones concerning so-called
"horror porn," as he notes that in this genre, the "object is assumed to
be 'real' rather than contrived, the viewer's pleasure and/or disgust
arising from the 'unseen' being put on display ... It is vital to understand the interplay between users in examining such imagery – not only
because an appreciation of context is required in order to construe its
significance, but because the image only comes into meaning in con-
junction with a viewer" (Jones 2010, 125). Amy Louise Wood (2009,
33) traces this same phenomenon with regard to public executions by
telling the story of a woman in attendance at a hanging. The woman

could not take her eyes off of the hanging because: she had come all this way to see it; had to tell her neighbors who were not in attendance about it; have nightmares about it, and to never want to see it again. In this way, the spectacle derives its status from the context in which the image circulates, from the relationship between the spectator and the image. This relationship produces the spectacle as that which presents itself as indisputable.

Second, accounts of the spectacle share an emphasis on desire as a key component in the functioning of the ocular politics under consideration here. The beheading image comes into being related not to the viewer, as we see with the pornography example, but rather to the purported non-viewer, as these images are not shown. Yet, they are seen in spectacular ways. Such spectacular politics is not simply the existence of body horror, but that the taboo, the sacred/uncanny, is rendered viewable. The taboo then invokes the desire/disgust nexus. There is pleasure in the repression of the image, which is a way of representing it by way of its denial. The fact that we desire the transgression of the *Bilderverbot* is part of what sustains it in the first place, whether it is transgressed or not. The desire for something one is not supposed to have is part of what sustains that thing as sacred. In this sense, my focus is not on the transgression of the *Bilderverbot,* but the dynamics of the *Bilderverbot* itself. Because a dynamic of erotism exists surrounding the severed head, this is precisely what allows the invocation of the *Bilderverbot,* which is what allows for the representation of the severed head through its absence and the regulation of its images.

Here it bears probing the story of the Western severed head to explore precisely this relationship between the spectator and the image. More specifically, what is the difference between the ocular politics of the Iraqi severed head discussed in the previous section, and the spectacular politics when the severed head "looks like us"? Francois Debrix has explored this logic in the operation of modern security politics. He has drawn attention to the way in which the killed body of the other and the hundreds of thousands of victims of "our" wars justifies the fall of "our" heroes, mostly Western soldiers. This

reveals that contemporary security politics as well as the logic of terror it supposedly confronts can only conceive of the body as an amalgamation of parts or bits that can be dismantled, dismembered, or disseminated in some cases (for example, when looking at enemy or terrorist bodies) but never when "our" own (Western) bodies and their assumed integrity/unity is at stake. (Debrix 2017, 59)

That is, the story of the spectacle of ISIS beheadings is of a very precise spectacle and a very precise beheading: one that involves a Western victim, and, correlatively, one that is too obscene to be shown, so that it generates the absent spectacle. Perhaps this is because, as Debrix argues, "metaphysical statements about humanity (and about the West as humanity's champion) are conveyed each time IS cuts off a Westerner's head" (Debrix 2017, 93). Beheadings as horror, as Debrix imagines them, are thus a form of unrepresentable violence that is still represented in particular ways.

There is a key component here to the functioning of this ocular politics: desire. In our fear of ISIS, we take for granted that in expressing horror we aren't also aware of or acknowledging the related enjoyment/fascination that coexists within the invocation of the *Bilderverbot*. Simultaneous to the horror of the image is the pleasure of its repression, a compensatory enjoyment built into the spectacle of a horrific and apotropaic image. Indeed, fear itself often invokes this dual desire and disgust, the very reason why the genre of horror film is so popular. Zizek (2008, 131) captures this in his discussion of Lacan's dialectic of desire, where the "paradoxical sentiment of being angry or ashamed at oneself when one desires something that one considers unworthy of one's desire, introduces the character of the taboo."

The curiosity surrounding beheading videos and images that are deemed unwatchable enacts this paradox. As beheading videos have been released, they have in specific instances been widely circulated.[3] People want to see them. After Nicholas Berg was executed in 2004, all of the top ten searches on Internet search engines involved his beheading (Larson 2014, 79). Michael Ignatieff (2004) refers to the desire to look at the taboo images as "terrorism as pornography" in the

---

[3] It is difficult to quantify this, though. Measuring the number of Twitter shares about them is difficult, for example, because Twitter and Facebook and YouTube all took down videos of ISIS beheadings (Newman 2014). Frances Larson, an expert on beheadings, noted that "it's difficult to calculate. But a poll taken in the UK, for example, in August 2014, estimated that 1.2 million people had watched the beheading of James Foley in the few days after it was released. ... A similar poll taken in the United States in November 2014 found that nine percent of those surveyed had watched beheading videos, and a further 23 percent had watched the videos but had stopped just before the death was shown" (Larson 2015b).

following sense: "[A]t first making audiences feel curious and aroused, despite themselves, then ashamed, possibly degraded and finally, perhaps, just indifferent. The audience for this vileness is global." Documenting this desire to look, Ignatieff goes on to describe a specific website that posts beheadings, and so increased its visitor counts from 200,000 to 750,000 after posting one video. Similarly, authors of analytical news pieces explored their own desire/disgust paradoxes with headlines such as "Why I Can't Stop Watching Horrifying ISIS Decapitation Videos," and "ISIS beheadings: Why we're too horrified to watch, too fascinated to turn away." Writing under the former headline for *Wired* magazine, Brianna Snyder commented on her own viewing of ISIS decapitation videos in the following way:

I'd like to say it's not my fault, that a sickness inside me made me watch. That as a writer and editor, knowing about violence and death is, you could say, part of my job. It's my duty to find and face the details. Except my beat is not international terrorism. And it wasn't until I'd seen the screenshots – and the warnings about how graphic the video was – that I started to think about it, what it might look like . . . .I turn my laptop away from my husband, mute the volume, and let the horror make my head go dizzy and my stomach turn upside-down . . . It's hyper-reality and it is devastating . . . I like to think I'm not like the commenters on BestGore – who call murdered women "bitches who deserved it" and LOL at "incompetent" Mexican drug lords who have to switch knives partway through a decapitation because theirs aren't sharp enough to cut through the neck tendons of their victims. But I am like them. I am clicking. I am driving traffic. I am letting the creators of these videos know their headlines are SEO-engineered effectively. I'm part of the problem. Am I "informed"? Am I, like Piers Morgan, enraged beyond reasonable argument? Am I going to enlist in the military? I think not. I'm just scared. (Snyder 2015)

While there is a substantive sense of danger underpinning the fear associated with viewing the severed head, the other part of the *Bilderverbot* is the pleasure. The taboo image/absent spectacle recalls the apotropaic image by way of its absence. It represents what is not to be seen in the form of its ban. This helps explains why the initial response to the beheading image/video is in fact disgust: this disgust enacts the performance of the taboo, with its underlying paradoxical narratives of both fear and desire, particularly when the disgust is turned back on ourselves at the breaking of the taboo. As Slavoj Zizek (2008: lxxiii) has articulated,

Is not the ultimate embodiment of the passion for the Real the option one gets on hard-core porn websites of observing the inside of a vagina from the vantage point of a tiny camera at the top of the penetrating dildo? At this extreme point, a shift occurs: when we get too close to the desired object, erotic fascination turns into disgust at the Real of the bare flesh.

In the play of pleasurable fascination and disturbance, from a certain distance, beheadings are fascinating to us; they lead to increased google searches, image sharing, and mass media coverage. Yet, when we get too close, when we see the mechanisms of production of the spectacle of the beheading, this becomes disturbing in a very embodied sense. We are revolted, not by the beheading itself, but by our proximity to the mechanisms of its creation, its conditions of possibility, which can be productive of fear, as exemplified by Snyder's reflection earlier. In this instance, the beheading functions as the sublime object of ideology, described by Zizek (2008, xlix) as "an object which starts to function as the empirical stand-in for the impossible-noumenal Thing." That is, fear becomes taken for granted precisely because of these twin components: the image ban exists because fear of ISIS is taken for granted, yet it is taken for granted precisely in the naturalization of the sublime object standing in for what is assumed to be the impossible, the unimaginable, the unspeakable. This follows with Zizek's notion that "the subject can enjoy his symptom only in so far as its logic escapes him" (Zizek 1989, 21). In other words, ISIS beheadings are posited as unknowable precisely because in their characterization the desire/disgust paradox functions as the assumed normal.[4]

And yet, the beheading videos *do* in some sense invoke an imputed "unimaginable." Responding to James Foley's beheading on August 20, 2014, US Secretary of State John Kerry said: "[T]here is

---

[4] This does not imply that we know nothing about the beheadings. Indeed, there has been much effort to understand who is carrying them out, alongside ISIS's mechanisms of recruitment and their use of technology. When I use the terminology of beheadings as unknowable, what I mean is that such violence is depicted as destructive of the human, a motivation that purportedly cannot be understood within a Western context posited as superior in values. Francois Debrix has argued something similar, in that the way beheadings are depicted as primitive violence allows the West to orient itself geopolitically, culturally, and morally by deploying "imaginative geographies about what oriental people are and do" (Debrix 2017, 91). This allows for the argument that humanity is what is at stake in ISIS beheadings.

evil in this world and we have all come face to face with it once again. Ugly, savage, inexplicable, nihilistic, and valueless evil." ISIS violence is depicted not only as atrocious, but as fundamentally inexplicable and unexplainable. At the same time, that violence is also invoked as something already-known: a familiar and confirmed threat to humanity. As President Obama explained in a contemporary speech, the beheading of James Wright-Foley was an act of violence that "shocks the conscience of the entire world" (cited in Friis 2015, 735). This implies then that, as Obama noted, there is "no reasoning, no negotiation with this brand of evil" (Friis 2015, 737). This violence is already presumed to shock our conscience, placing ISIS in the realm of not just the inhumane but the *inhuman*. Thus, a paradox emerges: we both know ISIS (and that is why we fear it), yet ISIS's evil is fundamentally unknowable to us (and that is why it is to be feared).

The very notion that we should discuss whether it is appropriate to view ISIS beheading videos already invokes an aura of fear surrounding them. With each beheading video, a spectacle is generated both by ISIS itself, but also by the way that the question of representing "body horror" is debated. Yet each of these spectacles invokes a fear that is presumed to be in place already. ISIS knows the release of the videos will be spectacular, because beheadings are scary, and we know we shouldn't look at certain things, even if we ultimately do, because beheadings are scary. Fear then comes to be taken for granted in the message that ISIS violence must be represented in certain ways. Zizek has detailed a similar process with regard to the wreck of the *Titanic*, which he calls a "kind of petrified forest of enjoyment" (Zizek 1989, 71). He argues that the wreck functions as a sublime object

> elevated to the status of the impossible Thing. And perhaps all the effort to articulate the metaphorical meaning of the Titanic is nothing but an attempt to escape this terrifying impact of the Thing, an attempt to domesticate the Thing by reducing it to its symbolic status, by providing it with a meaning. We usually say that the fascinating presence of a Thing obscures its meaning; here, the opposite is true: the meaning obscures the terrifying impact of its presence. (Zizek 1989, 71)

The same could be said of the beheading image, its own "petrified forest of enjoyment." The meaning of the image is invoked as already known even without looking. This is how the horror of the image is managed: the narrative, the meaning, obscures the image itself, hence my reference to ISIS beheading images as seen but not shown. The invocation of this "already known" character of the images, as Mitchell describes in reference to the Abu Ghraib photos, serves to sustain the narrative of dismissal: "move along, nothing to see here. Or if there is something to see, it is 'already known'" (Mitchell 2011, 118).

This is why prior interpretations of Medusa's head matter. They suggest that what remains spectacular about Medusa is the inherent threat involved in the gaze, and that viewing is itself already dangerous. What is to be viewed is already known as a threat even before it is seen. There is a near-epidemiological fear of watching ISIS beheadings. In that sense, the visual regulation of these images is performed precisely in such a way as to depict them as contagious, as too real. The mimetic taboo, or *Bilderverbot*, is replicated in the discussion of the spectacle generated by ISIS beheading videos. Specifically, this happens when one considers the very definition of a spectacle as something joining the real and the fantastic together in a hyper-visible and yet uncanny way. There is more to the Medusa story, though. The legend of Perseus's beheading of Medusa has been replicated in various art forms, most notably sculpture (Hertz 1983). In many of these representations, Perseus is depicted holding the severed head of Medusa, and wearing the helmet of invisibility and carrying the mirrored shield. Both of these tools enabled him to defeat Medusa: the mirrored shield allowed him to see her reflection without being turned to stone from her gaze, and the helmet allowed him to be invisible to Medusa, so she did not anticipate his attack.

Let us pause for a moment to consider the relationship of visibility here. Medusa is the naturalized threat: simply looking at her is dangerous. Yet, the only way to engage this threat is to participate in a visual paradox: to both look at her without looking at her, while oneself remaining invisible. There must be a double relationship of asymmetry: looking at her without her being able to look back, but looking at her without actually looking at her. So we ensure that there is nothing to see, just as one guarantees that one remains unseen. Indeed, it is precisely the fact that the Medusan head is not *watchable* that renders it disturbing. Cavarero notes that Medusa represents the unwatchability of one's own death, but more than that, the "unwatchability of the spectacle of disfigurement, which the singular body cannot bear" (Cavarero 2009, 8). Here, the *Bilderverbot* functions as an image ban, but this image ban is not total in the context of ISIS beheading videos, as the website hits statistics I cited earlier attest to. Rather, the *Bilderverbot* functions as a complex visual paradox: ISIS is evil, so simply looking at their handiwork is dangerous, yet to engage this threat, we must both see them for what they really are (or what we assume them to be), and do so without them seeing us (hence the ocular politics of drone warfare). In other words, these acts are seen in order to be proclaimed unwatchable by those representatives charged with enforcing the ban.

Indeed, in order to be able to speak about ISIS beheadings, perhaps WJT Mitchell's (1986) language of iconoclasm is most useful here. He notes that "we have made a fetish out of our own iconoclastic rhetoric projecting the very idols we claim to be smashing" (113). This is similar to David Campbell's (2016) argument that we should be paying more attention to the mechanisms of production of ISIS beheading videos, not in terms of how ISIS produces them, but in terms of how they are spliced, edited, and framed by our own Western media outlets. Furthermore, iconoclasm assumes that the other is "involved in irrational, obscene behavior from which (fortunately) we are exempt" (Mitchell 1986, 113). That is, though ISIS is often described as iconoclastic in its own right, ISIS is also depicted as turning the severed head into an idol of sorts. In the assumed fear that motivates our iconoclasm, we invoke the idol itself. This highlights the power of the image that is projected into it but which it may not possess without that invoked fear. Indeed, as Daniel Bertrand Monk has noted (2016): in order to be able to speak about ISIS beheadings, what we actually reference are beheadings practiced by iconoclasts, who in those moments make icons. He argues that when they cut off the heads we aren't supposed to see separated from bodies, and so cause horror, they also meet the demand that the threat to us is mitigated in symbolic acts.

Stitching Two Stories: Some Conclusions

The previous sections have examined the political status of given positions associated with the representation of beheadings. Taking the structure of these commonplace arguments into account, I have traced the existence of a particular paradox according to which ISIS beheadings are both a spectacle and operate under the image ban of the *Bilderverbot*. When beheadings are shown, the media commonly acts as a visual intermediary so that the wider public is spared the viewing, and in the process dissuaded from watching. In the process, since we know the image exists, but we cannot look on it, a taboo quality is created to the footage. Further attributable to ISIS then is an iconic status which becomes something to fear in itself. This acts to justify the need for trigger warnings associated with this material. Not viewing these has also been couched in the language of security, where viewing and circulating the images is a win for the terrorists or makes us less secure (Kayyem 2015; Snyder 2015). In other words, the schema of visuality I have traced here regarding the regulation of the spectacle is precisely the predispositive judgment concerning what must be judged in and about conflict to begin with.

Francois Debrix has noted that the iconic status of the severed head might be "about making horror – what some may think of as the unrepresentable – into something that can or should be represented, at least at times, depending on who is doing the cutting or on what the cutting of heads may enable or justify" (Debrix 2017, 88). That is, the story of the severed head is never only one story. It is about how the unrepresentability of the head, the taboo, is navigated. To get at this, this chapter has focused in on two stories in which the unrepresentable was represented: the story of an Iraqi severed head, which was shown but not seen, rendered background, banal to the story of excesses of war, and the story of a Western severed head, seen but not shown, around which an absent spectacle was constructed via the relationship between the image and its viewers. These seem to be very different stories at first: in the first account, the head is displayed by someone different than those who did the act of beheading, while in the second, ISIS videos are released by those who did the beheading. Yet, this may be a function of how we understand ISIS imagery: their double production is elided. Indeed, as David Campbell has noted, the media ends up producing the imagery of ISIS, because the (beheading) images that become iconic have been cut from an original video with the larger ISIS-produced narrative and context removed: we ourselves have played a role in constructing the threat of the visual icon (Campbell 2016).

As I have noted, there is a politics of production in these videos even after they are released by ISIS, in the way they are managed by the media and the general public, Debord's very idea of a spectacle as not simply an image or a collection of images, but a "social relation among people mediated by images" (Debord 1983, 4). There are indications then that the image ban is always already leaky, that the official discourse of evil and unique violence might be failing, and that there is something to be found in investigating these excesses. The chapter has traced the simultaneous mobilization of desire and disgust related to beheading images, which may be a signal both that beheadings are not always horrifying, as seen in the story of an Iraqi severed head, and that those who seek to watch beheading videos might enjoy the horror, as seen in the second story the chapter told.

Some scholars, most notably Stephen Walt (2016), argue that fear-mongering as a political strategy can erode liberty. Walt notes: "a frightened population tends to think first about its own safety, and forget about fundamental liberties." But if the beheadings teach us anything, it is that the security versus liberty nexus is not the one we should be focused on. Rather, what we need to ask ourselves is what this fear already invokes about how "our" safety and security are produced and defined to begin with. While the focus on liberty may be important, we should also be focused on what political work this fear does, based on what it invokes and how, as I have traced earlier, to make us believe that fear itself is what actually makes us safer. Such invocation of fear is intimately linked then with the positing of particular understandings of security.

Yet there is no discussion about whether we should be afraid: instead, fear is the assumed, unquestioned horizon against which the political assessment of ISIS is framed. As Bataille (1986 [1957], 38) notes, "if we observe the taboo, if we submit to it, we are no longer conscious of it." The regulatory mechanism of the taboo then has naturalized fear of ISIS even to the extent that it leads to a very real threat inflation in the world of policymaking, a topic that several security studies scholars and media analysts have drawn attention to (Brooks 2014; Frank 2015; Gillespie 2014; Layne 2015). This chapter has raised initial questions about what politics this invokes, about what appears in this process of claims for the need to visually regulate or withhold, and about what gets assumed without even looking. It has posited an alternative way of considering images, not in terms of what they are used for, but in terms of how fear of these images, and the visual politics this invokes, becomes common sense.

4 | *Dead Terrorists and Dead Dictators*

As I began thinking about this book project, something happened that raised questions about the way we think about, look at, and otherwise visually consume or render displayable dead bodies. I had the television on, flipping through channels, and a breaking news story of a car chase caught my attention. Car chases always make for a newsworthy story, especially if television news can capture them while they are ongoing. In this instance, after a relatively brief chase, it ended with the driver of the car pulling off into a field, aimlessly walking away from the car, pulling out a gun, and shooting himself in the head. In the United States, where I reside, television stations broadcast their news coverage of this type of live event on a slight delay, so that they can avoid the Federal Communications Commission fines associated with showing violence of this nature by accident. That is, showing an event like the man shooting himself is prohibited. But the news network I was watching made an error, and instead of delaying the broadcast of the footage to the public, they delayed the screen the news anchor was watching and narrating for the viewer. It created an odd disconnect, whereby the viewers saw the man shooting himself, followed by the panicked statements of the news anchor to cut the feed as he realized the shooting was imminent, and then the realization that the viewers had in fact already seen the footage. That night I had a nightmare about this shooting that I had witnessed.

This man's death, and indeed his body, depicted by video footage from news helicopters, was deemed obscene: unfit for display, for viewing, as a result of its disturbing nature, hence the prohibition on broadcasting footage of this sort. Indeed, I found it disturbing. But this made me wonder about why I felt this disturbance in a way that I did not necessarily feel under other circumstances of body display. Why is this deemed so offensive to human dignity, in a world where dead bodies are placed on display under specific sets of circumstances and dead body images often circulate in the media? Indeed, I had around the same time viewed media images of a dead Qaddafi, and rather than feeling disturbed as I felt with the car chase, I had experienced feelings of relief at the death of a dictator, turned into a spectacle for publication in Western media.

This encounter, with a particular death and dead body image, occurred within the mediatized spectacle of the television car chase. Yet it also existed within a larger context that this chapter examines, of how the existence of, or the viewing of, an image can be posited as a threat to security. This exists within a dynamic wherein displaying some dead bodies impacts how others are hidden, while hiding some bodies impacts how others are viewed (Sentilles 2018). The contemporary visual technologies of the war-on-terror are as much about invisibility as visibility, as much about what is moved out of sight or rendered visually taboo, as about what images are circulated and rendered hyper-visible. In this sense, while this chapter addresses the idea of the *Real* and the notion of the image ban, it focuses explicitly on the dimension of security associated with obscene images of dead enemies. In this sense, it seeks to elucidate the visual grammar of images that are overtly related to foreign policy actions such as counter-terrorism or democracy promotion. These larger policy discourses are supported and reinforced by the production and circulation of images of dead enemies in particular ways. By the rupture of the dead body taboo, viewers are instructed to engage with images in specific ways, and thus to engage the policy subjects of those images in particular ways, sustaining a larger narrative of security.

Rather than focus on soldier bodies, as often form the basis of such analysis related to the war-on-terror, I seek instead to understand the framing of what is seen and unseen in dead enemy bodies. I illustrate this by telling two stories in this chapter. First, I examine the absent spectacle of a dead Osama bin Laden, to examine the interplay of the real and the taboo with regard to dead body images in the wider context of a national security narrative. Here I articulate the interplay of images as depicting reality with the notion that a dead body image can itself be a significant security threat. Second, I tell the story of the display of the dead body of Muammar Qaddafi, deposed dictator of Libya, in 2011, circulated in Western media stories about the event, to elucidate the complex dynamics of the broken taboo governing dead body images in this case. The display of Qaddafi's dead body and the framing of him via the rhetoric of madness inculcate a particular visual grammar that instructs viewers that it is acceptable to look at non-normative dead bodies in the service of larger foreign policy successes and triumphs. In other words, the display of Qaddafi's body advanced a particular notion of security in the face of the threat of dictators that is key to how the West understands itself in terms of its security, which may necessitate the deaths of others.

These cases illustrate the ways in which obscenity is mustered as a visual and political tool, to both place a taboo on the viewing of certain dead bodies and invite the viewing of others. Obscenity here provides the framing concept for visual engagement, precisely because what constitutes or is suggested to constitute the obscene is a political decision, one that generates particular erasures and legitimates particular narratives. In other words, the difference between a dead dictator image and a dead terrorist image can tell us something about the role these two archetypal figures play in narratives about international security. Our purported emotional responses, which dictate and constrain policy choices, emerge from our encounters with images and from the way they are regulated with reference to the taboo governing dead body images.

I draw out these examples to make two main arguments in this chapter: first, that those instances when taboos are ruptured can tell us a lot about how they are constituted and reinforced, and second, that the war-on-terror has inaugurated new visual norms related to the obscenity taboo. Specifically, dangerous enemy bodies are rendered invisible as part of a larger security narrative (dead terrorists), while dead dictators are rendered hyper-visible as a means to circulate a wider narrative about security threat that legitimizes the rhetoric of democratic revolution.

In other words, it is through comparing these cases and drawing out the logics that underpin the circulation of dead body images in these cases that larger narratives can become evident. It is important to do so because dead body images are often painted with a broad brush. Moeller, Nurmis, and Barforoush, for example, note that the inhibitions on showing gore in the media are lifted for coverage of the death of an enemy: "All too often a blood lust rises among those who consider themselves to be the enemy's victims, even victims by proxy. Audiences want to see the formerly all-powerful persecutor 'taken down', and that often means wanting to see unexpurgated photos of corpses" (Moeller et al. 2015, 114). While I do trace what this looks like in the context of Qaddafi, this is an overly simplistic characterization, as we don't see the display of Osama bin Laden's dead body in the same way, despite many of the same triumphalist narratives of defeat of an enemy. The story is more complex: even the bodies of American soldiers have been dehumanized by being rendered invisible and ungrievable via mechanisms of statecraft such as the Dover Ban (Purnell 2018). Additionally, as I describe in Chapter 5, often the gory images of bodies of victims of atrocity are shown, with the taboo against graphic images lifted for larger humanitarian ends. In other words, there is not one rule for the rupturing of the taboo regarding dead enemy body images; this chapter seeks to complicate this picture by considering two cases in depth alongside one another.

The Visual Politics of Osama bin Laden: Securing the Dead Terrorist

In 2011, a dead body was produced, but we were not allowed to look at it. The death of Osama bin Laden after a long search was celebrated as a victory for the United States and indeed global security, and was broadly couched within a rhetoric of justice, though as Cox and Wood have noted, it can perhaps be situated as an act of state revenge (2016). Photos of bin Laden's face, or what was reportedly his corpse, mutilated from the shots that killed him, began to circulate. But those were soon discredited, and photographs of the body, and indeed the body itself, were not released to a demanding public. The body was buried at sea so as to avoid creating a shrine for Osama bin Laden. The body was disappeared in the service of a particular security narrative: we were told that to be secure, we must not look upon this particular corpse, that this dead body was itself still a security risk due to the power it held as a symbol. As US President Barack Obama noted shortly after the mission that killed Osama bin Laden: "It is important for us to make sure that very graphic photos of somebody who was shot in the head are not floating around as an incitement to additional violence, as a propaganda tool" (McConnell and Todd 2014, unpaginated). In other words, images can be dangerous in and of themselves, both because of the content and because of the context surrounding them. As Mitchell (2011, xvii) notes with regard to the Abu Ghraib images, some in the US military noted that these images were "more dangerous to American interests than any weapons of mass destruction." The bin Laden image was imbued with a similar power in the realm of security.

The creation, and then disappearance, of this dead body generated an absent spectacle: a spectacle that is publicized by virtue of its absence. This section seeks to consider this case as exemplary of how the dead terrorist figures into wider media and political narratives of the war-on-terror. While my focus here is on bin Laden's dead body itself, and the photographs taken of it by the SEAL team responsible for his death, I should note that his death is part and parcel of a larger spectacle of counter-terrorism. As Jeffords and Al-Sumait (2015, x) note, "[T]he final raid of bin Laden's house in Abottabad was itself a carefully orchestrated media event. The highly controlled nature of the mission by the now-famous Navy SEAL Team 6 included a mindful decision about how to confirm bin Laden's death through a series of photographic images taken on-site before the team left Abottabad." Priya Dixit (2014) has similarly noted that the visual politics of bin Laden's death can shed light on the new Orientalism inherent in the American narrative about the event. In other words, the dead body image is part of a larger visual discourse, in which visual images such as the bin Laden Wanted posters and the iconic destruction of the Twin Towers also play a key role.

The Image, the Real, and the Freedom of Information Act

After Osama bin Laden was killed, the US government claimed it had fifty-nine images of his corpse (Jeffords and al-Sumait 2015, x). Yet none were released to the public. Indeed, internal orders were given to destroy the photographs. "In an e-mail dated May 13, 2011, then-Vice Adm. William McRaven wrote the following: 'One particular item that I want to emphasize is photos; particularly UBLs remains. At this point – all photos should have been turned over to the CIA; if you still have them destroy them immediately or get them to the [redacted.]'" (McConnell and Todd 2014, unpaginated). President Obama himself argued that releasing the images would generate an immediate security risk.[1] Visualizing bin Laden's body became

---

[1] Dixit notes that "Obama is correct in saying a photograph of the dead bin Laden would be a national security risk, but not in the way he (presumably) meant. Instead, making bin Laden's body visible could interrogate the practices of US

securitized, "and so looking at him became something that could lead to (state) insecurity" (Dixit 2014, 346).

Yet there was a demand to see the photos. This demand was often couched in terms of providing clear evidence, as if photographs are equivalent to brute fact, the notion that bodies themselves are equated with the *Real* (Hill 2009, 15). Indeed, the justification for showing images of dead public figures tends to appeal to the notion of their evidentiary value, such as the bodies of Uday and Qusay Hussein, sons of Saddam Hussein. Yet there also seemed to be a strong desire to see bin Laden dead as a mechanism of vengeance. The demand to see the photos was a demand for an icon of the conquest of the enemy. This then manifested in a series of online games such as "Bend Over bin Laden." Additionally, in the online game "Kill Osama bin Laden," once the target is killed, the player has the opportunity to cut off his head "for proof to the government" (Jeffords and al-Sumait 2015, xxviii). In this virtual realm, the demand for the body as evidence manifests in the way it did in reality (with the US soldiers doing DNA tests on scene and taking the body with them as evidence until his identity could be established) but also in a way it didn't in reality (the public demand for bin Laden's body to be manifested was not realized). Similarly, the fake photo of a dead bin Laden and the frequency if its circulation also assuaged the bloodlust of a viewing public who wanted to see him taken down a notch.

Several Freedom of Information Act (FOIA) requests were filed to get the photos released. Judicial Watch, a conservative watchdog group, sued the Obama administration to get the photos released, claiming that it was not a security risk for US intelligence services to release the images (Wing 2014). They argued that "the government had failed to demonstrate how all of the images, even the non-graphic ones, would reasonably be expected to 'cause identifiable or describable exception-ally grave damage to national security,' as the government suggested they would" (Reilly 2013, unpaginated). A US Appeals court ruled that the government did not need to release the photos. The decision to go against the FOIA lawsuit was legitimized by reference to security: the imminent security threat to US "interests, citizens, and personnel" around the world that would be created by releasing the images, and

self-making as well as provide a different standpoint for analyzing 'security'" (Dixit 2014, 346).

presumably the assurance of their security by not releasing these images. As the panel decision notes, "this is not a case in which the declarants are making predictions about the consequences of releasing just any images. Rather, they are predicting the consequences of releasing an extraordinary set of images, ones that depict American military personnel burying the founder and leader of al Qaeda" (Reilly 2013b). The images themselves, in a very material sense, as a frozen capture of a moment in time, and the invocation of reality associated with that, are assumed to hold a particular power precisely because they are images of the dead.

Justice Department lawyer Robert Loeb, in stating the case of the administration, noted a difference between the photos of Uday and Qusay Hussein, which were ultimately publicly released, and Osama bin Laden. "While the U.S. was concerned that releasing photos of the bodies of Saddam Hussein's sons could spark riots, officials determined the release was necessary to assure the Iraqi people they were dead, said Loeb. That wasn't the case with the bin Laden photos, he argued" (Reilly 2013a, unpaginated). What is interesting about the Uday and Qusay Hussein case is that the image of their bodies that was released was taken after they had been touched up by a mortician, "making them look not quite real" (Moeller et al. 2015, 123). Yet the stated goal of releasing the images was to provide evidence that they were indeed dead to a skeptical Iraqi public, thereby justifying the apparent American hypocrisy of releasing these dead body images while criticizing the release of dead body images of American soldiers by Iraqi militants. US Secretary of Defense Donald Rumsfeld justified the release of the Hussein images on the grounds that it could "save American lives" and that while photographs of prisoners of war is a violation of the Geneva Convention, showing enemy bodies is not (Torriero and Spolar 2003). Though, Iraqis remained skeptical that the Uday and Qusay Hussein dead body images were in fact authentic.

Indeed, contrary to Loeb's argument, there was precisely such a demand for evidence of bin Laden's death in the days following the raid that killed him, and widespread disbelief among Afghans, and indeed Americans, that he was in fact dead. Indeed, as ABC News noted about the release of the images: "The argument for releasing them: to ensure that the public knows and can appreciate that he is dead ... the argument against releasing the pictures: they're gruesome. He has a massive head wound above his left eye where he took a bullet, with brains and blood visible" (as cited in Moeller et al. 2015, 123). Setting aside that that description is also gruesome, and that it describes something we have seen numerous times on television shows such as *CSI* (does the reality of it make it worse?), this isn't the reason the US government cited for not releasing the images – that was about national security, not the obscene nature of the images. In that sense, unlike the images of Qaddafi I will discuss in the next section, this was a government decision not to release images, not the decision of a particular media outlet about the tensions between obscenity and public information. Indeed, some members of the US Congress did see the images of bin Laden's body (Schlag 2019, 9), so the debate over the release of the image is very much about the creation of a *public* spectacle and the need for communal catharsis related to seeing the body.

As Jeffords and al-Sumait (2015, x) note, "the 'real' bin Laden continues to be elusive even after his death." Indeed, the lack of images led some to ask whether bin Laden had actually been killed. Conservative American talk show host Glenn Beck asked the day after bin Laden's death was reported: "[W]ere poll numbers involved, or are we seeing a show? It is possible that Osama bin Laden has been ghosted out of his compound, and we're seeing a show at this point? Watch the other hand" (as cited in Jeffords and al-Sumait 2015, x). While Beck is right that the death was a carefully orchestrated public spectacle, even though his intent was to invoke a conspiracy theory, this also raises the dilemma of the *Real* in the image. Indeed, though her focus is on the missing of 9/11, Jenny Edkins's theorization of the politics of the person as missing notes that when someone goes missing, what happened doesn't seem possible, and as a result, we are often left with the ambiguity of photographs from when they were alive/present (Edkins 2011, 1). In applying this to the case of bin Laden, what we can see is that while audiences were being told he was dead, the visual grammar was in fact presenting his body as missing from this wider narrative of his death, invoking the dilemma of the *reality* of his death. While previous chapters have discussed how the obscene image can seem to be *unreal,* this case instead raises the notion that the image's obscenity is the only thing seen to stand in for the *Real.*

Yet even this notion is fraught with problems. After bin Laden's death, an image began circulating on the Internet that seemed to depict a dead Osama bin Laden with a bruised and bloody face (Figure 4.1). The image, however, had been doctored and was a fake. Indeed, the

Figure 4.1 Iraqis in Baghdad watch a news broadcast on Al-Arabiya showing an image purporting to be the dead body of Osama bin Laden after US forces killed bin Laden in a raid in Pakistan. The image was later debunked and does not in fact depict a dead bin Laden. May 2, 2011, SABAH ARAR/AFP via Getty Images

American Dover Ban, which meant that images of American soldiers' coffins were not allowed to be photographed (Purnell 2014), led to the emergence of both illicit images in 2004, and fake images in the following years of soldier coffins (Perlmutter 2005, 120), both cases where visual regulation led to the manufacturing of the obscenity image. The fake bin Laden image was a composite between a real image of a live bin Laden that had circulated in global media, and a photo of an unknown dead man (Schlag 2019).

The production and circulation of this fake dead bin Laden image emphasizes the demand for images of bin Laden's body. Indeed, purported images of a dead bin Laden were used as bait for a computer scam, where an email message would invite recipients to view bin Laden's dead body, and when they would click on the link, it would download a computer virus (Jeffords and al-Sumait 2015, xxix). This allure that the image had, particularly in the fact that Americans were told it did not exist for them to see, emphasizes the fascination associated with viewing the taboo. The taboo was transgressed in some ways, due to the demand to see the image as a mechanism of revenge, and reinforced in others, since the images were not actually released. But this generated an absent spectacle of sorts, where the taboo was in fact transgressed without the public even needing to see the images in many ways, because all of the pleasure and salaciousness associated with the viewing was fulfilled by the larger narrative surrounding the photos and the manhunt itself.

It also created a dilemma because many events are impossible to imagine without the photographic images associated with them (Lyford and Payne 2005, 119). As a result, if some images are too gruesome, or too much of a security risk, then how do we understand these events, or visualize events that are too obscene to be visually depicted? Richard Jackson emphasizes a similar point when he refers to bin Laden's death as a simulacrum: "an event that at first appears to be a real, meaningful moment in world politics, whereas, in fact, closer analysis reveals that it is merely a symbolic imitation of a meaningful event" (Jackson 2015, 4). In this vein, the absent spectacle of the image is correlated with the absent spectacle of the death itself, the fact that bin Laden's death in fact had no meaningful changes on global counterterrorism efforts, as Jackson notes. The death played out like an espionage movie (Jackson 2015). As a result, the key question here becomes what the reality of the event was, and how reality is determined. Dixit (2014, 337) makes this point when she notes that bin Laden's death was narrated from a US perspective in a way that literally made him disappear from his own story: "this has implications for how (in)security is depicted and understood in that others – usually raced others – are often missing even in narratives about themselves," thus functioning to maintain bin Laden as the ultimate racialized, invisible Other.

Identifying bin Laden Onscreen: Zero Dark Thirty *and the bin Laden Tapes*

Because the image of the body was not released, the narrative became shaped through other images. Schlag (2019, 10) has detailed how the image of the Situation Room functioned as a stand-in for the lack of images of bin Laden's body to the American public, shifting the story to one of government control of the death, and, later, the image. Though there are no images of a dead bin Laden that were released to the public, two mechanisms of videotape gave access to a similar visual representation: the film *Zero Dark Thirty* and the tapes of bin Laden's speeches released by Al-Qaeda. While I will mainly examine the former here, it bears mentioning the latter briefly. Andrew Hill notes that the videos present bin Laden in "disembodied, dematerialized form, allowing him to retain an absence at the hard Real (as a physical, embodied being) – which is precisely his presence at the latter that constitutes a precondition for his capture or killing" (Hill 2015, 37). Characterizing bin Laden as a "ghostly presence," Hill notes that the videos emphasize bin Laden's uncertain ontological status (2015, 38), similar to the debate about whether bin Laden was actually dead that I discuss above. Hill draws on Lacan to label bin Laden "objet petit a," "the thing that the subject is at once drawn toward and repelled by – that exists in the 'beyond-of-the-signified' of the Real and as such remains unknowable and unreachable" (Hill, 2015, 38). He goes on:

The unobtainability of the objet petit a derives in part from its rooting in the Real – a position that at once overlaps with the conception of bin Laden as a type of ghostly or monstrous presence … indeed, while the objet petit a serves to provoke a scopic desire, as Lacan outlines, it remains beyond the field of the visible. (Hill 2015, 39)

Though Hill's focus is mainly on the manhunt for bin Laden and its play of visibility, the same dynamic can be said to be true after his death.

Bin Laden lingers as a ghostly figure, one that motivates the ongoing war-on-terror. Indeed, while Jackson (2015) notes that nothing changed in counter-terrorism efforts, and thus bin Laden's death was a non-event, I would argue that is precisely the point – that the image of bin Laden's body was never released partly to allow the ghostly threat of terrorism to linger. Representing the threat allows it to end, so bin Laden's death must remain unrepresentable, and objet petit a must always remain constantly present but just beyond our reach. WJT Mitchell notes this point more broadly with regard to the war-on-terror: "prohibit something from being shown, hide it away from view, and its power as a concealed image outstrips anything it could have achieved by being shown" (Mitchell 2011, 63). Showing an image or video can render it banal, precisely because it is displayable and viewable (Bennett 2010, 215). Hill argues that by not releasing the image of bin Laden's body, the Obama administration wanted to limit the ability of bin Laden to continue to haunt, to kill him in the Symbolic as well as the *Real* (2015, 46), but I think it is precisely the opposite. Bin Laden haunts precisely because no images were shown, so bin Laden has only died in the Symbolic, not in the *Real*, at least for the audience.

Indeed, the film *Zero Dark Thirty* depicts this tension nicely. It both satisfies the demand for a visual representation of the death of Osama bin Laden, to presence his body on screen to posit a counterpoint to the invisibility of his dead body, as the film centers on finding and identifying, indeed *visualizing* Bin Laden, thus making his death *real*, and yet offers lingering questions, as the body's identifying features remain off screen in the scene where bin Laden's dead body is depicted. In that sense, it both assuaged the desire to see, and maintained the dominant narrative that the American public did not actually want to encounter the obscenity of the overly recognizable death of Osama bin Laden.

One of the important features of this case is the multiplicity of ways the dead body functions. That is, it has sentimental value to loved ones, political value to various states and the international community, and evidentiary value to those demanding to see it. Indeed, according to court papers from the suit mentioned above, one of the main reasons the photographs of Osama bin Laden's corpse existed in the first place was so that the Central Intelligence Agency (CIA) could conduct facial recognition analysis to confirm that it was indeed bin Laden rather than a body double ("Bin Laden death photos" 2013). As in other instances where the dead body is made visible, there is a tension between the dignity often attributed to the dead human body, and the potential value it can have to tell the story of its own death. This dead body was central to political stories about the heroism of American Special Forces, the lack of cooperation with Pakistani authorities, and as evidence of the fact that this powerful figure was in fact dead and thus no longer a threat to global and American security. The dead body, then, acted as the symbol that insecurity was alleviated, that the world had been made a safer place.

This recurred in the court narratives with the decision about the release of the photographs. A US Appeals court ruled that the CIA did not need to release the photos. The decision to go against FOIA was legitimized by reference to security: the imminent security threat to US "interests, citizens, and personnel" around the world that would be created by releasing the images, and presumably the assurance of their security by not releasing these images. As the panel decision notes, "this is not a case in which the declarants are making predictions about the consequences of releasing just any images. Rather, they are predicting the consequences of releasing an extraordinary set of images, ones that depict American military personnel burying the founder and leader of al Qaeda" (Reilly 2013b, unpaginated). Thus the debate is one about the security risk of an *extraordinary* dead body. In a context where the dead body is both the product of a mission to secure (the Abottabad raid that killed Osama bin Laden) and the nexus for potential future insecurity (a propaganda tool for future terrorist recruitment), what the singular dead body means remains hotly contested.

It is impossible to fully conceptualize the relationship between terrorism and security without addressing the way the dead body of the terrorist is produced. That is, labeling terrorism as a key threat to security implies a policy to end terrorism; this has taken the form of targeting terrorists, of causing their deaths. Their dead bodies thus become the symbols of the end of a security risk or threat, but at the same time, their dead bodies are complex things: they are sites for generating future terrorist recruitment, bodies enmeshed in religious discourses about proper body disposal, someone's loved one, the material evidence that a security threat has been eliminated. This raises important questions about who is being secured, and whose dead bodies represent the achievement of additional degrees of security.

Ultimately, these images play with notions of how bodies are rendered visible and consumed. I return to the scene of Osama bin Laden's death in the film *Zero Dark Thirty*. The scene takes place in the dark, and the face of bin Laden is never shown, as at the point he is shot the camera pans to display instead the bullet holes on his body The mismatch of not actually being able to see the face, even while the obscenity, the graphic part of the death, is shown works to construct a narrative about threat and death and security with regard to the dead terrorist. The dead dictator, in the body of Qaddafi, is enmeshed within its own stories about visibility and threat, but both take place within a visual and cinematic context that is not intended to cultivate empathy for the dead, but rather to inculcate a certain type of seeing in the war-on-terror, a contemporary technology of seeing war that instructs the viewer via framing mechanisms how to see and consume certain kinds of dead bodies. As Schlag notes, "political and normative issues are at stake whenever images of dead bodies are either displayed or banned" (2019, 9).

"Mad Dog" on Bloody Display: Viewing Qaddafi's Dead Body

When Muammar Qaddafi,[2] Libyan dictator, was killed, his corpse was displayed lying on a sheet on the floor, for a parade of global media. The video of his bloodied body being carried through a crowd and the display thereafter reinforced the idea not only that is it acceptable to kill a dictator, but that it is acceptable to show his corpse. His dead body was enabled as a display. As I have noted elsewhere, dead bodies are generally not displayed: as a matter of dignity, photographs of bodies are blurred, and it is considered a question of humanity and international law to properly bury the enemy's dead during wartime (Auchter 2015a).

Yet, after Qaddafi's death, his corpse, along with that of his son, was displayed for viewing, almost as in a traditional funeral where mourners parade past the casket, except in this case, those walking past were celebrating his death, and he was not displayed as a sanitized clean corpse with flowers, but rather bloodied and ragged laying on a sheet on the floor, with the bullet hole in his head evident. Thousands of Libyans and foreign journalists lined up to see Qaddafi's body, displayed in a cold storage unit in Misrata. Even after removal, photographers were permitted to take pictures of his rotting corpse on its way to be buried.[3] One photograph of Qaddafi's dead body, taken by media sources, shows his bloodied corpse with hands in the foreground of the shot holding cell phones to take photographs of it: a photograph of photographing, a re-production and re-presentation of the logic of image-creation that revolved around this singular figure.

This brings up the issue of the ethics of a body on display. The etymology of the word display speaks to its meaning: scatter, unfold, spread out, reveal, exhibit. Thus, Qaddafi's body is not simply rendered visible, it is also unfurled in such a way as to convey its essential

---

[2] I have chosen to maintain consistency in the spelling and thus use Qaddafi throughout, following on the *New York Times*, "because the letter Q is typically used to render the glottal stop that is so common in Arabic and that begins Qaddafi's name" (Fisher 2011).

[3] One example can be found in the article "Ignominious End for Dictator Gaddafi" in London's *Daily Mail*.

meaning as the body of a dead dictator, subject to portrayal as a bloody corpse. There is an ethics associated not only with the display but also with the viewing that must be acknowledged. My analysis must engage with this ethical dilemma then: of how to assess a particular set of discourses surrounding this display, draw attention to the way they were replicated and circulated by traditional and social media, yet myself avoid replicating and re-presenting the meanings that are potentially ethically problematic. That is, even as I look at the photographs of Qaddafi's corpse, I am implicated in its display and the ethical questions therein.

As Susan Sontag (2003: 42) notes, the gruesome invites us to be either spectators or cowards. If I too am a spectator of the gruesome image, then the onus is on me to be self-reflexive on the silence, invisibilities, asymmetries such a relationship engenders. Yet there is also something problematic about this dichotomy that I hope to interrogate: the notion that if not looking is cowardice, there is something courageous about looking at the obscene, or the idea that not looking is representative of a fear of engaging with the image rather than a denial of such an engagement. Indeed, as Sontag herself notes (2003: 95), "images of the repulsive can allure," thus the relationship of viewing must be further complicated than the dichotomy between spectating and cowardice. Exploring how, when, and why images of Qaddafi dead or dying were circulated is the first step toward problematizing this dichotomy.

This story can be situated within a wider history of deposed leaders, perhaps. Scholars have identified the way in which communist and post-communist regimes display leaders to give the regime a sense of immortality (Buck-Morss 2002; Verdery 1999). Indeed, more recently, media outlets debated whether to show images of Saddam Hussein after his hanging. The images of Saddam Hussein that became notable were of a disheveled man emerging from an underground hiding place, the dictator beaten down by the necessity of running from his inevitable overthrow and ultimate death sentence. Still, these images were situated within a wider visual discourse that included the iconic toppling of the large statue of Saddam Hussein in Firdos Square in Baghdad, marking the deposition of the dictator and his individual dehumanization. The *New York Times* published a photograph of Saddam Hussein's dead body on its front page after his execution. Indeed, the goal was to captivate Western viewers, while in Arab media, the goal was to provide evidence of Hussein's death without inflaming sectarian tensions (Moeller et al. 2015, 115). In a similar sense, Qaddafi's death was itself retroactively articulated by the display of his dead body as the condition of possibility for bringing democracy to Libya.

Qaddafi's Death in the Headlines

It is important to examine how various media sources portrayed and depicted Qaddafi's death. *The New York Post* had perhaps the most creative, though not entirely accurate, headline, which would appeal to their viewership: "Khadafy Killed by Yankee Fan: Gunman Had More Hits than A-Rod." Along with the headline was a photograph of Qaddafi's bloody face as he was dragged through the streets before his death (Fisher 2011). Many news sources chose similar photographs to show in the wake of the death announcement on October 20, 2011, including *The Guardian*, with its headline: "Death of a Dictator," Washington, D.C.'s *Express,* New York's *Daily News*, *The Washington Post*, and others. It was only later that the images of his dead body on display appeared, mostly on Internet media sources, indicative of the dispersion of viewing in an era of democratized technology access. On the day after Qaddafi's death, only 7 out of 424 print newspapers in the United States used large images of his dead body on the cover, for example, though additional ones printed smaller photos of his dead body (Moos 2011). On October 21, the United Kingdom's *Mirror* was one of the international papers that showed a picture of Qaddafi's dead body on their cover, with the headline: "Don't shoot, Don't shoot," Qaddafi's alleged last words. His face is bruised and bloody, swollen with death, and his chest is marked with traces of his own blood. The text that accompanies the photo reads, "For 42 years Colonel Gaddafi terrorised his own people ... and the world. Yesterday, he died as he lived, shown no mercy as he pleaded for his life." Supplementary text refers to him as "Mad Dog," which recirculates connections between obscenity and madness that tell us it is more acceptable to look at a non-normative corpse and fetishizes madness so as to cultivate a distance between the viewer and the obscene corpse.

There is a key strain running through media coverage: headlines that refer to Qaddafi as "Mad Dog." This notion of "Mad Dog" recirculates connections between obscenity and madness that were also depicted in the photographs of Qaddafi being taken out of his hiding place before he was killed, which is quite similar to those from a similar context when Saddam Hussein was captured. Qaddafi looks "mad": his hair is unkempt, his face puffy, his eyes wild. This is true of the photographs of his corpse as well. There is something important about the connection between madness and display here that tells us that it is more acceptable to display and to view a "mad" or non-normalized obscene corpse. It is objectified as a curiosity in the same way madness is in other social contexts. Elizabeth Dauphinee (2007) has explored the way pain was inscribed in the Abu Ghraib photographs, and then fetishized through the recirculation of the images. In this context, it is not pain that is being fetishized and circulated, but rather madness, a madness that is viewed as a continuation of the narratives of madness surrounding Qaddafi's life, including his support for the Lockerbie perpetrators, his penchant for a female cadre of guards, and his unconventional fashion choices.

That is, in Qaddafi's case, imaging and understanding pain is not focused on empathy, but on distancing via a schema of "madness," both rhetorically, via news headlines, and visually, where his matted hair and wild eyes reinforce this perspective and perception. This distancing instituted a schema of dehumanization that was also evident via a variety of media descriptions: one such example is an Australian newspaper that described Qaddafi as being "killed like a dog in the gutter" (Usborne et al. 2011), and another is the rumor that Qaddafi was sodomized after his death ("Ignominious end" 2011). There is an interesting culturally specific dimension to this that must be addressed. Qaddafi's madness is part and parcel of how a dictator is viewed and constructed by Western and American perceptions to legitimate specific policies. In this sense, decisions to display Qaddafi's body are culturally specific, and my own interpretation of the visual cultures of dead body display also stem from my own cultural contexts, one that is perhaps reflective of the intended consumer of these circulated images. But Qaddafi also has a particular legacy of anti-colonialism, which heightens the depiction of Qaddafi as the mad dictator, rendering his body simply a failed (post)colonial subject on display for the colonizer. Indeed, as Stuart Allan notes, "Gaddafi's status as a dictator and war criminal meant he would not be accorded the respect that might be otherwise expected for a slain political leader" (Allan 2014, 181).

To return to media coverage of Qaddafi's death, the *Daily Mail* reiterates Qaddafi's last words in its headline on October 21, 2011, and displays a bloody picture of Qaddafi before his death. The text reads, "Battered and bloody, the tyrant of Libya pleads for his life. Moments later, he was dead – executed with a bullet to the head." The United Kingdom's *Independent* shows a montage of photos of a bloody Qaddafi being dragged through the street before his death, with the headline "End of a Tyrant." *The Times* and *The Daily Telegraph* have a similar headline and photo. *Metro*'s image is of the same heavily filmed and photographed journey Qaddafi took from his hiding place to his death. The language of its headline is illuminating: "A mad dog in life but a cowering rat in his last, brutal moments." The reference to a rat dehumanizes Qaddafi after his capture, justifying the measures taken to kill him. The *Daily Express* shows the same iconic picture of Qaddafi, bloody, in the streets, before his death, and the headline and subheading read: "Gaddafi gunned down in sewer: Murdering rat gets his just deserts." But *The Sun* is perhaps the most dramatic in terms of justification of Qaddafi's death, with its October 21 headline over a picture of Qaddafi's bloody face: "That's for Lockerbie." The preview of the table of contents at the bottom of the front page alludes to a story about Qaddafi in hell with Hitler. This fits with some of the statements made by Lockerbie family members. Kathy Tedeschi, whose husband was killed in the Pan Am plane, said in response to Qaddafi's death: "I hope he is in hell with Hitler" (Usborne et al. 2011). Figure 4.2 illustrates some of these.

A variety of American news programs offered up their own interpretations of the display described above. Fox News America's Headquarters on October 22, 2011, had a guest who described Qaddafi on display: "now he is laying here like a mad dog." This language speaks to the way in which the corpse of Qaddafi was dehumanized, but this is done in the service of a particular construction of the dead dictator. CNN's Anderson Cooper interviewed Middle East expert Fouad Ajami on October 20, 2011, on the news of Qaddafi's death, and Ajami focuses on "the oddity, if you will, of getting rid of these dictators, that on the one hand it's such a moment of exhilaration, and on the other, there is a kind of disappointment, anti-climactic, if you will, when discovered that these great figures, that these tyrants, these despots, whom we thought about all the time and wondered about, were actually cowards." He goes on to say, "this is the fate of

Figure 4.2 A selection of Britain's daily national newspapers reporting on the death of Muammar Qaddafi, October 21, 2011, BEN STANSALL/AFP via Getty Images

the despots. This is what they do and this is the end they deserve."[4] He thus makes a moral statement about the end of a dictator. It also promulgates the idea that dictators are in fact not a threat to democracy, but are actually at heart cowards. Or, as Barry Rubin notes, Qaddafi's death teaches us that "dictators must fight or die" and gives credit to Western intervention or military involvement rather than popular revolt as the motivation for revolution (Rubin 2011). He characterizes the philosophy of Middle Eastern dictators as "repress or die," and notes the implications of this for the Syrian case, which has, at least at the time of this writing, proven to be a true adage for Bashar al-Assad. That is, Qaddafi's death and the display of his body demonstrates that the only end for a dictator is death, and that despite the repression that characterizes the reign of dictatorships, they can be relatively easily overthrown with the interference of the West in the name of democracy, but only if the West chooses such an intervention option. This minimizes the very real threat to their own people that dictators can pose by positing dictatorship as easily overcome by democratic ideals.

[4] Transcript available at http://transcripts.cnn.com/TRANSCRIPTS/1110/20/acd .02.html

The relationship to narratives about democracy was clear when US President Barack Obama commented on Qaddafi's death and the display of his dead body on the Jay Leno show. He stated:

Well, this is somebody who, for 40 years, has terrorized his country and supported terrorism. And he had an opportunity during the Arab Spring to finally let loose of his grip on power and to peacefully transition into democracy. We gave him ample opportunity, and he wouldn't do it. . . . Obviously, you never like to see anybody come to the kind of end that he did, but I think it obviously sends a strong message around the world to dictators that people long to be free, and they need to respect the human rights and the universal aspirations of people. ("Ignominious end" 2011)

Being anti-democracy, then, means that one is denied the standard privileges accorded to human beings, both in terms of cultural norms surrounding dead bodies, and Geneva Conventions on POWs and dead enemy bodies. But aside from the discursive construction of the "dead dictator" figure, such remarks also serve to make it seem as though defeat of dictatorship is not only noble but also easy. Dictatorship, then, is posited as weak in the face of democratic movements.

It is useful to contrast these English and American headlines and images with those from around the world, to emphasize the cultural specificity and postcolonial dimension noted above. English and American newspapers were more likely to use the images of Qaddafi, bloody, being dragged through the streets, or even his dead body, whereas papers from other regions of the world were likely to use similar headlines about Qaddafi's last words, but to include old photographs of him before his capture and death. Such papers include *Pakistan Today*, and a selection of Sri Lankan and Chinese newspapers ("Gaddafi dead" 2011). France's *Le Figaro,* Portugal's *Publico*, Poland's *Gazeta*, and Canada's *National Post* all showed an old picture of Qaddafi, some in military uniform and others not (Moos 2011). Tabloid-type papers were also on the whole more likely to show photos of his dead body, which legitimates the notion that there is something prurient about viewing the obscene body (Tait 2008). This is also framed by the textual warnings surrounding the images themselves, which depict the fantasy of the dead dictator and allow the reader to become a privileged witness to the obscenity of Qaddafi's violent death. Even descriptions of Qaddafi's death in the media utilized dramatic descriptions of his death and body, whether they chose to show the images or not. One example would be *Newsweek,* which wrote on its website: "Warning: this is video of Muammar Gaddafi's corpse being dragged through the streets of Sirte. No way to whitewash that. We're posting it because many others have, and at this point, it's a video asset in the history books" (as quoted in Allan 2014, 183).

In other words, the image of a dead Qaddafi was seen as so *real* it needed to be shown, regardless of how obscene it was. Moeller et al. (2015, 119) note that in this case, because the images did not appear staged, and many were taken by amateur photographers, this lent credence to the reliability of the images and to the idea that they depicted something "brutal, raw, and almost unbearably true." In this sense, the images were not distributed solely for the purpose of celebrating Qaddafi's death, but also for the purpose of establishing the *reality* of the death of a dictator.

Qaddafi on Social Media: Caricaturing a Dictator

In a recent article, I analyzed Twitter accounts that purported to be Qaddafi (Auchter 2015b). While that project was a comprehensive analysis of all of these English-language accounts, one account is worth drawing out here, which specifically addresses the display of Qaddafi's dead body. @GhostGaddafi's account begins on October 20, 2011, the date Qaddafi is killed, with a tweet exclaiming "I'm dead." Later tweets speak to the images of Qaddafi's death that are emerging. He tweets, "I deserved to be showcased in HD, shitty cell phone quality," and tweets to CNN, "@CNN I demand you take down those unflattering pictures at once!" This is the only account that specifically references the photographs of Qaddafi themselves. This account's response to Qaddafi's death and the images of his dead body lead us to ask what the impact of his death was on this larger analysis of his portrayal on Twitter.

NM Incite analyzed the reactions to Qaddafi's death on Twitter and found that 76 percent of tweets were information sharing, revolving largely around photos of dead Qaddafi. Online site Mashable highlights the results of the analysis. "19% of tweets express a sense of justice for what was considered Gaddafi's dictatorship over Libya" (Hernandez 2011). Most interestingly, however, was the number of tweets that expressed concern about Qaddafi's death or the display of photos and imagery. Only 4 percent of tweets on Qaddafi were negative, meaning that these users indicated it was wrong to celebrate death. When this is contrasted with Osama bin Laden's death, wherein negative tweets accounted for 11 percent of the tweets, what emerges is the conclusion that more Twitter users felt uncomfortable with celebrating the death of Osama bin Laden than did with the death of Qaddafi. That is, the most wanted global terrorist received more sympathy in death than Qaddafi. This is highlighted even further when one thinks about the display of Qaddafi's body, and the fact that bin Laden's body was not on display in the same manner. Surely if anything were to prompt a negative reaction, it would be the display of a corpse in violation of international law and cultural norms as to what is done with a dead body, even a dead enemy body. Why did it not provoke such a reaction?

Comedian James Adomian remarked on the difference between Qaddafi's death and Osama bin Laden's, particularly in terms of what was done with their bodies. He tweeted: "Is it too late to dump #Gaddafi's body on the ocean and make everybody take our word for it?" (Wabash). This is an implicit commentary on the politics of display surrounding Qaddafi, and the contrast with bin Laden is illustrative. That is, what politics makes a dictator's dead body eligible for display and for that display to be dispersed, continually passed on, as the majority of tweets surrounding Qaddafi's death were retweets and passing on the news he was dead or the images surrounding his death. How does a dead dictator differ from a dead terrorist? A dead terrorist is obliterated, his body removed from public display, as in the cases of Osama bin Laden and Anwar al-Awlaki. But Qaddafi is a different story. There is a qualitative distinction in the grievability of certain lives labeled as "other" or "enemy," and it speaks to the discursive construction of threat.

As Robert Wabash details, the highest-rated Gaddafi post on Reddit, a social news website, was the Disney reference to King John from the animated film Robin Hood. The image depicts the character of King John, a lion who is outfitted in jewels and a crown, sucking his thumb. The character in the film is known for his childlike irrational behavior and the aggressive way in which he engages in both a grab for power and targeting his enemies. The image of King John has written at the top, "Muammar Gaddafi 1942–2011." King John's character is a quintessential Disney villain, evil for evil's sake. In this case, he also represents the dictator who has no concern for his people. But, at the same time, he is a cartoon character, and speaks to the way "the dictator" has become a caricature. Qaddafi's own behavior played into this idea, as when he famously wanted to stay in a tent when attending the General Assembly meeting at the United Nations in New York. Similarly, @DepressedDarth, intended to refer to Star Wars villain Darth Vader, writes, "Apparently Muammar Gadhafi has been killed. In related news, Ewoks have already begun celebrating in the Libyan forest," a reference to the celebration of Ewoks in the movie *Return of the Jedi* after the explosion of the Death Star. This type of rhetoric paints Qaddafi as a quintessential Hollywood-style villain, and interestingly, the Libyan people into characters akin to the primitive Ewoks, furry childlike creatures who are beloved by Star Wars fans largely for their cuteness and visually depicted via imagery that reinforces their lack of development, such as forest dwellings and strange religious rituals. By this comparison, the Libyan people are turned into primitive passive instruments of a triumphant NATO democratization of their country, accomplished by deposing an evil dictator. Similarly, by turning Qaddafi into a character it renders him less-than-human and thereby morally enables him to be subject to treatment that violates the norm of what is and should be done to dead bodies, including displaying them. That is, referencing Qaddafi alongside King John and Darth Vader not only makes room for depictions of the Libyan people as passive non-agents in the overthrow of Qaddafi and the subsequent democratization of Libya, it also dehumanizes Qaddafi himself, in both a material and discursive sense. It changes the frame of reference of visually consuming a dead body from one of pity to a larger political context, where we are instructed by the images themselves to engage with them in specific ways, enhanced by the larger popular culture context in which Qaddafi has been situated.

Celebrating Death, Commodifying the Dead

Renee Marlin-Bennett, Marieke Wilson, and Jason Walton (2010) discuss the role of dead bodies by exploring commodified bodies and the politics of display. They explore the exhibition of plasticized human cadavers in museums for educational purposes, arguing that in these exhibits, dead bodies are being depoliticized and commodified in a morally troubling way. Though regulations exist for dead bodies and body parts, plasticized bodies are couched in discourses of specimens rather than human beings. They argue that spectacle of their display in often provocative positions invokes scientific authority to legitimate a specific representation of these bodies that silences and depoliticizes their histories. Spectators walk through scenes in which the plasticized bodies enact a particular moral economy that is only possible with the base assumption that they are no longer considered to be human. Viewers are instructed not to engage emotionally with the bodies, and this, coupled with the disbelief that what is being exhibited is actually a human body, creates a cognitive dissonance that is coopted by the exhibit to condone objectification of things whose difference we cannot understand (Marlin-Bennett et al. 2010, p. 172).

When this schema is applied to the case of Qaddafi's body, we can envision almost the opposite: the images instruct the viewer to emotionally engage with the corpse, yet in such a way as to dehumanize it. After all, only non-normative bodies can be displayed within very particular contexts, such as the scientific ones above. But aside from this, a corpse outside of the funeral industry represents a failure of sorts, and must then be managed within other narratives that situate it. In this context, Qaddafi's corpse may bring up feelings of pity that may be quickly squashed when it is contextualized within discourses of vengeance or justice associated with the end of a dictatorship. While rationally we may acknowledge it as a person, the corpse is rendered a figure, a character, and perhaps a caricature by the manner of display, and thus no longer qualified for the standard rules governing the disposal of the dead body. This is particularly the case given the audience who is expected to consume these images, and indeed consume the afterlife of Qaddafi. Intended for a primarily Western audience, the circulation of images of a bloody and dead Qaddafi were intended to cultivate particular sentiments among a particular audience, one that could engage with the death, and take away from it a picture of the "dead dictator" rather than engage with discourse of humanity and mortality.

Several news stories and commenters drew attention to the ethical discomfort in viewing Qaddafi's body. For example, Chloe, from London, in a comment on the *Daily Mail* website on the story that shows the picture of a dead Qaddafi, remarks, "Is it necessary to see these visuals? What are we teaching our children as justice? It's medieval! Kill the man, but don't splash his bloody corpse all over the papers" ("Ignominious end" unpaginated). This comment is an interesting one because it separates Qaddafi's death from the display of his dead body, implying that justice can be an extrajudicial killing, yet cannot be a visual engagement with the result of such an act, a notion that recurred in the context of the display of the image. Indeed, both were situated within the same larger logic. It is precisely the notion that it was acceptable to kill Qaddafi that rendered the display of his body the logical next step. It is precisely the display of his body that reinforces the justification for killing him: that he is less-than-human and thus not entitled to the same cultural and even legal protections, when alive or when dead.

The very display of the body in this instance evokes a certain paradox about death itself. Death is usually mourned, but what are the politics when a death is celebrated? Jonathan Jones aptly critiques the responses by Western media as hypocritical in that they rushed to publish photographs even while claiming to be concerned about the ethics of displaying the photographs of a dead body. Though it should be noted that not many of the newspapers that published images explored the ethical dilemma of publishing them. Rather, Qaddafi was visual fodder for the story of revolution, and the viewers of the images drew attention to the ethical questions at hand. The display of the body has also coopted the democratic revolution itself. He writes:

The Arab Spring became The Autumn of the Patriarch, as his dead body haunted the new era. No wonder a Libyan was quoted as saying he has given more trouble dead than alive. Yet the main trouble dead Gaddafi has given is to expose the fundamental shallowness and sentimentality of the western democracies' support for Arab revolution and in particular our military intervention in Libya. To get upset by photographs of the dead Gaddafi is to pretend we did not know we went to war at all. It is to fantasise that our own role is so just and proper and decent that it is not bloody at all. (Jones 2011, unpaginated)

Thus Libyans are ultimately painted as bloodthirsty even in their struggle for democracy, while Western democracies can consider themselves to have clean hands in the matter, reaping the benefits of democratization without paying the bloody cost, or as Jones says, enacting a fantasy of war based on just war theory that depicts war as "utterly righteous, from which we emerge with no guilt on our hands, not even the killing of a brutal dictator." Thus, we can claim both the triumph of democracy over dictatorship yet also distance ourselves from the brutality of war that led to the death of Qaddafi and is represented by his body on display: "a day in the life of hell, also known as war: a corpse photographed for souvenirs, displayed to satisfy the oppressed, in a moment of violent gratification." Yet I disagree with Jones on the matter of widespread concern about the photographs of Qaddafi's body. Indeed, most of the responses amounted to the fact that he got what he deserved. And even those that considered the photographs problematic attempted to disassociate that from the death itself.

That is, there is a politics behind the notion that we are not horrified by the rotting corpse of the dead dictator. In fact, this imagery sustains democracy itself by positing the dead dictator as display-able. This is a politics/ethics of horror, which is biologically grounded in the human body. We are not horrified by the dead bodies of international politics, even when they are rendered overtly visible to us, perhaps because of the politics of visibility at play. If certain bodies do not count as bodies, if certain deaths are not considered grievable (Butler 2010), then perhaps the standard rules of corpses do not apply? That is, the death itself is not any less obscene than viewing it. Encountering the obscenity of the image is one way of deferring the obscenity of the death itself, of making the image the iconic representation so as to not have to reckon with the larger context of the event.

Harry Mount (2011) asks the appropriate question here: "is it wrong to feel pleased at Gaddafi's death?" There is, then a moral question involved in celebrating a death. He notes that feeling conflicted, both pleasure and pity, is a luxury of those with no personal stake, and that for those who were oppressed under Qaddafi, rejoicing seems the only appropriate emotion. It seems, though, that for those who were not oppressed under Qaddafi, for the audience of these English-language tweets, rejoicing at a death is a political statement about the legitimacy of particular actions taken by democracies against dictators. They circulate wider meanings that tell us that obscenity can be part of the triumphs and successes of war.

It bears mentioning here an interesting paradox that is part of the display of Qaddafi's body. It is displayed both as a symbol of dead dictatorship and the triumph of democracy in Western discourse, as in the way it was circulated, yet also as morally problematic, as if to reinforce the notion that even when celebrating, Westerners feel pity the way Libyans do not. Similarly, the notion that "we in the West" are revolted by the display of the body, when in actuality the photo was widely circulated and there is no evidence of this general revulsion, operates to construct Libyans, even when democratic, as somehow still backward and primitive. Thus, even as Western news sources circulate the photographs of Qaddafi's dead body, they also note the controversy over its display, and criticisms surrounding the circumstances of his death (Boffey 2011). They thus claim the moral high ground while circulating very specific understandings of the meaning of Qaddafi's death.

Jonathan Jones (2011) has described the "fuss and bother" around the photographs of Qaddafi in that they display the "face of war, washed in blood, bathed in cruelty." It is precisely the idea that it is the face of war that renders it frightening and perhaps even spectral, as if the spirit of the crazy man lingers in the smeared blood and tattered hair. Jones describes the photographs as haunting, and indeed they are disturbing, but it is further significant precisely because of the way they are haunted by the specter of the construction of democracy. That is, dead Qaddafi is not simply a dead man, but a "dead dictator" and all that that entails, and enmeshed within the discourses that enable the display of his corpse as a "mad dog" rather than as a human being, and a very specific story about his death and its broader significance for the triumph of democracy.

The satirical framing associated with the popular culture of Qaddafi allows for these stories and understandings. The way Qaddafi's death was turned into a joke, rather than a political event, exemplifies the figuration of the popular politics of a dead dictator. After he died, @domknight tweeted, "When Gaddafi gets to the top of Twitter's trending topics list, it'll be the first democratic contest he's legitimately won" (Downs 2011). Similarly, comedian Jeff Ross tweeted, "Moammar Gaddhafi is dead. He's survived by his brothers Larry Gadhafi and Curly Gadhafi" (Malec and Garvey 2011). The mingling of invocations of Qaddafi as a political figure with Qaddafi as the butt of the joke reinforce understandings of the figure of the dead dictator as one both legitimately killed and rendered dehumanized by the satire accompanying the popular representations of his death. The way Qaddafi is turned into a character and caricature invokes a particular audience who is part of the joke, and it is this same audience who becomes responsible for determining and legitimizing policy interventions in Libya, and the way in which democratization there is portrayed and depicted in Western media accounts even at the time of this writing.

The portrayal of dictatorship as already non-normative, as an assumption, that circulates in policymaking circles, was both reflected in and shaped by popular culture circulations of Qaddafi as the "mad dog," madness being the apex of non-normativity, and then following on this, legitimized by it, the dead dictator, able to be displayed, paraded past, and visually marked as an exception to the taboo of looking at the dead body.

Conclusions

Tiffany Jenkins draws attention to the contrast between Qaddafi's dead body and Osama bin Laden's. Bin Laden's body was not displayed, photographs were not shown, and his burial at sea was intended to keep his gravesite from becoming a shrine. Qaddafi, on the other hand, was displayed and paraded past, photographs were splashed around the Internet, and his bloodied body was dragged through the streets. As Jenkins (2011, unpaginated) notes, "the contrast between the careful concealment of Bin Laden's body, and the public parading of Gaddafi's tells us something. The weakness of Gaddafi's position before he died meant he was easier to dominate when dead; Bin Laden, on the other hand, was feared until the end, and his supporters are still considered extremely dangerous. Even in death, he remains a threat." However, what Jenkins omits from her assessment is the discursive work at play here. Osama bin Laden needed to continue to be a threat even from beyond the grave in order to legitimate an ongoing war-on-terror and the broad criteria for carrying out drone strikes in Pakistan and Yemen, and his body was enmeshed in a wider story about Al-Qaeda revenge for the death. Thus bin Laden's body is disappeared within a narrative enabled in the service of a particular policy. Qaddafi, on the other hand, is not a dead terrorist, but a dead dictator, and his dead body and its display enable a different conversation about the illegitimacy of the dictator and the lack of threat he poses to democratic forms of governance. In this sense, obscenity as a framing concept becomes particularly useful because it can be imagined both as the obscenity of seeing too much, and as the obscenity of seeing too little. Osama bin Laden was the body that was too obscene to be shown, while Qaddafi's was just obscene enough to shock on display, and cause some ethical discomfort and debate, while still acting as a triumphant display of a win for Western democracy.

The rules of body display are not set in stone: each dead body story offers up one visualization of the technologies of erasure, in service of a particular narrative. The existence of a dead body can be a failure of the system, as in natural disasters where bodies crop up in places they should not be, demanding to be managed and reincorporated within mechanisms of body management. However, the existence of a dead body can also be indicative of a success of the system, that a body has been rendered into a corpse so as to enhance security, as with the death of Osama bin Laden, and the demands to materialize his corpse a means to narrativize the security threat itself.

As I have described, images of violently dead bodies have been circulated and mobilized in the service of the war-on-terror. Some bodies are rendered hyper-visible, such as that of Qaddafi, so as to enable a story about the triumph of democracy over dictatorship, and the madness of a dictator that continues beyond his death. Other bodies are displayed in a complex schema of visuality, as in the command to look at Syrian victims, or to look at pieces of blurred images of atrocities committed by soldiers. Still others are deemed too volatile to be displayed, as in the case of the corpse of Osama bin Laden. The images are part of a wider discourse, used strategically and to specific effect. Circulating images of Qaddafi reinforced the notion of the inevitable failure of dictatorship, supporting a policy of democratization. The body of Osama bin Laden, on the other hand, represented a success of the war-on-terror, but its visibility was considered a security risk that could further heighten tensions and provoke retaliatory attacks by Al-Qaeda.

Judith Butler, in the context of the Abu Ghraib photos, has argued that what we see when we look at these photos is ourselves seeing. To paraphrase, she notes that we are the photographers to the extent that we live within the visual norms in which the prisoners are rendered abject and beaten. But the individuals depicted are indifferent to us (Butler 2005, 826). This is similarly the case in the photographs I have described here, most importantly because in a structural sense, there is no way the dead body can see back at us as we consume it visually. Butler has argued that this sort of depiction tells us that certain kinds of seeing are memorialized in the photograph. These ways of seeing do not depict human suffering because the visual framing does not conceive of the subject of the photograph as human. She lays the framework, then, for considering images of suffering and obscene atrocity that are not intended to, or are unable to, provoke moral outrage precisely because they represent a rupture in symmetric seeing.

The visual asymmetry of viewing the dead inculcates a particular relationship of consumption such that specific non-normative bodies are consumed rather than simply viewed. Beyond this, the privileged act of seeing at a distance is often equated with witnessing, yet it also inculcates a model wherein we experience modern war by proxy, and this framing shapes understandings of what war is via which images of war are deemed legitimate grounds for visual consumption. Obscenity provides a means of generating a spectacle out of dead enemy bodies, both in their display and in the way they are visually erased. It does so through technology: the editing of images, the pixellation of parts of obscene images as a means to blur and remove certain images, thereby visually managing them and their meanings. That is, in thinking about the technologies of erasure in the war-on-terror, what matters may be questions surrounding who is *seen* and how, but also who is *seeing* and how.

5 | Proof of Death
Evidence and Atrocity

In March 2015, photographs defined as "graphic" depicting the tortured, bloodied, and bruised dead bodies of civilians killed by the regime of Bashar al-Assad in Syria went on display in the halls of the United Nations (UN) building in New York, as can be seen in Figure 5.1. They are accompanied by warning signs to indicate the graphic nature of their subject, and some have argued that they are too graphic to be displayed. However, their display occurs in a context of awareness, which seems to be accompanied by an impetus to look. "'We know that it is far easier to walk rapidly down this corridor, far easier to look away', Michele J Sison, the US deputy representative to the UN, told the gathered crowd of diplomats and journalists. 'These images are the graphic depiction of how the Assad regime treats its citizens. It is imperative that we at the United Nations not look away'" (Jalabi 2015). The images, part of a collection taken by a former Syrian military photographer who defected, were originally taken to act as evidence within the Syrian government that the regime had indeed killed the person it had reported as dead.

In describing the exhibit, UN representatives emphasized the moral imperative associated with looking. In a world where cultural norms often dictate that dead bodies should not be viewable outside of the funerary industry, especially when they are graphic by virtue of a bloody and violent death, these images of dead and tortured bodies are instead accompanied by a command to look. The images are themselves imbued with some sort of humanitarian power, implying that simply by looking, we can make things better, thereby inculcating a particular relationship between the viewer and the image, placing the viewer in a position of power to effect change. Such a framing tends to assume that buried deep within us is our empathy for other human beings, if only it could be uncovered by the right word, slogan, news, or image.

Figure 5.1 Visitors look at the images of dead bodies at the UN headquarters in New York on March 12, 2015. Images of torture carried out by the Syrian regime forces are on display in the halls of the UN. CEM OZDEL/Anadolu Agency via Getty Images

Even as we are instructed to look at and engage with these images, portions of the images considered too graphic for display have been blurred. That is, even as the obscenity of the images provides a basis for their power to effect change, there is also the notion that some things are simply too obscene to be shown. Again, the audience here matters, as the viewers of these images at UN Headquarters are those visiting this building in New York, many of whom are classified as humanitarian actors with the power to bring about change simply via their visual consumption. Other viewers include Western audiences of the media outlets that circulated these images.

In this sense, there are dead body images we are "supposed" to engage with, such as those in this UN exhibit. The undercurrent of this narrative, of course is the images we are not supposed to look at (those parts of the torture images not shown, the falling bodies of 9/11, the coffins of US soldiers from the wars in Afghanistan and Iraq, as some examples). There are dead bodies we should look at and those we shouldn't. The images of Syrian torture victims are intended to spur action on the part of the international community by making obscenity visible, leading us to perceive the situation as sufficiently extreme to transgress visual norms. On the other hand, images of dead American victims of 9/11 are characterized as too obscene to be part of the visual spectrum of the war-on-terror.

This chapter takes the paradoxical nature of responses to obscene images depicting dead bodies as a starting point to consider the display of dead bodies in the context of humanitarian awareness campaigns. My focus is not on these campaigns themselves, but rather in the way dead bodies, and the photographic representations of them, often function for the purpose of bringing hard evidence to claims of atrocity and as an affective instrument that can spur a response on the part of the viewer that may then lead to policy action. In doing so, we must struggle with the dilemma of the *Real* associated with images of the dead as evidence, particularly as evidence of things we would prefer to see as *not real* or that we find to be unbelievable: large-scale human rights violations. While my empirical focus here is mainly on the Syrian case I introduce this chapter with, many of these same points can be generalized to other empirical examples as well.

The chapter first examines the tensions at play between obscenity, dignity, and evidentiary value, with display of dead bodies for humanitarian purposes, examining the functioning of obscenity to drive awareness and policy change, and the functional rupturing of the dead body taboo. It then takes on the case of images of torture victims in Syria from 2013 to the present, which provided evidence in two ways: they were initially taken by an Assad regime photographer to act as proof that these individuals had actually been killed, and then, when the photographer defected, they acted as evidence on a global scale of the atrocities of the Assad regime. It considers these images alongside the image of a different dead Syrian: the toddler Aylan Kurdi, whose body washed up on a Turkish beach became iconic of the vulnerability of the refugee. Then, the chapter explores the cases of Kayla Mueller and Giulio Regeni. Mueller was an American aid worker working in besieged Syria held captive by ISIS, who was ultimately killed in an American airstrike. Her family refused to believe she had been killed, and ISIS sent them a photo of Mueller's dead body to act as evidence, as "proof of death." Similarly, Giulio Regeni was an Italian student working in Egypt who was arrested and killed by the Egyptian police, and his body dumped on a street. When the Egyptian government refused to acknowledge their role in his death, his family threatened to send them a photo of his dead body, to act as proof of the truth surrounding his death.

The chapter examines the various ways death images and dead bodies themselves act as evidence, raising questions about how and when the dead are too obscene to be viewed, and when they are situated within a logic about what must be viewed. In other words, I am not interested in bodies as forensic evidence in their own right, but rather in the ways in which images of the dead can act as evidence in larger political discourses, thus justifying their publication or display for particular purposes, contravening the taboo that typically governs viewing dead bodies and dead body images.

The Obscene Body in Pain: "How Do I Know if It Is Real"?

This section focuses on the narratives through which particular bodies are rendered visible in the context of humanitarian awareness. I argue that the obscene suffering dead body is made visible in the service of two main purposes: first, to make the audience aware of distant suffering in an attempt to change the policy outcomes for the suffering, and second, to acknowledge the reality of the suffering of others. I focus specifically on the relationship between the taboo and the *Real*, as a means of contextualizing the larger politics of visualizing human suffering. To do so, I first detail the taboo surrounding viewing pain and the larger questions of compassion and empathy that exist in the context of humanitarianism in a way they have not arisen in the previous chapters.

Prior to the eighteenth century, pain was considered in a Western Judeo-Christian context to be either a mechanism of God's punishment or a redemptive opportunity to emulate Christ (Halttunen 1995). Indeed, much religious art depicted the body in pain (Sontag 2003, 41). But in the era of philosophy that bred John Locke, pain became redefined as something unacceptable and eradicable. Yet along with this comes the notion that pain is "obscenely titillating precisely because the humanitarian sensibility deemed it unacceptable, taboo" (Halttunen 1995, 304). The twinning of desire and disgust motivated the emergence of the literary genres of voyeurism and sadism. We often see rhetoric in the literature of this time that combines pleasure and pain: "dear delicious pain," "pleasing Anguish" (Halttunen 1995, 308). By the eighteenth century nearly all pornography had become about pain because of the shock value associated with the nature of pain as forbidden (Halttunen 1995, 318). In other words, the suffering human body is taboo precisely because our Enlightenment-based philosophies tell us suffering is preventable, and thus *inhumane*. Yet there is also a notion that atrocity images arouse prurient interest (Sontag 2003), and much of this stems from the perception that atrocity images can be beautiful.

This emerges at the same time as a culture of salaciousness surrounding gory crimes such as murder. Similarly, we see the emergence of a humanitarian genre focused on depicting suffering in a graphic manner to draw attention to it, with *Uncle Tom's Cabin*'s opening scene of Uncle Tom being flogged a key example of this so-called reformer literature that sought to focus on pain as a means to argue against its existence. The idea was that the "spectacle of pain was a source of illicit excitement, prurience, and obscenity – the power to evoke revulsion and disgust" (Halttunen 1995, 325). In other words, such graphic descriptions and sometimes illustrations in literary works were seen to have a material effect on the ongoing existence of practices causing human suffering. Indeed, the purpose of shocking obscene images of suffering is to create guilt and shame in the viewer as a mechanism of advancing an idea of social justice (Chouliaraki 2010, 111). We are thus called to look at images that we are not supposed to look at, and feel shame looking at.

The moral failure associated with such images is seen to "foster ethics of recognition of the humanness of others" (Kozol 2014, 19). Much of the origins of images of suffering come from a wartime context, though it should be noted that after World War I such images became recategorized as potentially pornographic, reducing "men's sacred bodies to objects of excitement, pleasure or domination and thereby further violated the dead" (Dean 2003, 91).

Debates about the ethics of depicting suffering continue to the present day. In the modern era, such pain becomes primarily narrativized through images, and specifically photographs: "[I]nfluenced by Locke's understanding of the primacy of vision among the senses, eighteenth century moral philosophers treated sympathy as a sentiment stirred primarily through sight" (Halttunen 1995, 305). This is intimately connected to the notion that visual experience is the only authentic way to experience events (Lyford and Payne 2005, 123). Yet, Western modernity has also been characterized by a larger effort to move dead bodies out of the public eye, managed through a funerary industry that privatizes death and its visibility (Mitford 1998; Papailias 2019, 1050). Additionally, the viewing of obscene images of suffering and death in particular has at various times been framed as pornographic and as extending the suffering of the humans therein (Prosser 2012; Sentilles 2017). Yet invoking pornography as a metaphor for this type of suffering conceals the way they are different, namely that the subjects of porn are typically consenting, while that is not the case for documentary footage of suffering, and that the latter is *a priori* connected to cultural traditions of evidence and bearing witness in ways pornography is not (Tait 2008, 96).

Thus, we begin with a paradox: rendering pain visible stirs an affective response in the viewer that may motivate political action, yet it also raises an ethical dilemma about which bodies are seen and about how and whether we can ethically engage with dead body images. I should remind the reader here that my focus is primarily on a Western context and Western audience, though I do acknowledge the limits of such a focus. Indeed, As Hochberg notes, different audiences tend to have different perceptions of the need to show particular images. Israeli media, for example, tends to see graphic photos of death and injury as voyeuristic and pornographic while Arab media considers them to be necessary for accurate reporting. He details this as less about a cultural difference and more about the different positions Israelis and Palestinians hold with respect to sovereign power (Hochberg 2015, 9).

Sarah Sentilles (2017) has framed many of these questions via her work as a journalist: "What should one do when faced with images of violence? Do these images harm their subjects? Is it an ethical violation to make a photograph of suffering beautiful? Do I have a right to look at other people's pain?" There is also a larger dynamic at play here, related to the specific images that are rendered visible. Perceptions of vulnerability come into play with who counts as a victim, with children often becoming exemplary of victimhood in such images (Berents 2019). Race also becomes an issue with these perceptions of vulnerability and visibility, with some of the rhetoric around the James Wright Foley beheading image focused on his position as a white journalist. James Ball, for example, compares the outrage about the Foley image to the image of a dead Palestinian child shown on the cover page of the *New York Times*. As he notes, depictions of civilian men massacred by ISIS are often shown, and there is very little controversy about it: he writes, "to see an outcry for Foley's video and not for others is to wonder whether we are disproportionately concerned over showing graphic deaths of white westerners – maybe even white journalists – and not others" (Ball 2014). These debates matter because the images that become icons tell us something about our identities; they are ways in which "people and communities make sense of themselves" (Bleiker 2018, 8).

In short, there is a political and ethical question about which bodies should be rendered visible, yet such a framing posits some bodies as worthy of visibility precisely because such visibility is equated with some sort of action, shifting the focus to the viewer, their emotions, how they see, and how they engage with the content of the image. In other words, visibility functions as a precondition for awareness and policy change, or at least it is posited as such. This becomes the mechanism for breaking the taboo governing viewing the dead: it functions to draw awareness to deaths that matter and as a result must be made visible so that they can be redeemed through the acknowledgment that they matter and are deserving of something more, some action, some response. Yet the tension remains precisely because of the taboo, the notion that trauma itself is unrepresentable (Baer 2005), and that the body in pain specifically defies attempts at visual representation (Dauphinee 2007, 139). Despite this, iconic visual images of pain and death seem to capture attention precisely because of this ethical gap in representations.

This ethical issue of representation draws on social norms about what should not be seen, connecting such visual grammar to notions about a civilized viewer. When the body of Aylan Kurdi washed up on a Turkish beach after a boat capsized as his refugee family attempted to flee for Europe, the image was widely published in global media. It symbolized a rupture in civilized society: "[A]ppearing in ways that might be considered taboo – images of dead children are not 'meant' to be seen as they are not 'meant' to occur – images of children's dead bodies ask the viewer to be outraged" (Berents 2019, 150). Susie Linfield also describes images of suffering, contrasting them with pornographic images: while the latter show something that we shouldn't see, the former show us something that should not exist (2010, 41).

In the case of atrocity images, it is the process of rendering these bodies visible that reconfigures the ethical space occupied by the viewer, demanding the viewer then act as a witness to atrocity. Images of the dead presented in a humanitarian context place demands on viewers: outrage, action, and so on, and the breaking of the taboo governing viewing the dead becomes narrativized and justified in the context of the evidentiary value of these bodies, a notion I take up later in this chapter with regard to the case of the bodies of Syrian torture victims.

Humanitarian campaigns specifically have often mobilized images as a means to raise awareness of distant suffering, and the main purpose seems to be resistance to violence (Sentilles 2017). Sontag notes that for a long time, people thought if suffering could simply be sufficiently vivid, people would realize the nature of war (2003, 14). There is also a wide-ranging assumption that death images have a "documented ability to influence viewers" (Winkler et al., 2019, 248; see also Kozol 2014; Moeller 1999; Rose 2001, 10; Shim 2014, 24; Sliwinski 2011). Ranciere notes this as the "dream of photojournalism" that an image will spur an audience to action (Ranciere 2011, 103). Yet this response may not always emerge, "seeing does not necessarily translate into believing, caring, or acting" (Linfield 2010, 33), and it is also the case that responses to vulnerability can be heavily gendered (Moeller 1999, 38), where having an affective response to the suffering of others is deemed emotional rather than rational, and thus not an effective precondition for policy. In many instances the very thing that makes an image obscene is the excess of affect in the viewer's response.

Lilie Chouliaraki characterizes the approach to humanitarianism that seeks to spur action in the viewer as "shock effect," noting that it can serve to fetishize the bodies depicted (2010, 110). As she notes about a 1961 Red Cross campaign: "[T]hey do not reflect real human bodies but curiosities of the flesh that mobilize a pornographic specta-torial imagination between disgust and desire" (Chouliaraki 2010, 110). In this vein, the effort to depict the reality of starvation paradox-ically renders the bodies *unreal,* and the activation of the twin impetuses of desire and disgust associated with the taboo governing viewing bodies like this results in the rendering iconic of the image. The image becomes an icon precisely because of its departure from the *Real* at the same time as depicting it. This can remove from consideration the specificity of the pain depicted in one single image, as the symbol of collective pain becomes more important than the reality of that pain or trauma itself (Dauphinee 2007, 146).

Indeed, just as many news outlets justified showing images or video of ISIS beheadings because it "was important not to hide from reality" (Meade 2014), the display of images of the dead in the humanitarian context is often seen to be about exposing the reality of human suffering: the evidentiary function. Images are increasingly used as a key way to understand human rights crises (Ristovska 2019, 333). This is premised on the notion that photography lends itself to the incorruptibility of the image and that which is contained therein, due to its referential nature (Moeller et al. 2015, 121), an assumption key to the evolution of the modern genre of humanitarian photography and the relationship between photography and human rights consciousness (Twomey 2014). Indeed, the origins of some of the first human rights campaigns coincide with the development of the genre of atrocity photography, as in the Congo Reform campaign, which was premised on photographs of the mutilated bodies of Congolese that functioned both as evidence and to suggest that Africans were possessed of human dignity (Twomey 2012, 39). Elizabeth Dauphinee has noted that the concentration camp survivor was not believed because of the notion that he had mistaken a nightmare for reality (2007, 142), and she argues that if war is about injury and death, we should not hide such images from the public eye precisely because of this evidentiary function (2018, 32). Some even argue that "to not picture atrocity is therefore to omit what's there, to fail the truth of a situation, to withhold that proof" (Prosser 2012, 7). Viewing then is equated with a particular truth, a way of accessing the *Real* of a human suffering that also at the same time seems *unreal* to us.

The image of the suffering other and the evidentiary value it holds also implicates the viewer in a certain responsibility to do something in response to this reality. "Beholding the corpse of the Other confronts us with the limits of representation and our responsibilities for the dead/dying Other" (Papailias 2019, 1051). In this sense, there is a dilemma at play here: dead body images hammer home the reality of human suffering, yet because this suffering is not proximate to us, it does not seem *real* to us, thus complicating the framing of such images as evidence of atrocity, while also complicating our emotional responses to them, not to mention the fact that emotional responses are often delegitimized in the realm of hard policy. Even in Plato's *Republic,* he discusses how emotional images can confuse reality, which emphasizes the duration of the existence of the binary often set up between the emotional and the real (Perlmutter 2005, 109). Levi-Strauss context-ualizes this in his notion that "it is not that we mistake photographs for reality; we prefer them to reality. We cannot bear reality, but we bear images" (2003, 185).

Chouliaraki also introduces the dilemma of the *Real*, in the "'How do I know this is real' sensibility further amplified by the public's awareness of the capacity of the media to manipulate images of suffer-ing" (Chouliaraki 2010, 114). This may be the case, despite the media trafficking in the claim to factuality and showing things as they really are, substantiated by photography's claim to veracity (Chouliaraki 2006, 159). Sontag also draws attention to this idea, noting that "the real thing may not be fearsome enough, and therefore needs to be enhanced or reenacted more convincingly" (2003). Indeed, one of the most famous images from the Congo Reform campaign was of Nsala with the remains of his daughter (hand and foot), which he brought to the missionaries because he knew as an African that he would not be believed without the material evidence (Twomey 2012, 43). In that sense, there are some bodies that are needed to act as evidence precisely because some lives, stories, and deaths already matter more than others. Others have also drawn attention to the notion of hierarchies of suffering, which centralize suffering proximate to us or by those who look like us, as in the idea of "Missing White Woman Syndrome" (Jones 2013).

This may be particularly true because Western audiences tend not to be responsive to suffering in and of itself. Indeed, for its seventy-fifth anniversary, *Time* magazine compiled a list of its ten worst-selling covers, and on that list was coverage of Bosnia in 1993 and Somalia in 1992 (Moeller 1999, 18). Moeller (1999, 235) has also noted as an example the donations coming in to Oxfam during and after the Rwandan genocide. During the genocide, as pictures emerged of atro-city, Oxfam called for donations and none came. When images of the cholera outbreak at the refugee camp later were published, thousands donated, and spikes in donations could be directly traced to associated media coverage. Perhaps viewers do not sufficiently care and do not want to be revolted by the encounter with the image, as in the case of the *New York Times* reader who wrote a letter to complain about the 1998 photo of a Kosovar massacre victim, noting that "this is not something I wish to see alongside my breakfast" (as quoted in Rushdy 2000, 74).

Indeed, at times the suffering depicted seems too bad to be real, as we often see in the language of responses to genocide (Power 2002). Indeed, during the Rwandan genocide, CNN anchor John Holliman noted that "the pictures from Rwanda are reminiscent of those from the Holocaust. Perhaps too horrible to believe" (as quoted in Moeller 1999, 222). In other words, extreme embodied violence and death suspends *reality*. While Moeller blames this on compassion fatigue, I see more to this. Indeed, many photojournalists characterize their work as functioning to deny the viewer the luxury of disbelief (Kennedy 2016, 124). The very idea of what is *real* is rendered moot in the face of the obscene death image. Instead, what we see and how we respond is mediated by what is too obscene (because it is *too real* – i.e. genocide), and what is obscene enough (because it is a reality we can digest, conceptualize, and empathize – i.e. famine). Indeed, it is often precisely because of the reality of the image that the taboo is seen to be justifiably broken: it is those situations where the trauma cannot be adequately represented that it becomes important for the trauma to be witnessed (Lowe 2014, 212).

The *unreal* nature of suffering becomes vital through a narrative of distance associated with the pain of others that derives from the problem of adequate representation of trauma. Dauphinee specifically calls images of the body in pain "an obscenity" because the experience of the body in pain cannot be easily accessed even by the viewer of the photograph, noting the problem of representation associated with the suffering of others that can enhance this spectatorial distance (2018, 34). The idea of spectatorial sympathy rests on social distance and the ability of the viewer to be grateful they are not in the circumstances of the other (Halttunen 1995, 309), paradoxically making it so that those depicted in humanitarian images actually seem further away from us rather than more proximate, and seem more different than us, even as it may cultivate sympathy for their plight. Much of the humanitarian campaigns from the 1960s to 1980s draw on the idea of the distant sufferer, and "establish(ed) a social relationship anchored on the colonial gaze and premised on maximal distance between spectator and suffering other" (Chouliaraki 2010, 110). The choices and frames about which bodies become rendered visible or symbolic of the violence is a decision fraught with the functioning of power, and "the victims that are seen to illustrate humanitarian disaster often look different from the predominantly white consumers of these images in the Global North" (Berents 2019, 155, see also Prosser 2012). Indeed, Papailias (2019, 1055) has demonstrated with regard to images of refugees that trigger warnings often serve to shift the focus from the person depicted to the often-Western viewer: "[T]hey shift the emphasis to their potential harm, not that already inflicted on the photographed subject. Ironically the image of precarious subjects appears to be protected more than their own lives."

Indeed, what we see is often a viewer-centric notion of visual culture or visual politics. Yet this is missing a part of the politics of visibility because it focuses primarily on the affective orientation or response of the viewer, which already presumes a particular power relationship. Parashar notes that even the connection between showing dead body images and action is premised on a problematic affective orientation toward the Other. The desire to do something, she notes, "lays bare our encounters with the 'Other' for whom compassion must first be visually manufactured (through photographs) and then made available only by mitigating differences" (Parashar 2015, unpaginated). Indeed, if "the act of 'seeing' appears to confirm the existence and reality of what one sees" (Moeller et al. 2015, 121), it is important to ask after the reification of seeing as a precondition for global political action. Indeed, we should also ask ourselves what suffering we are not seeing and why (Casper and Moore 2009, 3; Robinson 2018, 66).

It should also be noted that images of the suffering other, displayed in a humanitarian context, offer up a particular notion of lethality. Nisha Shah (2017) has discussed the evolution of the calibration of lethality with regard to weapons, particularly the damage that can be caused by bullets as a mechanism of military effectiveness. In this sense, while lethality became an indicator associated with the debates about military weaponry, in the instances I discuss lethality often becomes a justification for outside attention or intervention: the more lethal, the more terrible, the more objectionable, the more obscene the violence against the innocent, the more worthy it becomes of attention and action. In this sense, the images must justify themselves, and their framing must justify them, as worthy enough of the breaking of the taboo toward a particular political end. I examine what this looks like in action in the next section. I attempt to shift the focus from the decisions about which bodies are visible to an examination of how particular bodies are rendered visible and the politics this is in the service of.

The Dead Bodies of Syrians: Narratives of Vulnerability and Evidence

The hallmark of an atrocity photo is the "intentional crossing of a certain threshold of the intact body which has been trespassed by various degrees of harm, possibly even becoming a dead body" (Azoulay 2012, 250). In this sense, the intentionality of the transgression of the taboo of bodily integrity is the key to this framing. Unlike most atrocity images, the images of Syrian torture victims were photographed not by photojournalists cataloguing the event but by a Syrian regime photographer – by the perpetrator. War trophy photographs, of which these could perhaps be conceived of as example, are a souvenir for the victors precisely because they are titillating. They are both pornographic and evidentiary, because they can serve as proof of atrocity (Roberts 2012, 203).

While scholars debate "whether human beings abhor or enjoy reading about and viewing the suffering of others" (Mieszkowski 2012, 3), the functioning of the obscenity taboo is actually the simultaneous desire and disgust, the way in which we feel compelled to view photographs that we then are horrified by. The twin functioning of this is what sustains the taboo in its very rupturing. In other words, when we are instructed to view dead body images, particularly gory ones such as those of Syrian torture victims, we break the taboo that governs the viewing of the dead, but we do so in such a way, via such a framing of the reasons for viewing the images and the ways in which we should engage with them as a form of political action, that sustains the taboo itself, that reinforces the exceptional nature of this particular viewing in this moment and no other. We do not go from viewing images of Syrian torture victims to a rupturing of the taboo governing viewing the dead, but rather to a sense that the taboo is there for us to avoid encountering the things we shouldn't, but that there are rare occasions where we should in fact encounter those very things: when they occur when they shouldn't. Indeed, Shah (2017b, 552) notes that bodies on display related to war exhibitions tell us that there are acceptable ways in which bodies can be killed in war, but these are soldier bodies, and in the humanitarian context, the framing instead tells us that these bodies should not have been killed in war. Because these deaths should not have occurred, they occupy an exceptional space where they can, indeed should, be viewed, so long as they spur the appropriate feelings and emotions in the viewer. The story about what and how one should see then becomes just as important as what one does see (Mieszkowski 2012, 69).

A point of contrast here is useful. Nisha Shah (2017b) has drawn attention to the (lack of) display of corpses at the Canadian War Museum as a means to illustrate the point that the exhibit tells us that war is not about the production of corpses as a main event. Indeed, though there are some images of the dead on display, in general we are left with the notion that war does not produce very many corpses. She particularly draws attention to a painting from World War I called "A Corpse, Evening" that does not depict any corpses (Shah 2017b, 550). Her point then is that the dynamics of corpse display not only illustrate a story of corpses as evidence of what occurred but also frame our interpretations of the event in a substantive way. In this vein, looking at which corpses are displayed and why, and how this fits into a larger story about an event, can tell us about how death is calibrated, to borrow Shah's words.

Torture Photographs

The images of tortured Syrian dead bodies were not meant to be made public, but they were intended to be part of government records kept by the Syrian government of atrocity carried out on their own citizens. The photographs, more than 55,000 in total, were taken by a Syrian government forensic photographer who gave himself the code name Caesar (Nichols 2015). He smuggled them out of Syria between 2011 and 2013. In 2015, some of the images went on display at the UN building in New York, as I discuss at the beginning of this chapter. The photographs are gruesome. The bodies are bloody, with bones protruding. They look starving. Some show children: Human Rights Watch has identified a fourteen-year-old boy in one of the images. The images come from a detention center where these individuals were tortured and killed. Caesar, who is now in witness protection somewhere in Europe, describes how his work shifted from photographing crime scenes and accidents to the tortured protesters, as the antigovernment protests spread:

I had never seen this before. Before the Revolution, the regime would torture people to extract information. Now they were simply torturing people to death. I saw the candle burns ... some people had deep knife wounds, eyeballs ripped out, broken teeth, whip marks ... sometimes the bodies were covered in blood, and the blood was still fresh ... they knew they were going to die ... they had their mouths open in pain, and you could sense the humiliation they had suffered ... I had to take breaks so that I wouldn't start crying ... I could picture my brothers and sisters as one of those corpses. It made me ill ... we couldn't avert our gaze. The detainee came back to life in front of us. We could really see the bodies, imagine the torture, feel the blows raining down. Then we had to write the report. (As quoted in Linfield 2019)

Linfield (2019) situates these images within what she calls the resurgence of perpetrator photographs: "[I]n this war, the perpetrators themselves – both in the Assad regime and in the terrorist groups opposing him – have photographed, indeed advertised their *own* atrocities, of which they are apparently proud. So while documentation of war crimes is still vital, the classic function of photography is now sorely tested." She connects the Caesar images to ISIS's propaganda videos, including beheading videos, such as those I discussed in Chapter 3, and the al-Kasasbeh footage I discussed in Chapter 2.

As Moller notes, "it seems odd or even wrong to look at torture photographs with the same clinical attitude, the same analytical interest" as any other routine photograph (Moller 2013, 12). Indeed, they replicate the schema used by the Assad government to turn these corpses into numbers rather than names, something that Caesar himself speaks of (Linfield 2019). Moller specifically notes that torture images cannot/shall not be represented. In other words, they are firmly placed in the realm of the taboo, in the injunction against representation that we find in the *Bilderverbot*. Linfield (2019), in this same vein, refers to the photographs as "unbearable." Though much of the debate in visual politics centers on whether we should look, characterized well by Moller's (2013) point that looking is morally unacceptable because it prolongs suffering, but not looking is morally unacceptable because it denies suffering, my focus here is not on the choice to look itself, but rather on what the ethical dilemma surrounding looking tells us. In other words, the very debate governing images considered to be obscene frames the question as one about how to engage suffering (look at it or look away). My question here is rather how obscenity functions as a regulatory mechanism to instruct us to engage in particular ways, to set the very terms of the debate about looking in the first place. In the words of Francois Debrix (2019, unpaginated): "[W]hat becomes intolerable or unacceptable is not so much what the image shows but rather that it shows."

These images were shown within a wider narrative of the necessity of action. Britain's UN ambassador noted that "we hope that this exhibition will serve as a reminder of the imperative to pursue a political solution to the conflict with utmost urgency to end the suffering of the Syrian people" (as quoted in Nichols 2015). The affective response of the viewer is linked with a particular type of action. The role of images then is seen to be presencing the subject material, materializing a particular kind of suffering, a narrative that renders necessary the viewing of such atrocity images for a larger political purpose of making suffering itself politically visible. Susie Linfield also discusses these images in light of the "traditional hope of photojournalists ... that, in revealing the cruelty of war, the world would take ... saving action" (Linfield 2019). Images of torture then are seen to be able to spur an affective response of horror that can achieve something positive. Wendy Kozol describes this with reference to the Abu Ghraib images: "[T]here can be pleasure in being appalled, horrified, and disgusted, a pleasure in the sense of being right or good" (Kozol 2012, 33). Her focus here is on reclaiming the idea of the pleasure of voyeurism and torture porn for the empathetic spectator who can feel good about their engagement with a torture image, if, and only if, they acknowledge their own complicity in the suffering depicted (in the case of Abu Ghraib, American complicity in the acts of the American government). In this vein, she also justifies publishing the images of Abu Ghraib in her article – that the workings of visual practices to shape our understanding of torture should be made visible. In this sense, she frames viewing and recirculating torture images as a form of ethical witnessing – many of the same arguments made about the importance of looking at Caesar's torture images.

Abir Hamdar (2018) has noted the way the Syrian corpse acts as an agent of post-mortem resistance. Indeed, this is also how Caesar himself views his photos: he thought that their release would topple Assad, and thus were worth risking his own life to release to the global public. But they didn't topple Assad. The author of a book about Caesar noted that "Caesar is disappointed by the international community's inaction. He is wondering why he put his own life and those of his loved ones at risk and caused them so much fear" (as cited in Linfield 2019). People were horrified, but nothing changed. Debrix (2019) notes about Caesar's photographs of Syrian torture victims that the US public has made a point not to face the images of horror emerging from Syria. He suggests that the "dead and mutilated human faces like these captured by Caesar's camera are today's Muselmann." He takes issue with the notion that the display of these images at sites like the UN or the US Holocaust Memorial Museum serves the function of rehumanization. Instead, he notes, "the realism/reality of the image simply points to faces of individuals who have been killed, and perhaps there is no more to be seen than this." In this, Debrix gets at the complex visuality surrounding an image: it is not simply what it depicts or even how it is framed in its display. It is also about what we choose to see, as the viewer. We may choose to see an ongoing atrocity that is in need of action, but we may also choose to see a dead body, and only a dead body.

The last component of these images I want to discuss here is the verification process when they were released in the West. When Caesar presented the images, they were not taken at face value. US intelligence agencies including the FBI and other forensic experts verified the authenticity of the images (Linfield 2019). Human Rights Watch also sought to independently verify Caesar's claims about the images, including where they were taken. As its 2015 report notes:

Caesar told both an international team of lawyers investigating the photographs and the U.S. Congress that they were taken at Syrian government military hospitals. "What you see here is the garage of the military hospital," he told Congress. "We used to use the morgue, but they were bringing way more bodies, so we decided to start using the garage." Using satellite imagery and geolocation techniques, as well as the evidence of a defector from Military Hospital 601, Human Rights Watch confirmed that the courtyard photographs were taken in the courtyard of Military Hospital 601 in Mezze, Damascus. Folder names in the photograph collection, as well as photographs of medical reports and military judicial system orders included in the collection, indicate that Syrian military police photographers, in coordination with the military's forensic medical officers, took the photographs at Military Hospital 601 and Tishreen Military Hospital, also in Damascus. ("If the Dead Could Speak" 2015)

In addition to the geolocation matches, and analyzing the metadata embedded in the images, Human Rights Watch also sought to establish the identities of some of the individuals as a way to confirm the images as authentic. This is partly in response to Bashar al-Assad's interview in 2015 with *Foreign Affairs* in which he argues:

You can bring photos from anyone and say this is torture. Who took the pictures? Who is he? Nobody knows. There is no verification of any of this evidence, so it's all allegations without evidence. . . . It's funded by Qatar, and they say it's an anonymous source. So nothing is clear or proven. The pictures are not clear which person they show. They're just pictures of a head, for example, with some skulls. Who said this is done by the government, not by the rebels? Who said this is a Syrian victim, not someone else? ("Syria's President Speaks" 2015)

Human Rights Watch takes his remarks as a starting point, and in its report notes that it "set out to answer three key sets of questions about the photographs of the dead detainees: 1) Are the photographs authentic? Are they really images of dead detainees? 2) If so, what caused so many to die? and 3) How did the bodies end up in military hospitals and what happened to the corpses afterwards?" It focused on twenty-seven cases, examining evidence from family members and comparing photographs of the dead bodies to images of the individuals before they were arrested (the side-by-side photos appear in its report) ("If the Dead Could Speak" 2015).

As I have noted, the content of the images is gruesome. Human Rights Watch offers a trigger warning about the distressing content even in the middle of its report when one is given the opportunity to click on a gallery of images, which include the side-by-side comparisons that it used to authenticate the images. One of the issues that made it take so long for the individuals to be identified was that when the images were first published by media outlets, the faces of the dead were blurred. While this was done as a mechanism of dignity, and is fairly common as a media practice, in this case ironically it made it more difficult to verify the photographs and for them to act as evidence: it was only later when the full images were made available without the redactions or blurring that family members were able to identify their loved ones, information which Human Rights Watch was able to use in its verification process. In this sense, because the images themselves were seen to act as evidence of atrocity, without showing the full image, they occupied an ambiguous status that dehumanized the victims by depriving them of their names and individuality, and that rendered them less reliable forms of evidence of atrocity.

What I want to draw attention to here is that amid the assumption of photojournalism's ability to tell the truth that proliferates, the immediate response to these images was that they were not real, claimed both by al-Assad as a means to undermine the claims of government violence against civilians, and by viewers of the images who did not want to believe that they were *real*, precisely because they were so obscene. The US deputy representative to the UN noted that there was "no vocabulary" to describe the images (Kobos 2015). Comparisons were made to images from Bosnia and the Holocaust, and a source close to the French Foreign Minister at the time suggested that they were "images we haven't seen since the Jewish genocide and the crimes of the Khmer Rouge" (Linfield 2019). In other words, just as the Holocaust generated the philosophical debate I traced in Chapter 2 about the inability to represent, these images also lead us to question what is *real,* and how it can be represented if it is unrepresentable?

The images of Syrian torture victims push the boundaries of our connection between photography and the real they purports to represent. They act as the stand-in for the impossible *Real*, which is posited as too horrible to contemplate: both *too real* and *unreal* at the same time, and defer our encounter with the *reality* that is in fact depicted in the photos: a government that is killing its own citizens while we stand by and do nothing. While the focus of the discussion is on authentication and horror, these responses focus on the *Real* of the medium (authentication via geolocation and metadata) and the *unreality* of the content (the gruesome deaths). Understanding how obscenity acts as a regulatory mechanism for these encounters allows us to excavate the way these narratives function to sustain particular modes of politics that allow for the unrepresentable to lead to the paralyzing.

A Dead Body, an Icon: Aylan Kurdi

While the images of Syrian torture victims were displayed to a particular audience at sites like universities, the United Nations, and the US Holocaust Memorial Museum, another image of a different Syrian dead body emerged on the scene, was widely circulated, and achieved iconic status. In 2015, Syrian toddler Aylan Kurdi was fleeing with his family on a boat, and when their boat sank, he drowned and his body washed up on a Turkish beach. It immediately became emblematic of the European refugee crisis.

The image became a contested site of public mourning (Papailias 2019, 1063). Aylan Kurdi's body was evidence of something, but no one could quite agree on what that should be. Many saw it as representative of the failure of the international community to protect refugees. European right-wing anti-immigration parties saw his death as evidence of the invasion onto European shores, and the willingness of desperate refugees to flout laws and borders (Parkhill 2015). Others viewed the image as the ultimate icon of refugee vulnerability. Still others saw the image as displacing the larger conversation about precarious subjects. Abir Hamdar (2018, 84) has noted the various uses of the image: *Dabiq,* ISIS's English-language propaganda publication, used the image to issue a warning of what would happen if people abandoned Islam by fleeing ISIS. Controversial French publication *Charlie Hebdo* published cartoons depicting a grown-up Aylan Kurdi sexually assaulting women, to emphasize the danger posed by refugees. His body became symbolic of a political order (Hamdar 2018, 84).

I teach an undergraduate course on human security, and in class we discussed the impact of the photograph when it was first published. The image had already become iconic of the global refugee crisis and human vulnerability. Yet several of my students had not seen it, had intentionally avoided the encounter with the image, having already conditioned themselves as to their presumed emotional response, and seeking to avoid that. When we looked at the image together in class, I posed a question of responsibility. Who is responsible for this child, for this death? Are we, looking on this image, avoiding looking at this image, responsible? One student noted that the image was not graphic or gory. Indeed, the lack of gore in the image is a mismatch with our preconceived perceptions of the deaths that matter in global politics. The deaths that come to matter are soldiers who die in explosions, political figures who are assassinated. The child whose body lies peacefully on a beach: his body has been instrumentalized as the story of the refugee crisis, and to do so, a trigger warning has been set up surrounding this. Articles including the photograph note that they include a "disturbing image" (Paraszczuk 2015). But the image itself, without knowing its context, without knowing that it depicts the dead body of a young child, without being warned that it is disturbing, may not in fact be all that disturbing.

This was also within the context of an ongoing debate about whether the image itself should even be shown, or whether it was coopting the vulnerability of the refugee for ratings. Penelope Papailias notes that "the debate about showing/not showing the image and prescriptive injunctions regarding moral spectatorship ultimately deflected attention from what this global media event might tell us about the formation of contemporary affective networks in the context of public bereavement and the place of the dead body-image of precarious subjects in this process" (Papailias 2019, 1057).

The conversation surrounding Kurdi's body was also suffused with the question of reality and authenticity. Indeed, some news outlets couched their choice to show it in this vein, with *The Independent* noting that it published it "because, among the often glib words about the 'ongoing migrant crisis,' it is all too easy to forget the reality of the desperate situation facing many refugees" (Withnall 2015). It was seen to depict the reality of the dangers faced by refugees. Many noted that it was difficult to conceive of Kurdi as doing anything but simply sleeping since the photo was not itself graphic. I should note that some may even argue that the photo was not obscene, and thus wonder why I consider it here in this project. I would argue that obscenity is a socially constructed notion, and evidence of the obscenity of the image can be found in the decision made by many publishers to apologize for publishing the image and revoke its publication: in other words, it was determined to be too obscene to publish. The outrage about the instrumentalization of his body for political purposes and the notion that the images would perhaps hurt his family led editors to change their decisions about publishing the image: "[T]hese acts of repressing the corpse-image were coupled by attempts to engineer a way of unseeing an image that 'everyone' had already seen and reversing supposedly 'primal,' 'unthinking,' and 'spontaneous' gestures of sharing with others the experience of seeing this image" (Papailias 2019, 1055). The emphasis on the language of primal and unthinking gestures to the idea that the immediate reaction to the image was emotional rather than rational.

To return to the notion that the image itself was not graphic or gory, Parashar also speaks of the need to show more and more suffering of the Other, more and more graphically and detailed, in order to authenticate the *reality*, emphasizing the problem it poses when we seek to authenticate the *reality* of Aylan Kurdi to awaken our own conscience (Parashar 2015, unpaginated). This occurs when the focus is on the Western viewer and cultivating awareness rather than on the dead body depicted in the image. Papailias notes that what was most disturbing about the image of Kurdi was not the corpse itself, but the "inauthentic" and "inappropriate" mourning by Western witnesses who were implicated in the very circumstances that led to Kurdi's vulnerability in the first place (2019, 1057). Here the question arises of the authenticity and reality of the affective response to death in the humanitarian context. Much of the framing of these images seems to suggest that viewers will be jolted into a new *reality* simply by virtue of viewing what is characterized as a powerful image. But the image's power may in fact rest in how it is perceived, not only how it is framed, and those may not be the same. Linfield argues that despite Caesar's hope that the photographs would end the Assad regime and the hope held by many that the Aylan Kurdi image would have an impact on global policy, these photographs "didn't do that because they couldn't. Photographs cannot overthrow dictators" (Linfield 2019).

Kayla Mueller and Giulio Regeni: The Image as Proof of Death ... or Is It?

This section examines these two cases to explore the workings of images as evidence of death. In the former case, the image was not made public but was supplied to the family of Mueller by ISIS. In the second case, the demand for the presencing of Regeni's body and the larger story surrounding his death by Egyptian security forces acted in concert with the visibility of his dead body and its functioning as forensic evidence. In other words, these two cases illustrate the notion, both cultural and political, that presencing the dead in a material or visual sense is a predicate to accepting and narrativizing the loss. Materializing the dead body is also seen as a key feature that allows the truth to come out about what happened in the midst of competing stories, as if the dead body holds the sacred secret of the *Real*. Beyond this, materializing the image is seen to give "instant and rapid entry into events and experiences" and to represent "certificates of death" (Maclear 1999, 17).

Jenny Edkins notes about the missing from 9/11 that the absences associated with not knowing if someone was dead dehumanized the victims. They were treated as bare life, "deprived not only of their lives but also of their deaths. They were not the dead. They were the missing" (2011, 26). She notes that the ongoing reminders of the missing in the form of posters emphasized that "there are no remains, they are not 'dead,' – the dead have corpses" (Edkins 2011, 35). She emphasizes the inability to process loss without a body (Edkins 2011, 126). Grief is linked with a body: Sledge (2007, 4) notes that while losing a family member is horrible, it is even worse not to have a body to lay to rest. He argues that seeing the dead body is what brings home the reality and finality of death, including its irreversibility (Sledge 2007, 23). In this sense they fulfill an important evidentiary role. Edkins also notes the double nature of the missing bodies in the 9/11 case, in that they are missing both in a material sense (and may never be recovered), and as there is no place for them in our politics, except as they may be coopted into larger political projects (2011, 35).

Using the framing of the missing body, I now explore the missing body of Kayla Mueller, an American aid worker who was working in Syria, captured by ISIS, and held in ISIS-controlled territory until she was ultimately killed, purportedly in a Jordanian coalition airstrike. Her body and the story of its absence and later the way it was rendered visible and present illustrates the significance of manifesting bodies as a form of evidence, but also the difficulties in particular dead bodies coming to the fore of our politics. While her family ultimately saw an image of her dead body as evidence, in the wider American political narrative, she remained absent. As David Shim notes, "images determine both who is visible and what remains out of view, they allow only limited and specific kinds of seeing" (Shim 2014, 2). In this sense, the image of Kayla Mueller depicts one version of the larger story.

Mueller was a high-profile victim of ISIS kidnapping, and video and images of her were released by ISIS, who initially demanded a prisoner exchange. She was held in the city of Raqqa. In early 2015, in retaliation for the killing of pilot al-Kasasbeh, whose story I told in Chapter 2, the Jordanian government stepped up their involvement in airstrikes against ISIS in northern Syria. After one such raid, ISIS released a media statement claiming Mueller had been killed, with a photograph of the destroyed building (Callimachi and Gladstone 2015). At that time the Pentagon confirmed that coalition airstrikes had targeted that building but denied that any civilians had been inside. The Jordanian government referred to it as a "PR stunt" (Campbell 2015), and many news sources drew attention to the lack of a body released by ISIS. As CNN noted, "it did not show a body or provide any proof of death" (Botelho et al. 2015). There was thus a debate about whether she had actually died, or whether her death was being faked by ISIS. What was so interesting about this is that the media expected an image of her body as proof of death. In fact, it was precisely because they didn't release a photo that analysts were skeptical about the authenticity of claims she had been killed, because of ISIS's hallmark of releasing grisly beheading videos. As Moeller et al. note, "How do you know someone is dead unless you see the evidence? If the fact of a death really matters – politically, militarily, even emotionally – is it enough to take someone else's word for it, to just simply hear (or read) a narrative account of that death? Does a waiting audience want – or need – visual confirmation?" (Moeller et al. 2015, 112). In this case, the answer was a firm yes.

After the statement by ISIS, Mueller's family released a statement: "After going to extraordinary efforts to keep Kayla's name out of the media for so long, by securing the cooperation of journalists through-out the world, her name was released today. This news leaves us concerned, yet, we are still hopeful that Kayla is alive. We have sent you a private message and ask that you respond to us privately" (Ritchie 2015). The Pentagon did not investigate her death, as their policy is only to investigate credible claims of civilian casualties, and ISIS casualty claims do not count as credible (Harris and Youssef 2015). ISIS then responded to Mueller's family's request to send them a message privately and sent Mueller's family an email with three photographs of her dead body (Callimachi and Schmitt 2015). "Two showed Ms. Mueller, who was 26, in a black hijab, or Muslim head covering, that partly obscured her face. Another showed her in a white burial shroud, which is used in traditional Muslim funerals. The images showed bruises on the face" (Callimachi and Schmitt 2015). In the email, ISIS claimed that they had treated her body with dignity, noting that they had shrouded the body according to Islamic custom.[1] The images were authenticated by American intelligence agencies, thus offering forensic proof of Mueller's death.

Except they didn't. Several years after Mueller's death, the US raid that killed Abu Bakr al-Baghdadi, the leader of ISIS, was named after Mueller. At this time, the focus shone on Mueller again. Information around this time had emerged from an ISIS-affiliated prisoner, Umm Sayaf, whose husband had been killed by American forces, that Mueller

---

[1] See www.youtube.com/watch?v=tRO-R3llKy0

had been held by al-Baghdadi himself and that it was possible he had had her killed. Mueller's parents even met with Umm Sayyaf "to try to find out what happened to Kayla's remains or even if she was possibly still alive" ("US military raid" 2019). Even the picture, the proof of death from several years earlier, was insufficient. "Even after the announcement of her death, the Muellers continued to look for her. Ms. Mueller's mother described herself as tormented by images of her daughter that the Islamic State sent the family, which showed Kayla Mueller lying on her back in a shroud with bruises on her face and a large gash on her right cheek – wounds that experts told them were inconclusive regarding her manner of death, or even whether she was dead at all" (Goldman and Callimachi 2019).

As of 2020, Mueller's family is also carrying out their own investigation. Mueller's mother noted in a 2020 BBC documentary that "other than those three photos, we don't really have any proof yet," alluding to the distrust of these proof-of-death images ("Kayla Mueller's parents" 2020). They have also demanded that the US government prioritize finding her remains if indeed she is dead. As they note about Mueller and other ISIS captives who were killed: "Their bodies belong in their native land" (Mueller and Mueller 2019), drawing on traditional conceptions of the body in wartime as a key national symbol that needs to be repatriated. The United States maintains that Mueller was killed by ISIS terrorists.

I tell this story because it complicates the picture often painted of the role of images as proof of death. As I noted earlier in this chapter, images are endowed with a particular weight and sacredness if they are of the dead, and this has tremendous evidentiary power. It is worth returning here to the Syrian torture victims I discussed earlier. One of the purposes of these photographs to begin with was so that the Syrian intelligence agencies could "inform families of the fate of their loved ones without having to produce an actual, mutilated body" (Linfield 2019). The Mueller case is similar: while the production of the body itself is infeasible, the image, once authenticated, becomes proof of death, or at least it would seem to. But death is not so easily bound in a photograph, and even when authenticated, forensics are not the incontrovertible truth that television shows often depict them to be. Deep emotional attachments to the dead as vibrantly continuing members of our political communities structure the way we interpret evidence.

In the context of Giulio Regeni, we see a similar demand to materialize the body as a means of accounting for a wrongful death. Regeni was an Italian graduate student conducting research in Egypt on the history of labor unions in the country. His body was discovered in 2016 in the street in Cairo. Egyptian police claimed that his death was not the cause of foul play, but rather that he had been killed in a car accident, then later said he was a victim of a robbery (Stille 2016). Egyptian police then sought to bury evidence, including from his phone and from security cameras in the area. His body, sent back to Italy for his funeral, became a key piece of evidence that was seen to materialize the truth of what had occurred. Italian prosecutors obtained a "vital piece of evidence: Regeni's battered corpse, which, after an extremely thorough autopsy in Italy has told them volumes about the final nine days of his life, from the time of his disappearance to the time his body was dumped in a concrete channel beside the road from Cairo to Alexandria" (Stille 2016). The Egyptian medical examiner had noted that it appeared he had been hit on the head, but this evidence was quickly covered up by Egyptian authorities in service of the accident or robbery narratives.

When the body was returned to Italy, this autopsy indicated that he had been killed as a result of a broken neck. Additionally, it showed that

he had been hit repeatedly on the head, but that these blows were not fatal. Blood had coagulated around the points where he had been hit, and other cuts, bruises and abrasions on his body showed different stages of healing. This indicated that Regeni had been tortured more than once – and that days had passed between his initial torture, later sessions, and the moment of his death. He was covered with cuts and burns, and his hands and feet had been broken. Even his teeth were broken. His torturers appear to have carved letters into his flesh, a well-documented practice of the Egyptian police. (Stille 2016)

Regeni's mother, who had identified his body, noted that due to the torture, she could only identify him from the tip of his nose ("Egypt tried" 2019). Upon establishing time of death from forensic examination, the medical examiners in Italy noted that "he was alive for at least six or seven days and tortured repeatedly during that time" (Stille 2016).

The evidence from this autopsy led the Egyptian government to revise its story and claim he had been killed by a criminal gang as part of a conspiracy to harm Egypt's reputation as a tourist destination and weaken relations between Egypt and Italy. The supposed perpetrators were killed in a shootout with police. Yet as clear evidence of the involvement of Egyptian security forces continued to emerge, Regeni's family held his body up as clear evidence. They suggested that if Egypt kept going with these false narratives and failed to release evidence from its initial investigation, they would release the photo of Regeni's dead body to the public ("Italian Student's Family" 2016). This threat, to literally materialize the body in the form of the image-as-evidence, is worth probing further here. This is a different story of absence than told in the previous chapter. Here, the body is present, but the larger context of what happened to Regeni is absent. The death itself is absent, even as the dead body is present.

In this instance, the dead body image was seen to be imbued with the truth of what occurred, and the fact that Egyptian security forces were responsible, even though Italian medical examiners could not establish that definitively solely from Regeni's body. Yet the image was seen by his family as substantively more powerful than solely what it depicted. Publicizing it, breaking the taboo surrounding the dead body image, was seen as what may be needed to establish the reality of his death. The narrative of exceptionality surrounding the possible release of the image emphasizes the way in which absent images can also engender spectacles. In other words, the image does not even need to be seen in order to establish the *Real* – the obscenity of the dead body image only needs to be alluded to.

Conclusions: Presencing the Dead

Ariella Azoulay notes in her 2008 book *The Civil Contract of Photography* that she was spurred to write it during the second intifada, driven by viewing unbearable sights. While we may each have an experience of at least secondhand viewing of something unbearable, what constitutes the unbearability of an image? To what extent are the images of Syrian torture victims unbearable, and more or less unbearable than being emailed a private photo of your dead daughter who was in ISIS captivity and killed by an airstrike from "your side"? I have sought in this chapter to examine the issue of unbearability and the unreal associated with images of suffering and atrocity, which are often coopted into larger humanitarian narratives. I have suggested that the shock effect and compassion fatigue frameworks are both limiting and problematically viewer-centric, which leaves out some larger questions about how visual regulation functions based both on the content and context of images.

I have also problematized the "to look or not to look" binary as a means of considering the gray areas of absent and present images, following on the Osama bin Laden case from Chapter 4. Here I noted that bodies can be obscene even if not seen by the public, as in the case of Kayla Mueller and Giulio Regeni, and that materially and visually presencing the dead is often seen as inextricably linked to narratives of truth, which may be a false promise in terms of alleviating human suffering itself, as I noted with the case of Aylan Kurdi and the Syrian torture victims. We should also be asking ourselves: unbearable for whom? The two main justifications often given for not showing an image of a dead body is the instinct to give the dead dignity and the instinct to protect the viewer. This viewer-centric dynamic is also what privileges the shock effect idea that images can jolt the viewer into doing something about the suffering that they are witnessing, but it is problematic both practically (it rarely has such an effect) and ethically (obscenity is about the viewer and their subject-position, not about the image itself).

Images can be instrumentalized for political purposes, as this chapter has traced. Sontag (2003, 10) has drawn attention to the way photographs can be framed by their captions and the ways they are used, offering the story of the same image of children killed in a village bombing that was used by both Serb and Croat propaganda during the Balkan war. While I have raised skepticism about the evidentiary value of photographs, following on this previous work that has questioned the role of the image-as-truth, I have also sought to emphasize that we need to do more than simply examine whether the image accurately accounts for the event. In the context of dead body images and images of atrocity, we also need to ask ourselves how images account, or attempt to account, for the *Real,* the sublime in the taboo image that arouses both a disgust and a desire to look, framed by the complexity of image regulation governing what is shown. In other words, there are some images that are shown but not seen, such as the lack of attention paid to the images of Syrian torture victims, and some that could be said to be seen but not shown, such as the proof-of-death images of Kayla Mueller and Giulio Regeni.

Additionally, I have sought to elucidate the problem of representation associated with images of suffering, calling on the framing of the *Bilderverbot* that I laid out in earlier chapters. The problem of representation is at the heart of much of the debate over the ethics and politics of viewing images of suffering and death. Mitchell notes that "trauma, like God, is supposed to be unrepresentable in word and image. But we incorrigibly insist on talking about it, depicting it, and trying to render it in increasingly vivid and literal ways. Certain works of contemporary art are designed to transmit trauma as directly as possible, to rub the spectator's face in the unspeakable and unimaginable. The Holocaust industry now combines trauma theory's cult of the unrepresentable with a negative theology discourse to produce a virtual liturgy of the unspeakable and unimaginable, all rendered in an outpouring of words and images, objects, installations, architectural and monumental constructions" (Mitchell 2011, 60). In this chapter, I have asked after the politics of this unrepresentability, examining how and why it works in the ways that it does.

This chapter has also sought to complicate the question of bearing witness beyond the debate over whether one should view graphic images of suffering. Following Sue Tait (2008, 94), it is important to acknowledge the ways that "the bearing witness position assumes a liberal pacifist gaze. Other modes of looking are produced, and indeed required, within violent and warring cultures." While I do not necessarily subscribe to the idea that this is premised on a cultural difference, we would do well to attend to the assumptions at the heart of the narrative of bearing witness associated with the framing of obscene images. Attending to this would help us attend to the suffering bodies that are "incapable of returning the gaze that we direct at them, too many bodies that are an object of speech without themselves having the chance to speak" (Ranciere 2011, 96). This narrative of the necessity of viewing particular suffering bodies justifies the breaking of a taboo, and in doing so reinforces the taboo at the moment of its rupture as a means of constructing the exceptional in the suffering Other. In other words, obscenity acts as a regulatory mechanism to frame deaths that matter, but this is premised on a particular assumption that already modulates our gaze and the agency theoretically contained within it.

6 | *Displaying the Dead Body*
Some Conclusions

I started this book by telling the story of my encounter with the tortured bodies of Syrian protesters, who dissented against their government and paid the ultimate price. These images, heavy with emotion for the viewer, were also significant ways that Human Rights Watch and other human rights organizations mustered evidence to counter the Syrian government's claims that it was not targeting, torturing, or killing civilians. My encounter with these images was laden with layers of social meaning: I first saw them through a trigger warning about their obscene nature, then passed this along to others. In translating them for you, the reader, I have made choices about how to describe these images, including how much to show and tell. These same dilemmas have suffused the other dead body stories in this book that make up a complex web of what I have labeled "global corpse politics." This book is the culmination of many dead body stories, only some of which I have told here, and many dead body images, and the discourses and narratives that structure and regulate them.

This book has argued that examining the functioning of the obscenity norm to regulate dead body images can shed light on the political communities we form and the structures in place that preserve them, such as taboos that regulate purported obscene images in specific ways. In other words, obscenity matters precisely because it is applied inconsistently across multiple cases. While some have suggested that the rules of this application are precise and illustrate a self/other dynamic, I have argued that it is not as simple as saying that we view dead enemy bodies but refuse to look at the corpses of our own. I have sought to complicate this picture and argue that the visual grammar of the dead body image is more multilayered and complex, by moving beyond solely the identity of the bodies depicted in dead body images and focusing on larger questions about the un-representability of trauma, the taboo governing viewing the dead, and the narratives of exceptionality at play when particular dead bodies are made visible.

In Chapter 1, I argued that previous work has failed to adequately account for the global dead, and began to frame my own approach as one that speaks to both the burgeoning literature on visual politics and other focal points such as embodiment/the body and emotions/trauma in IR. I focused explicitly on the problem of representing the dead, in light of previous work that has largely focused on dead body management. I began by telling two stories that outlined the empirical contexts I explored throughout the rest of the book: dead enemy bodies and atrocity victims. These stories were used to illustrate the argument that images of the dead can be human-making and disruptive of our humanness at the same time, with some images seeking to redeem the dead humans depicted, while others are shown explicitly to strip the dignity from the subjects depicted. I suggested that attending to the visual grammar of dead body images with this paradox in mind would allow for insights into the functioning of the obscenity norm.

In Chapter 2 I theorized a concept of obscenity that is itself a social construction, and asked what mechanisms sustained the very idea of obscenity. I focused here on the functioning of the obscenity taboo, which allows us to examine how obscenity may be applied inconsistently across multiple cases. While decisions about what is obscene are often depicted as culturally based, here I argued that they are fundamentally political in nature. I did so through the examination of several related concepts: the taboo, the *Bilderverbot* (image ban), the *Real,* the spectacle, and the horrifically graphic. Through these concepts I built a notion of obscenity and the obscenity norm focused on the political work such language does. I drew on previous work in the field of visual politics to articulate an approach to dead body images that considers them not simply as photographic depictions of reality but rather as part of a larger social context of visuality that involves a variety of framings: one in particular I focused on was the trigger warning. I also advocated considering the situatedness of the viewer. In considering the image, I focused on the tensions surrounding images, particularly their (in)ability to give us access to a presumed *Real,* connecting this to the way the taboo invokes both desire and disgust, and the larger paradox of representing suffering or death via an image that we see play out in the literature related to Holocaust trauma.

Chapter 3 took up the case of ISIS beheadings to examine the paradox according to which ISIS beheadings are both a spectacle and operate under the image ban of the *Bilderverbot.* To illustrate this,

I traced the way ISIS beheadings have become iconic, even when not viewed. This led to an examination of the dynamics of the unrepresentability of evil, which I connected to the larger politics of fear surrounding ISIS. I told two stories in this chapter to illustrate how the taboo governing the severed head was navigated in two instances by representing the unrepresentable: an Iraqi severed head, which was shown but not seen, background to the story of excesses of war, and the story of a Western severed head, seen but not shown, around which an absent spectacle was constructed via the relationship between the image and its viewers. I noted the ways in which the paradox that beheadings are represented as unrepresentable has entered the normal discourse, and sought to complicate the dynamics surrounding not only what we see but also how we see.

Chapter 4 sought to complicate the standard story often told about the desecration of and lack of dignity accorded to dead enemy bodies. To do so, I examined the cases of Osama bin Laden and Muammar Qaddafi. Both cases allowed me to trace the way obscenity was utilized as a political tool and to more specifically detail the ways in which what constitutes the obscene is a political decision. Yet the differences between the two cases also allowed me to explore the archetypal figures of the dead terrorist and the dead dictator. In the context of the former, I argued that not presencing the body of Osama bin Laden in the form of a dead body image generated a crisis of the *Real*, evidenced by the emergence of fake images of his dead body, and allowed the dead terrorist to linger as a spectral threat that served to legitimize the continuance of the war-on-terror, without much changing despite the ultimate manhunt. I examined some appearances of bin Laden in popular culture to briefly illustrate the ways in which his death generated an absent spectacle. In the case of Qaddafi, I argued that the display of his bloody body served to sustain a narrative of the "mad dog," a dictator who became uncanny in his madness, even in death, or perhaps particularly in death. His dead body image served the narrative of the Western triumph of democracy over dictatorship. In this way, particular dead bodies become iconic, and the choices made about which images to show (or none at all) and the stories those narrate can demonstrate the construction and functioning of cultural and political understandings about political communities and how they are used as the basis of securitization.

Chapter 5 returned to the humanitarian narratives I introduced in Chapter 1, to focus on the way dead body images function as proof of death, and how this relates to the dynamics of the suffering dead in humanitarian awareness images. I played with the notion of reality associated with dead body images as evidence: dead bodies, and the photographic representations of them, often function for the purpose of bringing hard evidence to claims of atrocity and as an affective instrument that can spur a response on the part of the viewer that may then lead to policy action. Yet, we must struggle with the dilemma of the *real* associated with images of the dead as evidence, particularly as evidence of things we would prefer to see as *not real*, including the deaths of civilians in global politics. I focused on the Syrian case, particularly the iconic image of Aylan Kurdi, which I used to illustrate the ambiguity surrounding images seen to speak for themselves, when in fact they may speak multiple narratives. I also examined the torture photographs released by Syrian defector Caesar, to examine how images become authenticated, both in the sense of human rights organizations and governments, and in the sense that they become authentically meaningful to the viewer because of their disruption of the taboo governing viewing the dead. I also focused on the cases of Kayla Mueller and Giulio Regeni, where their dead bodies were obscene even without being seen by the public. I argued that the shock effect and compassion fatigue frameworks are both limiting, and problematically viewer-centric, which leaves out some larger questions about how visual regulation functions based both on the content and context of images, and problematized the "to look or not to look" binary as a means of considering the gray areas of absent and present images, as the cases in this chapter illustrated.

Hamid Dabashi has argued that the posthuman body is the semiological sign of the event (Dabashi 2012, 6). In this same vein, the images of the dead I have analyzed in this text, and the dead bodies themselves, can be read semiologically in the frame of the visual regimes they inhabit, perform, sustain, and exemplify. While each of these bodies may mean something different in different contexts (to their loved ones, to sovereign state actors, to the media, to me as a scholar trying to interpret these cases), what they share is their embeddedness in complex political, social, and cultural narratives that can tell us something about the functioning of international politics. It is my goal in this conclusion to tie together these narratives and clarify what I see to be the main characteristics of the functioning of the obscenity norm. I here highlight five main conclusions that can be drawn from the points I have made across the previous chapters.

First, the dead body is vital matter. Examining dead bodies can not only shed light on cultural contexts, but it also blurs and complicates previous approaches to visuality and materiality in IR. Human remains in the context of scientific analysis and museum exhibition are considered to be sacred objects in terms of how they are treated in display, even if they are hundreds or thousands of years old. The Human Remains Working Group Report states that "human remains, irrespective of age, provenance or kind, occupy a unique category distinct from all other museum objects. There is a qualitative distinction between human remains and artifacts" (DCMS 2003, 166). As Edkins argues, rationally the corpse may be an inanimate object, but our cultures tell us otherwise: "the body may not be alive, but it is grievable" (2011, 126). Dead bodies are not objects or subjects, and in many ways, they invoke that line between life and death, by reminding us that they are our loved ones, yet at the same time they are not fully anymore. But they certainly remain imbued with some sense of the identity they held while alive, because we make pilgrimages to the gravesite to visit them. Dead bodies matter to us, precisely because they are not simply dead bodies. All living human beings have bodies, and all will eventually become dead bodies.

Dead bodies are ambiguous. Jane Bennett's (2010) theorization of vital materiality rests on acknowledging nonhuman materialities as participants and as agents. It enmeshes human beings in complex assemblages along with nonhuman participants in order to reenvision what it means to act and effect. But is the dead body human or nonhuman? What about the character of a being that was once vital in every sense but now falls into a much more complex categorization than nonhuman, particularly when dead bodies become so often revitalized, as in narratives of ethnic grievances or political maneuverings?[1] What about the character in the interstitial space: the dead body? The dead body poses particularly interesting questions for a materialist retheorization of agency. That is, if the dead body does not act in the way action is traditionally defined by our political communities, what is its

---

[1] Dabashi, for example, describes how thousands of bodies of Iran–Iraq war victims are kept in cold storage by the Iranian government to be rematerialized as martyrs of the revolution each time there are public protests against the government (2012, 183).

politics? What does it mean to look at things from the perspective of the dead body? Because dead bodies do not see, they disrupt traditional conceptions of visibility and self-recognition that form the basis of claims to agency and political viability. Dead bodies are enmeshed in material assemblages of human and nonhuman, but there is something unique about dead bodies because they are neither entirely human nor entirely nonhuman. In this sense, corpses are "ontologically multiple," in Bennett's words (2010, 8). Yet dead bodies are not these things that Bennett associates with her notion of ontological multiplicity: not lively, not alive, not vegetable, not verbal. They are a different complex ontology or ontologies: human yet dead, hyper-visible yet invisible, silent yet questioning, grievable person yet thing, subject yet object, subject of power and subject to power and object all at the same time (Auchter 2015a). The dead body "hovers uneasily between the animate and the inanimate, the past and the future" (Lovejoy 2013, xv). While death is the unrepresentable excess of humanity, it is also a creative synthesis of flows, energies, and perpetual becoming (Braidotti 2013, 131).

Beyond this, dead bodies pose different questions for images because of the status that they occupy. Norman Cantor (2010, 279) notes that "a dead person does not create the same image or leave the same visual memories as a living person." While he uses this point to illustrate the dignity of the corpse, it is also the case that images of the dead seem substantively different than images of the living, because of the sacred status corpses have. This also has some implications for the way theorists have begun to envision a posthuman era. As Braidotti notes, "[P]osthuman vital politics shifts the boundaries between life and death and consequently deals not only with the government of the living, but also with practices of dying" (2013, 111). I would go a step further and argue that we reside in a political context where what it means to live and die has become blurred. Braidotti also points out that "the body doubles up as the potential corpse it has always been" (2013, 119), and in this sense, considering the vitality of the dead in world politics can shed light on theoretical approaches such as biopolitics and necropolitics, and I have attempted to place these implicitly in conversation with materialist approaches to the body and embodied politics.

Second, and relatedly, it is worthwhile paying attention to dead bodies. Dead bodies are themselves the traces of political hauntings, both the invocation of death by the state in order to legitimize specific policymaking, and as the effects of the focal points we study as the key features of international conflict: war, genocide, economic inequality, famine, disease. How can we study these without looking at the dead bodies they create? Dead bodies are thus the material targets of power, but at the same time, the way in which dead bodies insinuate themselves into the project of radical questioning plays with the question of agency which we traditionally associate with living and breathing activity. In each of the cases this book has taken up, the particular dead bodies are inscribed with the workings of statecraft, but also resist their placement in linear narratives and complicate the picture of the workings of sovereign power and biopolitics.

Beyond being vital matter, they also tell us that our narratives of security are suffused with assumptions about who the subject of security is. As Priya Dixit has noted with regard to the deaths of Nepali migrant laborers in Qatar, "[T]he discussion of dead Nepali workers hopefully serves as an invitation to think further about the types of issues, objects, people and spaces we consider 'security', and others we leave out of our discussions" (Dixit 2015, 115). Dead bodies in general are left out of the discussion, but including them can shed light on the way political communities form and the structures and norms that sustain them in exclusionary ways. The triumphalist depiction of a dead Qaddafi sheds light on important ways the narrative of democracy promotion is substantiated through the deaths of others. Similarly, two severed heads can be imagined and narrativized in very different ways, depending on to whom they belonged, as Chapter 3 illustrated. They are presented to the viewer, or withheld from the viewer, in ways that signal the extent to which they matter or should matter, and how we should respond to them, based on our preconceived notions about how to interact with obscene images. Francois Debrix has pointed out that "contemporary security politics as well as the logic of terror it supposedly confronts can only conceive of the body as an amalgamation of parts or bits that can be dismantled, dismembered, or disseminated in some cases (for example when looking at enemy or terrorist bodies) but never when 'our' own (Western) bodies and their assumed integrity/unity is at stake" (Debrix 2017, 59). Following Debrix's point, I have sought to illustrate some of the rules that govern when and how images of particular dead are disseminated. While much scholarship focuses on dead enemy bodies (Sontag 2003), I have sought to complicate the binary picture often painted between dead enemy bodies and "our" bodies by focusing on the complexities of dead bodies of the "other" used for humanitarian purposes in Chapter 5, and by examining some cases where dead enemy bodies remained invisible, such as the case of Osama bin Laden in Chapter 4.

In this sense, the story this book tells is not simply that some dead bodies are visible and others are not, but that the process of visually manifesting and narrativizing particular dead bodies is a complex social, cultural, and political process that is worth looking at. It can tell us not only which dead bodies matter, but how they come to matter, and it can also lead us to rethink the intimate connection between making live or making die and the modern security performance. Though this book has not focused in on the conceptual framing of biopolitics or necropolitics, these ideas have remained an undercurrent that colors the way death is often perceived as relative to state sovereignty, as I have noted elsewhere (Auchter 2014). Yet this has been an attempt to move beyond the instrumentalization of the dead to examine something else.

As I noted in the Introduction, much of the work on the dead uses dead bodies or death as empirical contexts in which to examine the functioning of global governance, state sovereignty, the mechanisms of legal accountability, or the management of international institutions. Ben O'Loughlin, for example, focuses on state restriction of images (which, as I have argued, is only one component of image restriction, and perhaps even the least important), and emphasizes that it is not about the impact of images of dead bodies, but rather about what they signify, such as failures of governance (2011, 80). I disagree with this instrumentalization of the corpse image, which focuses solely on how it is used. I have argued instead that the content of the image, and particularly the way in which it is perceived and framed as obscene, can have a political impact in itself. Death need not signify a failure of the system or a warning sign for it to have a political impact, as I have noted elsewhere (Auchter 2013). It is for this reason that I have sought to complicate the evidentiary picture associated with the dead, particularly using the paradox posed by Zizek's notion of the *Real* or the sublime, and particularly with regard to the uses of images of suffering in humanitarian campaigns, as I discussed in Chapter 5. I have also sought to move beyond death-as-killing. Charlotte Heath-Kelly notes that interpreting death as such puts mortality in the control of the state (2016, 3). While she moves on to theorize mortality more broadly,

I take up her call to move beyond killing and have made as my focus dead bodies as material and visual artifacts. This allows for a broader conception of death and its impact, following what Steven Miller has argued: "death – the peaceful and proper arrangement of the dead in a graveyard – is both the aim and the limit of war's violence" (2014, 2).

Additionally, while this book has contributed to the literature in the burgeoning subfield of visual security studies (Vuori and Andersen 2018), I have sought to move beyond the notion that the visual only matters insofar as it relates explicitly to security. While such work does explain a key way in which the visual matters (enacting security, representing security, and investigating security [Vuori and Andersen 2018, 3]), I find it problematically limiting in our ability to examine the wide-ranging impact of visual politics. In other words, the dead do not simply matter because they are a sign of insecurity, but also because they are complex agents that blur the lines of what counts as a human worthy of participation, not just protection, in a political community. The dead linger as ghosts that can be disruptive of the binaries often associated with security and its enactment (Auchter 2014).

Third, what counts as obscene is a social construction. As Tait notes, "[T]he metaphor of pornography is plastic: it can be used to refer to war or violence itself, the culture which produces monstrous acts and practices, the representational process (as reductive, objectifying, or tainted by a profit imperative), the spectatorial position necessitated by graphic images (or their repetition), or the apathy or appetite of viewers" (2008, 95). The choices made by governments and media outlets about when to show graphic dead body images and how to contextualize them (with trigger warnings) function to realize a hierarchy of bodies that matter. Bodies are signs and signs are not signifiers (Dabashi 2012, 9). The context surrounding bodies shapes the meanings through which they are interpreted and interpellated.

Graphicness serves political ends: it "is a moveable, serviceable, and debatable convention, dependent on those who invoke it and for which aim" (Zelizer 2010, 22). What we refer to as obscene is premised on cultural and political contexts and serves those same contexts. Sledge has noted the long history of maltreatment of enemy soldiers, including war trophies made from their bones or stealing dog tags from dead Iraqi soldiers during the Gulf War so that their families could not identify them, operating on an Orwellian logic that some bodies are more equal than others (2005, 243). Particular images of death trigger the taboo function and cause delight precisely because they are the death of the Other (Taylor 1998, 29).

In this sense, it is more acceptable to view non-normative corpses, so it is worthwhile looking at the narratives surrounding particular dead. Chapter 4 traced this in the way discourses of madness legitimized the display of Qaddafi's corpse. Chapter 3 sought to illustrate this by telling the story of an Iraqi severed head that did not receive the same degree of global attention as the broad category of ISIS victims. Amanda Rogers, who personally knew James Wright Foley, one of the early victims of ISIS beheadings, notes that "it's important to understand the way people are being played by the framing of particular deaths ... they were framed to incite endless warfare. ... He was a person just like all the nameless massacred citizens of Syria. No matter how much we love Jim, we can't reduce him to a symbol" (as quoted in Mead 2020). Her point here is that we need to be aware of how particular dead bodies become icons, and what politics this serves. This also means attending to which bodies are rendered visible and which are not, and who is left out of the story of a focus on dead bodies. As Connerton notes, after World War I, there was a lot of commemoration of war dead, primarily because they were safely dead, which meant less focus on the 10 million wounded who were still a problem for political institutions (2011, 48). In this vein, we should be asking ourselves which dead are "safely dead" and what role this plays in how they are narrativized and imaged.

Fourth, embodied violence is often characterized in the language of the extreme or the exceptional, in line with the image ban associated with the *Bilderverbot,* and the notion that what can be depicted must necessarily be banal and that the sacred is beyond imagining, in both senses of the word. This is connected to wider ideas about death itself: Norris, for example, notes that "death shows what language can never say" (Norris 2005, 6). If death itself is beyond representation, when there is a representation or attempted representation of death via the dead body image, there is a discursive effort to justify or legitimate it, which is where we see such a reliance on the logic of exceptionality. This works to sustain the dead body taboo and its wider functioning. John Kerry, for example, referred to ISIS beheadings as the "most disturbing, stomach-churning, grotesque photos *ever displayed*" (as quoted in Debrix 2017, 87; my emphasis). This situates graphic violence firmly in the category of the unrepresentable by virtue of its extreme nature. This also often justifies its representation in the same vein.

We should be asking ourselves what politics this state of exception serves. Mitchell (2011, 129) has noted that fetishizing published images as radically exceptional cases functions as a powerful weapon on the side of secrecy, and specifically, to legitimate government powers of surveillance and targeting. If we follow Mitchell (2011, 152) and ask what the image wants from us, we must take into account the operation of the complex narratives of exceptionality that obscene images are situated in. In other words, while I have sought to move away from examining dead bodies as a tool to say something about governance, I must make a point about the workings of power, and at times sovereign power. The discourse of the extreme is a powerful one: it can evoke emotion via the mechanism of fear and horror and paint particular kinds of deaths as beyond the pale, as so extreme that they cannot be adequately represented and instead must simply be responded to (with more military strikes against ISIS, for example).

We should probe what larger political maneuvers and exercises of power particular narratives of obscenity hold. The viewable obscene is necessarily the exception, as I traced in Chapter 2. This is sustained through various aspects of textual and visual grammar, including trigger warnings and justifications of the importance of publication, as I noted in various examples throughout the book. As such, it can tell us about the process by which policymakers respond to excess and extreme, or do not respond, as we saw with Caesar's disappointment over the lack of effort to support regime change in Syria after the release of the photographs he took as a government forensic photographer, which I detailed in Chapter 5. It can also tell us about how images can both sustain and resist particular political orders, as visual politics scholars have also demonstrated.

Fifth, I have sought to complicate the picture often painted of what constitutes ethical witnessing. One of the hallmarks of the literature on visual politics is the debate over what should be seen, and the debate between the "shock effect" and "compassion fatigue" approaches to images of suffering that I detailed in Chapter 5. Yet there is nothing inherent that makes visibility either emancipatory or oppressive (Hochberg 2015, 164), so simply showing dead bodies, the victims of suffering, does not necessarily realize humanitarian ends or assuage the ethical imperative to witness atrocity. Witnessing, however, is often viewed as an ethical way to engage images of suffering and death. Ulrich Baer notes that there is a certain difficulty of relating to images of experiences that have dislodged the self-image of those depicted, of which dead body images and torture images are most certainly examples. Baer suggests that such images cannot be seen or understood, but instead must be witnessed (Baer 2005, 13).

Witnessing is often characterized as a radical expression of our humanity. Viewing dead body images is experiencing death by proxy. It enables onlookers to die and then return to the living (Taylor 1998, 30), and this emphasizes our own mortality, putting our humanity and its vulnerability into perspective. Yet as I have demonstrated, certain forms of witnessing death can be profoundly dehumanizing, both to the subjects of the image and to the viewers, something which came to light in the discussion of Muammar Qaddafi's death in Chapter 4. Kozol (2014, 12) details how "visual witnessing is not a one-way mirror but a relational process between the photographer or artists, subjects of the image, viewer, and surrounding contexts." There is a tendency with dead body images to focus less on the subjects of the image because we assume that dead bodies do not have agency, something which I have directly argued against, implicitly in this book, and more explicitly elsewhere (Auchter 2014, 2015a).

Yet the notion of witnessing has tended to privilege the connection between agency and sight, and often the idea of Western visuality as a framing both for understanding images and for regulating obscene images, where particular bodies of "others" are more likely to be shown. Indeed, as the viewer we often live within the visual norms in which the dead bodies of others are rendered objects (Butler 2005, 826). While some, like Kozol (2014), see the solution to this as the democratization of images (17), I would argue that the solution to this is not found in the images themselves, and the answer is not simply seeing broader categories of images. Neither, however, is it seeing fewer images or images of a different subject to represent death. It cannot be reducible to such a simple solution that is premised on the reification of the image and its power. Indeed, as Maclear (1999, 75) notes: "witnessing is the will to push at the limits of our looking." I would extend this further to note that it is also to push at the limits of what it means to look in the first place.

In the story that introduced the book, I noted that I was not sure how to respond to the dead body image, and that has been a thread that has continued throughout the cases I analyzed here. It has not always been easy to engage the content of these images. After working on Chapter 5, I had nightmares for quite some time about Syrian torture victims, for example. I have consistently tried to ask myself in this book what the right balance is between examining these cases as an academic interested in political processes and also acknowledging the individuals depicted in dead body images as profoundly human. I have sought to avoid treating humans as data, but I have also sought to problematize the notion that simply making such images visible is sufficient to dignify the victims of human suffering, or that simply looking or not looking is necessary for ethical engagement. Catherine Mills has noted that a hallmark of Giorgio Agamben's work is his notion of testimony and witnessing and the relationship between those and our humanness. She argues that "being human is fundamentally conditioned by an indefinite potentiality for being non-human" (Mills 2005, 201) and that human beings are only human insofar as they bear witness to the inhuman. This book has been an attempt to bear witness in its own right, in that it has sought to complicate claims that equate visibility with qualified political life, as well as complicating the underlying assumptions within security studies that life is a precondition for politics. By rendering and explicating death's politics beyond simply a focus on killing itself, as has been thoroughly taken up by the biopolitics literature, I argue that a key component to bearing witness is in focusing more attention not on what we see or even who we see (and don't), but on *how we see.*

This also has an important connection to the way in which emotion figures into our encounters with the global dead, but also with the way we study issues in global politics such as the ones I have addressed here. In other words, this book has modeled one way to engage the affective or emotional dimensions of world politics from a micro level. As Ty Solomon has noted, much of the previous work on emotion has focused on state-level emotions. But this prevents us from understanding the visceral and embodied politics of security, and the way in which "it is through the body that collective politics is experienced" (2015, 60). Roland Bleiker similarly notes that visual media can give the viewer a "visceral experience" and that this is why emotions seem able to capture the unimaginable (2018b, 195). I have also sought here to bridge the gap between the discursive and embodied dynamics of emotion. It also connects to the wider move in the practice theory literature to attempt to understand embodied everyday practices (McCourt 2016).

Lest these conclusions be seen as overly conclusive, I want to end here by pointing to some additional questions that this analysis has raised that could provide trajectories for future research. I have not posed here a definitive typology of images, but more can be said about the values images have: evidentiary, political, emotive, prompting action, performing a narrative, witnessing, and numerous others. I am not arguing that the taboo governing images can or should be overcome. The desire to look and to be seen is unlikely to change. What I have instead suggested is that it is worth examining the functioning of things we take for granted, such as the functioning of the obscenity taboo. One thing this analysis has pointed to is the way in which images are controlled and distributed not just by governments, but by non-state actors like ISIS and by family members like Giulio Regeni's mother. The actors involved in sustaining and resisting existing power relations are not simply states and governmental institutions; they are also a host of other agents and practices, ranging from dead bodies to images.

This text has focused on spectacular images: those that have become a public spectacle by virtue of being displayed (or not, but in a decisive, spectacular manner). Part of the reason for this is that these images are where the practices of regulation associated with the obscenity norm come into the sharpest view. One potential limitation then is that my analysis is exclusively focused on the spectacular image or death, and less on the everyday mundane nature of visual practices. Rebecca Adelman has encouraged visual politics scholars to reflect more on these mundane visual registers. She asks: on 9/11, was there anything to do but watch? As a result, there is less to be said about the mere act of viewing. She instead focuses on how visually mundane practices sustain statecraft in the war-on-terror (2014, 10). While I have argued here that we should move beyond the binary of simply looking or not looking, I do agree that the picture can be complicated with increased attention to the everyday nature of images, and to everyday visual representations, a potential direction for future research.

There is also more to be said about the dynamic of the Western audience that I have, to some extent, taken for granted in this text. Indeed, some argue that the desire to look at body horror that characterizes part of the taboo I have explored is not only fundamentally Western but also fundamentally American. Aaron Michael Kerner, for example, describes torture porn as a quintessentially American genre that emerges after 9/11 (2015, 22) and suggests that "torture porn reveals the American sadistic disposition that not only made the War on Terror possible but also desired it" (2015, 205). There is room for exploration here on the extent to which the mechanisms of viewing I attribute to Western audiences are directly connected to particular policies.

Indeed, it is perhaps no coincidence that, as I finish this book, racial issues have come to the fore in the West in the form of Black Lives Matter protests against racial inequality and police brutality. Such movements and protests raise many of the same questions I have here: in what ways are black bodies represented in the United States – as threatening, as non-normative, as killable? They focus on the visual politics of images of the dead, including the politics of their circulation. They raise questions about the assumptions at the heart of claims of community and point to its exclusionary processes that structure who belongs and argue that black lives have been excluded from the community and its processes of justice and development, among other things. Indeed, in the era where the deaths of black Americans proliferate on social media, some are concerned that this may further trauma for black communities while also inuring the general public to the deaths of black people (Dwyer 2016). It also plays with the obscenity taboo I have discussed here, with some suggesting that the black body has become "a spectacle for white pornography: the dead body as an object that satisfies an illicit desire" (Rankine 2015). In sum, the empirical cases I have discussed in this book have their roots in "our" understandings of death and visuality associated with internal violence such as lynching that is both projected upon and returned to the death narrative of overseas war.

While to some extent I have taken the "our" of the political communities I describe for granted as a mechanism of analysis, there is room to unsettle this, and these recent movements offer an opportunity to engage this. The "our" that informs the viewing public I describe rests on assumptions about black and brown bodies outside of Western borders that also has a deep impact on how these individuals are othered within those same societies. This project has been an effort to reckon with the use of obscenity as a strategic label that accords dignity only to members of our own political communities, yet the very idea of homogeneous political communities is a political construction that should be acknowledged as such. Political communities are precarious entities, engaged in an iterative process of identity construction that relies on making claims about who belongs, often a visual claim itself. While this book has traced the roots and effects of the obscenity norm, norms are not fully and finally fixed, and uncovering the assumptions at the heart of how they function is an important project to clarify the complex and fragile nature of identities and claims to political community.

Ultimately, my intent is that this book has raised more questions than it has perhaps answered. This is because I firmly believe that approaches to global politics must pay more attention to the material and emotional aftereffects of the things we tend to study, such as conflict, sovereignty, or governance. I also see the need to have more conversations across approaches, and this book has made the effort to speak across various recent turns including the visual, the material, the embodied, and the affective. My contention has been that global corpse politics is one way to take account of the complex narratives that structure our being in the international. We are all proceeding toward our deaths, yet the fear and anxiety associated with our own mortality have limited our ability to see the ways in which death and the dead are integral to uncovering the assumptions that structure the functioning of global politics, particularly narratives of security. Instead, choosing to engage global corpse politics can complicate the picture often painted of such discourses.

References

Adelman, Rebecca, *Beyond the Checkpoint: Visual Practices in America's Global War on Terror*, Amherst: University of Massachusetts Press, 2014.

Adler-Nissen, Rebecca, "Stigma Management in International Relations: Transgressive Identities, Norms, and Order in International Society," *International Organization*, 68, 1, 2014, 143–176.

Agamben, Giorgio, *Homo Sacer: Sovereign Power and Bare Life*, Palo Alto: Stanford University Press, 1998.

Agathangelou, Anna, "Bodies to the Slaughter: Global Racial Reconstructions, Fanon's Combat Breath, and Wrestling for Life," *Somatechnics*, 1, 1, 2011, 209–248.

Ali, Yashar, "Off With Her Head," *The Cut,* August 2017, available at www.thecut.com/2017/08/kathy-griffin-donald-trump-interview.html

Allan, Stuart, "Photo-Reportage of the Libyan Conflict," in Kennedy, Liam, and Caitlin Patrick, eds, *The Violence of the Image: Photography and International Conflict*, New York: IB Tauris, 2014, 167–192.

"American Admits Beheading Was a Hoax," *New York Times*, August 8, 2004, available at www.nytimes.com/2004/08/08/us/american-admits-beheading-was-a-hoax.html

Amoore, Louise, "Vigilant Visualities: The Watchful Politics of the War on Terror," *Security Dialogue*, 38, 2, 2007, 215–232.

Arnold, Jeremy, *State Violence and Moral Horror*, Albany: SUNY Press, 2017.

Auchter, Jessica, "Border Monuments: Memory, Counter-Memory, and (B)ordering Practices Along the U.S.-Mexico Border," *Review of International Studies*, 39, 2, 2013, 291–311.

Auchter, Jessica, *The Politics of Haunting and Memory in International Relations*, London: Routledge, 2014.

Auchter, Jessica, "Corpses," in Salter, Mark, ed, *Making Things International*, Minneapolis: University of Minnesota Press, 2015a, 129–140.

Auchter, Jessica, "@GaddafisGhost: On the Popular Memoro-politics of a Dead Dictator," *Journal for Cultural Research*, 19, 3, 2015b, 291–305.

Auchter, Jessica. "Caution – Graphic Images: The Politics of Obscene Dead Bodies," *Critical Studies on Security*, 4, 1, 2016a, 118–120.

Auchter, Jessica, "Paying Attention to Dead Bodies: The Future of Security Studies," *Journal of Global Security Studies*, 1, 1, 2016b, 36–50.

Azoulay, Ariella, *Death's Showcase: The Power of Image in Contemporary Democracy*, Cambridge: MIT Press, 2001.

Azoulay, Ariella, *The Civil Contract of Photography*, New York: Zone Books, 2008.

Azoulay, Ariella, "The Execution Portrait," in Batchen, Geoffrey, Mick Gidley, Nancy Miller, and Jay Prosser, eds, *Picturing Atrocity: Photography in Crisis*, London: Reaktion, 2012, 249–259.

Baer, Ulrich, *Spectral Evidence: The Photography of Trauma*, Cambridge: MIT Press, 2005.

Bajekal, Naina, "ISIS Mass Beheading Video Took 6 Hours to Film and Multiple Takes," *Time*, December 9, 2014, available at https://time.com /3624976/isis-beheading-technology-video-trac-quilliam/

Ball, James, "James Foley and The Daily Horrors of the Internet," *The Guardian*, August 20, 2014, available at www.theguardian.com/commentisfree/2014/a ug/20/james-foley-daily-horrors-internet-think-clicking-beheading

Bataille, George, *Erotism: Death and Sensuality*, San Francisco: City Lights, 1986 [1957].

Batchen, Geoffrey, Mick Gidley, Nancy Miller, and Jay Prosser, eds, *Picturing Atrocity: Photography in Crisis*, London: Reaktion, 2012.

Baquedano, Elizabeth and Michel Graulich, "Decapitation among the Aztecs: Mythology, Agriculture and Politics, and Hunting," *Estudios De Cultura Nahuatl*, 23, 1993, 163–178.

Baudrillard, Jean, *The Gulf War Did Not Take Place*, Sydney: Power Publications, 1995.

Bennett, Bruce, "Framing Terror: Cinema, Docudrama and the 'War on Terror'," *Studies in Documentary Film*, 4, 3, 2010, 209–225.

Bennett, Jane, *Vibrant Matter: A Political Ecology of Things*, Durham: Duke University Press, 2010.

Bentley, Michelle, "Scenes of a Disturbing Nature: Trigger Warnings," *Critical Studies on Security*, 4, 1, 2016a, 114–117.

Bentley, Michelle, *Syria and the Chemical Weapons Taboo: Exploiting the Forbidden*, Manchester: Manchester University Press, 2016b.

Berents, Helen, "Apprehending the 'Telegenic Dead': Considering Images of Dead Children in Global Politics," *International Political Sociology*, 13, 2019, 145–160.

Berger, John, *Ways of Seeing*, London: Penguin, 1977.

Berger, J. M., "The Decapitation Will Not Be Televised." *Foreign Policy*, July 3, 2016, available at http://foreignpolicy.com/2016/07/03/isis-roller-ball-hunger

-games-cinema/?utm_content=bufferc2ef8&utm_medium=social&utm_sour
ce=facebook.com&utm_campaign=buffer

Bernstein, J. M., "Bare Life, Bearing Witness: Auschwitz and the Pornography of Horror," *Parallax*, 10, 2004, 2–16.

Bleiker, Roland, "Mapping Visual Global Politics," in Bleiker, Roland, ed, *Visual Global Politics*, London: Routledge, 2018, 1–29.

Bleiker, Roland, ed, *Visual Global Politics*, London: Routledge, 2018.

Bleiker, Roland, "Visual Security: Patterns and Prospects," in Vuori, Juha, and Rune Saugmann Andersen, eds, *Visual Security Studies: Sights and Spectacles of Insecurity and War*, London: Routledge, 2018b, 189–200.

Boffey, Daniel, "Gaddafi's Death: Growing Revulsion at the Treatment of the Dictator's Body," *The Guardian*, October 22, 2011.

Bogard, William, "Empire of the Living Dead," *Mortality*, 13, 2, 2008, 187–200.

Borchers, Callum, "This *Der Spiegel* Cover is Stunning," *The Washington Post*, February 3, 2017, available at www.washingtonpost.com/news/the-fix/wp/2017/02/03/trump-beheads-the-statue-of-liberty-in-striking-magazine-cover-illustration/

Botelho, Greg, Steve Almasy, and Jomana Karadsheh, "Jordan Challenges ISIS Claim of U.S. Hostage Death in Airstrike," *CNN*, February 6, 2015, available at www.cnn.com/2015/02/06/world/isis-jordan/index.html

Bousquet, Antoine, *The Eye of War: Military Perception from the Telescope to the Drone*, Minneapolis: University of Minnesota Press, 2018.

Braidotti, Rosi, *The Posthuman*, Cambridge: Polity, 2013.

Brooks, David, "The Body and the Spirit," *The New York Times*, September 5, 2014, A27, available at www.nytimes.com/2014/09/05/opinion/david-brooks-the-body-and-the-spirit.html

Brooks, Rosa, "But This Threatiness Goes To 11," *Foreign Policy*, September 25, 2014, available at http://foreignpolicy.com/2014/09/25/bu t-this-threatiness-goes-to–11/

Brooks, Rosa, "The Magical Thinking of Killing Mullah Mansour," *Foreign Policy*, May 24, 2016, available at https://foreignpolicy.com/2016/05/24/t he-magical-thinking-of-killing-mullah-mansour-taliban-al-qaeda-obama/

Buck-Morss, Susan, *Dreamworld and Catastrophe: The Passing of Mass Utopia in East and West*, Cambridge: MIT Press, 2002.

Bunker, Pamela L., Lisa J. Campbell, and Robert J. Bunker, "Torture, Beheadings, and Narcocultos," *Small Wars & Insurgencies*, 21, 1, 2010, 145–178.

Butler, Judith, "Photography, War, Outrage," *PMLA*, 120, 3, 2005, 822–827.

Butler, Judith, *Frames of War: When is Life Grievable?* London: Verso, 2010.

Callimachi, Rukmani and Rick Gladstone, "ISIS Declares Airstrike Killed a US Hostage," *New York Times*, February 6, 2015, available at www .nytimes.com/2015/02/07/world/middleeast/isis-claims-american-hostage -killed-by-jordanian-retaliation-bombings.html

Callimachi, Rukmani and Eric Schmitt, "With Proof From ISIS of Her Death, Family Honors Kayla Mueller," *New York Times*, February 10, 2015, available at www.nytimes.com/2015/02/11/world/middleeast/parents-of-kayla-mueller-isis-hostage-confirm-she-is-dead.html

Callimachi, Rukmani, and Catherine Porter, "2 American Wives of ISIS Militants Want to Return Home," *The New York Times*, February 19, 2019, available at www.nytimes.com/2019/02/19/us/islamic-state-american-women.html?emc=edit_na_20190220&nl=breaking-news&nlid =66500985ing-news&ref=cta

Campbell, Colin, "Jordan Dismisses Claim of Killed US Hostage as an ISIS 'PR Stunt,'" *Business Insider*, February 6, 2015, available at www .businessinsider.com/jordan-claim-of-killed-us-hostage-is-isis-pr-stunt– 2015–2

Campbell, David, "Horrific Blindness: Images of Death in Contemporary Media," *Journal for Cultural Research*, 8, 1, 2004, 55–74.

Campbell, D. (2007), "Geopolitics and Visuality: Sighting the Darfur Conflict," *Political Geography*, 26, 357–382.

Campbell, David, "The Myth of Compassion Fatigue," in Kennedy, Liam, and Caitlin Patrick, eds, *The Violence of the Image: Photography and International Conflict*, New York: IB Tauris, 2014, 97–111.

Campbell, David, "Imaging Fear," Keynote address, "Who's Afraid of ISIS" Workshop, Colgate University, September 9, 2016.

Cantor, Norman, *After We Die: The Life and Times of the Human Cadaver*, Washington, DC: Georgetown University Press, 2010.

Casper, Monica, and Lisa Jean Moore, *Missing Bodies: The Politics of Visibility*, New York: New York University Press, 2009.

Cavarero, Adriana, *Horrorism: Naming Contemporary Violence*, New York: Columbia University Press, 2009.

Chen, Adrian, "The Laborers Who Keep Dick Pics and Beheadings Out of Your Facebook Feed," *Wired*, October 23, 2014, available at www .wired.com/2014/10/content-moderation/

Chouliaraki, Lilie, *The Spectatorship of Suffering*, London: Sage, 2006.

Chouliaraki, Lilie, "Post-Humanitarianism: Humanitarian Communication Beyond a Politics of Pity," *International Journal of Cultural Studies*, 13, 2, 2010, 107–126.

Cole, Teju, "Death in the Browser Tab," *The New York Times Magazine*, May 21, 2015, available at www.nytimes.com/2015/05/24/magazine/dea th-in-the-browser-tab.html

Conant, Eve, "Terror: The Remains of 9/11 Hijackers," *Newsweek*, January 2, 2009, available at www.newsweek.com/terror-remains-911-hijackers-78327

Connerton, Paul, *The Spirit of Mourning: History, Memory, and the Body*, Cambridge: Cambridge University Press, 2011.

Cosgrove, Ben, "Portrait from the Brutal Pacific: 'Skull on a Tank,' Guadalcanal, 1942," *Time*, February 19, 2014, available at http://time.com/3518085/life-behind-the-picture-skull-on-a-tank-guadalcanal–1942/

Cox, Lloyd, and Steve Wood, "'Got Him': Revenge, Emotions, and the Killing of Osama bin Laden," *Review of International Studies*, 43, 1, 2016, 112–129.

Crawford, Neta, "The Passion of World Politics," *International Security*, 24, 4, 2000, 116–156.

Cronin, Bruce, *Bugsplat: The Politics of Collateral Damage in Western Armed Conflicts*, Oxford: Oxford University Press, 2018.

Dabashi, Hamid, *Corpus Anarchicum: Political Protest, Suicidal Volence, and the Making of the Posthuman Body*, New York: Palgrave Macmillan, 2012

"Ignominious End for Gaddafi as He is Buried with Son Mutassim in Unmarked Desert Grave at Dawn," *The Daily Mail*, October 25, 2011, available at www.dailymail.co.uk/news/article-2053110/Gaddafi-burial-Dictator-son-Mutassims-dead-bodiesunmarked-grave.html

"Bin Laden Death Photos Will Not be Released as US Court Rules They Must Stay Classified," *The Daily Mail*, May 22, 2013, available at www.dailymail.co.uk/news/article-2328948/Bin-Laden-death-photos-NOT-released-U-S-court-rulesstay-classified.html

Danchev, Alex, *On Art and War and Terror*, Edinburgh: Edinburgh University Press, 2011.

Danil, Linda Roland, "Trigger Warnings: Lacanian Psychoanalysis and International Security: Making a Link," *Critical Studies on Security*, 4, 1, 2016, 121–124.

Dauphinee, Elizabeth, "The Politics of the Body in Pain," *Security Dialogue*, 38, 2, 2007, 139–155.

Dauphinee, Elizabeth, "Body," in Bleiker, Roland, ed, *Visual Global Politics*, London, Routledge, 2018, 30–34.

DCMS, *Report of the Working Group on Human Remains*, London: Department of Culture Media and Sport, 2003.

Dean, Caroline, "Empathy, Pornography, and Suffering," *Differences: A Journal of Feminist Cultural Studies*, 14, 2003, 88–124.

Debord, Guy, *Society of the Spectacle*, Detroit: Black and Red, 1983.

Debrix, Francois, *Global Powers of Horror: Security, Politics, and the Body in Pieces*, London: Routledge, 2017.

Debrix, Francois, "Confronting Horror: IR Beyond Humanity," in Edkins, Jenny, ed, *Routledge Handbook of Critical IR*, London: Routledge, 2019, 77–88.

Derrida, Jacques, *Specters of Marx*, London: Routledge, 1994.

Dixit, Priya, "Decolonizing Visuality in Security Studies: Reflections on the Death of Osama bin Laden," *Critical Studies on Security*, 2, 3, 2014, 337–351.

Dixit, Priya, "Let the Dead Speak! Mobility, Visibility, and (In)Security in Qatar," *Critical Studies on Security*, 3, 1, 2015, 112–117.

Dodds, Klaus, "Steve Bell's Eye: Cartoons, Geopolitics and the Visualization of the War on Terror," *Security Dialogue*, 38, 2, 2007, 157–177.

Dolan, Thomas, "Unthinkable and Tragic: The Psychology of Weapons Taboos in War," *International Organization*, 67, 1, 2013, 37–63.

Doughty, Caitlin, *Smoke Gets in Your Eyes: And Other Lessons from the Crematory*, New York: Noughton, 2015.

Downs, Ray, "Muammar Gaddafi Dead: Twitter Users Joke About Dictator's Reported Capture and Death," *Christian Post*, October 20, 2011, available at www.christianpost.com/news/muammar-gadaffi-dead-twitter-users-joke-about-dictators-reported-capture-and-death-58765/

Duca, Lauren, "On Kathy Griffin, Performative Outrage, and the Relativity of Shame," *Teen Vogue*, June 2, 2017, available at www.teenvogue.com/story/kathy-griffin-performative-outrage-relativity-shame-thigh-high-politics

Durand, Lauren, "Are NGO Agendas Dictated by Western Assumptions?," *E-IR*, September 26, 2012, available at www.e-ir.info/2012/09/26/are-ngo-agendas-dictated-by-western-assumptions/

Dwyer, Liz, "The Collective Trauma of Watching the End of Black Lives," *TakePart*, July 7 2016, available at www.takepart.com/article/2016/07/07/racism-and-black-ptsd

Edkins, Jenny, *Missing: Persons and Politics*, Ithaca: Cornell University Press, 2011.

Edkins, Jenny, "Politics and Personhood: Reflections on the Portrait Photograph," *Alternatives*, 38, 2, 2013, 139–154.

"Egypt Tried To Cover Up Student Murder, Italy Says," *BBC News*, December 18, 2019, www.bbc.com/news/world-europe–50835174

Epstein, Charlotte, "Guilty Bodies, Productive Bodies, Destructive Bodies: Crossing the Biometric Borders," *International Political Sociology*, 1, 2007, 149–164.

Fahey, Jamie, "*The Guardian*'s Decision to Publish Shocking Photos of Aylan Kurdi," *The Guardian*, September 7, 2015, available at www.theguardian.com/commentisfree/2015/sep/07/guardian-decision-to-publish-shocking-photos-of-aylan-kurdi

Fazal, Tanisha, "Dead Wrong?: Battle Deaths, Military Medicine, and Exaggerated Reports of War's Demise," *International Security*, 39, 1, 2014, 95–125.

Ferrandiz, Francisco, and Antonius Robben, eds, *Necropolitics: Mass Graves and Exhumations in the Age of Human Rights*, University of Pennsylvania Press, 2015.

Finnemore, Martha, and Kathryn Sikkink, "International Norm Dynamics and Political Change," *International Organization*, 52, 4, 1998, 887–917.

Fisher, M, "Fact Check: New York Post's Qaddafi Headline almost Certainly Wrong," *The Atlantic*, October 21, 2011, available at www.theatlantic.com/international/archive/2011/10/fact-check-new-york-posts-qaddafi-headlinealmost-certainly-wrong/247141/

Foltyn, Jacque Lynn, "Dead Famous and Dead Sexy: Popular Culture, Forensics, and the Rise of the Corpse," *Mortality*, 13, 2, 2008, 153–173.

Foucault, Michel, *Society Must be Defended*, London: Picador, 1997.

Frank, Jeffrey, "The G.O.P.'s Problem With Threat Inflation," *The New Yorker*, December 17, 2015, available at www.newyorker.com/news/daily-comment/the-g-o-p-s-problem-with-threat-inflation

Frankenberg, Gunter, "Torture and Taboo: An Essay Comparing Paradigms of Organized Cruelty," *American Journal of Comparative Law*, 56, 2, 2008, 403–422.

Friis, Simone Molin, "'Beyond Anything We Have Ever Seen': Beheading Videos and the Visibility of Violence in the War Against ISIS," *International Affairs*, 91, 4, 2015, 725–746.

Freud, Sigmund, *The Taboo of Virginity*, London: Hogarth, 1918.

Freud, Sigmund, *Totem and Taboo*, London: Routledge, 1919.

Freud, Sigmund, *Writings on Art and Literature*, Palo Alto: Stanford University Press, 1997.

"Gaddafi Dead: How Colonel Gaddafi's Death Made Headlines Around the World," *The Mirror*, October 21, 2011, available at www.mirror.co.uk/news/uk-news/gaddafi-dead-how-colonel-gaddafis–275437

Gillespie, Nick, "Why We Shouldn't Be Scared of ISIS: Threat Inflation and Our Next Dumb War," *The Daily Beast*, September 10, 2014, available at www.thedailybeast.com/articles/2014/09/10/why-we-shouldn-t-be-scared-of-isis-threat-inflation-and-our-next-dumb-war

Giroux, Henry, "Reading Hurricane Katrina: Race, Class, and the Politics of Disposability," *College Literature*, 33, 3, 2006, 171–196.

Goldman, Adam, and Rukmini Callimachi, "ISIS Leader al-Baghdadi May Have Had U.S. Hostage Executed, Witness Says," *The New York Times*, November 12, 2019, available at www.nytimes.com/2019/11/12/us/politics/kayla-mueller-baghdadi.html

172

Gourevitch, Philip, "Among the Dead," in Roth, Michael, and Charles Salas, eds, *Disturbing Remains*, Los Angeles: The Getty Institute, 2001, 63–73.

Grayson, Kyle, and Jocelyn Mawdsley, "Scopic Regimes and The Visual Turn in International Relations: Seeing World Politics Through the Drone," *European Journal of International Relations*, 25, 2, 2019, 431–457.

Gregory, Derek, "From a View to A Kill: Drones and Late Modern War," *Theory, Culture, and Society*, 28, 7–8, 2011, 188–215.

Gregory, Thomas, "Dismembering the Dead: Violence, Vulnerability and the Body in War," *European Journal of International Relations*, 22, 4, 2016, 944–965.

Gregory, Thomas, "Targeted Killings: Drones, Noncombatant Immunity, and the Politics of Killing," *Contemporary Security Policy*, 38, 2 2017, 212–236.

Groll, Elias, "Islamic State Releases Video Showing Jordanian Pilot Being Burned Alive," *Foreign Policy*, February 3, 2015, available at https://for eignpolicy.com/2015/02/03/islamic_state_releases_video_showing_jorda nian_pilot_being_burned_alive/

Guittet, Emmanuel-Pierre, and Andreja Zevnik, "Exposed Images of War," in Ahall, Linda, and Thomas Gregory, eds, *Emotions, Politics, and War*, London: Routledge, 2014, 195–209.

Hallam, Lindsay, "Genre Cinema as Trauma Cinema: Post 9/11 Trauma and the Rise of 'Torture Porn' in Recent Horror Films," in Broderick, Mick, and Antonio Traverso, eds, *Trauma, Media, Art: New Perspectives*, Newcastle Upon Tyne: Cambridge Scholars Publishing, 2010, 228–236.

Halliday, Josh, "Police Warn Sharing James Wright Killing Video is a Crime," *The Guardian*, August 20, 2014, available at www.theguardian.com/uk-news/2014/aug/20/police-warn-james-foley-video-crime-social-media

Halttunen, Karen, "Humanitarianism and the Pornography of Pain in Anglo-American Culture," *The American Historical Review*, 100, 2, 1995, 303–334.

Hansen, Lene, "Theorizing the Image for Security Studies: Visual Securitization and the Muhammad Cartoon Crisis," *European Journal of International Relations*, 17, 1, 2011, 51–74.

Hansen, Lene, "How Images Make World Politics: International Icons and the Case of Abu Ghraib," *Review of International Studies*, 41, 2, 2015, 263–288.

Hamdar, Abir, "The Syrian Corpse: The Politics of Dignity in Visual and Media Representations of the Syrian Revolution," *Journal for Cultural Research*, 22, 1, 2018, 73–89.

Hariman, Robert, and John Louis Lucaites, *No Caption Needed: Iconic Photographs, Public Culture, and Liberal Democracy*, Chicago: University of Chicago Press, 2007.

Harris, Shane, and Nancy Youssef, "US Won't Investigate ISIS Hostage's Death," *The Daily Beast*, February 6, 2015, available at www.thedaily beast.com/us-wont-investigate-isis-hostages-death

Hawley, Thomas, *The Remains of War: Bodies, Politics, and the Search For American Soldiers Unaccounted For In Southeast Asia*, Durham: Duke University Press, 2005.

Heath-Kelly, Charlotte, *Death and Security: Memory and Mortality at the Bombsite*, Manchester: Manchester University Press, 2016.

Heck, Axel, and Gabi Schlag, "Securitizing Images: The Female Body and the War in Afghanistan," *European Journal of International Relations*, 19, 4, 2013, 891–913.

Hellmich, Christina, and Andreas Behnke, eds, *Knowing al-Qaeda: The Epistemology of Terrorism*, London: Ashgate, 2012.

Hernandez, Brian Anthony, "25 Twitter Reactions to Gaddafi's Capture and Death," *Mashable*, October 20, 2011, available at http://mashable.com/2011/10/20/gaddafi-death-tweets-twitter/

Hertz, Neil, "Medusa's Head: Male Hysteria under Political Pressure," *Representations*, 4, 1983, 27–54.

Hill, Andrew, *Re-Imagining The War On Terror: Seeing, Waiting, Traveling*, London: Palgrave, 2009.

Hill, Andrew, "The Bin Laden Tapes," in Jeffords, Susan, and Fahed al-Sumait, eds, *Covering bin Laden: Global Media and the World's Most Wanted Man*, Chicago: University of Illinois Press, 2015, 35–52.

Hochberg, Gil, *Visual Occupations: Violence and Visibility in a Conflict Zone*, Durham: Duke University Press, 2015.

Hollander, Jenny, "Fox News Airs Images of Muath al-Kasasbeh Burning to Death 'To Bring You the Reality of Islamic Terrorism,'" *Bustle*, February 4, 2015, available at www.bustle.com/articles/62353-fox-news-airs-images-of-muath-al-kaseasbeh-burning-to-death-to-bring-you-the-reality-of

Huyssen, Andreas, "Present Pasts: Media, Politics, Amnesia," in Appadurai, Arjun, ed, *Globalization*, Durham: Duke University Press, 2001.

"If the Dead Could Speak: Mass Deaths and Torture in Syria's Detention Facilities," *Human Rights Watch*, December 16, 2015, available at www.hrw.org/report/2015/12/16/if-dead-could-speak/mass-deaths-and-torture-syrias-detention-facilities

Ignatieff, Michael, "Terrorist as Auteur," *The New York Times*, November 14, 2004, available at www.nytimes.com/2004/11/14/movies/the-terrorist-as-auteur.html?_r=0

"Ignominious End for Dictator Gaddafi," *The Daily Mail*, October 25, 2011, available at www.dailymail.co.uk/news/article-2053110/Gaddafi-burial-Dictator-son-Mutassims-dead-bodies-unmarked-grave.html

"Italian Student's Family Threatens to Show Body Photo," *BBC News*, March 30, 2016, available at www.bbc.com/news/world-middle-east–35923666

Jackson, Richard, "Bin Laden's Ghost and the Epistemological Crisis of Counterterrorism," in Jeffords, Susan, and Fahed al-Sumait, eds, *Covering bin Laden: Global Media and the World's Most Wanted Man*, Chicago: University of Illinois Press, 2015, 3–19.

Jalabi, R, "Images of Syrian Torture on Display at UN," *The Guardian*, March 11, 2015, available at www.theguardian.com/world/2015/mar/11/imagessyrian-torture-shock-new-yorkers-united-nations

Janes, Regina, *Losing Our Heads: Beheadings in Literature and Culture*, New York: NYU Press, 2005.

Jeffords, Susan, and Fahed al-Sumait, "Introduction: After bin Laden," in Jeffords, Susan, and Fahed al-Sumait, eds, *Covering bin Laden: Global Media and the World's Most Wanted Man*, Chicago: University of Illinois Press, 2015, vii–xxxvii.

Jeffords, Susan, and Fahed al-Sumait, eds, *Covering bin Laden: Global Media and the World's Most Wanted Man*, Chicago: University of Illinois Press, 2015.

Jenkins, Tiffany. "Gaddafi: Body Politics," *Prospect Magazine*, October 24, 2011, available at www.prospectmagazine.co.uk/magazine/gaddafi-body-politics/

Johnston, Patrick, "Does Decapitation Work?" *International Security*, 30, 4, 2012, 47–79.

Jones, J, "The West Wrings its Hands over Dead Gaddafi Photos, But War is always Hell," *The Guardian*, October 25, 2011, available at www.theguardian.com/commentisfree/2011/oct/25/dead-gaddafi-photos-war-hell

Jones, Owen, "Our Shameful Hierarchy – Some Deaths Matter more than Others," *The Independent*, April 21, 2013, available at www.independent.co.uk/voices/comment/our-shameful-hierarchy-some-deaths-matter-more-than-others-8581715.html

Jones, Ronald, "Terrorist Beheadings: Cultural and Strategic Implications," US Air Force Air War College, June 2005, available at www.au.af.mil/au/awc/awcgate/ssi/terr_beheadings.pdf

Jones, Steve, "Horrorporn/Pornhorror: The Problematic Communities and Contexts of Online Shock Imagery," in Attwood, Feona, ed, *Porn.com: Making Sense of Online Pornography*, New York: Peter Lang, 2010, 123–137.

Jordan, Jenna, "When Heads Roll: Assessing the Effectiveness of Leadership Decapitation," *Security Studies*, 18, 4, 2009, 719–755.

Jurkovich, Michelle, "What Isn't A Norm? Redefining the Conceptual Boundaries of Norms in the Human Rights Literature," *International Studies Review*, 22, 3, 2020, 693–711.

"Kathy Griffin Beheads President Trump," *TMZ*, May 30, 2017, available at www.tmz.com/2017/05/30/kathy-griffin-beheads-donald-trump-photo-tyler-shields/

"Kayla Mueller's Parents: We Can't Let Her Down Again," *BBC News*, October 4, 2020, available at www.bbc.com/news/av/stories–54386534

Kayyem, Juliette, "Airing Killings Makes Media a Tool." *CNN*, August 28, 2015, available at www.cnn.com/2015/08/27/opinions/should-media-show-killings-roundup/

Kennedy, Liam, *Afterimages: Photography and US Foreign Policy*, Chicago: University of Chicago Press, 2016.

Kennedy, Liam, and Caitlin Patrick, eds, *The Violence of the Image: Photography and International Conflict*, New York: IB Tauris, 2014.

Kerner, Aaron Michael, *Torture Porn in the Wake of 9/11: Horror, Exploitation, and the Cinema of Sensation*, New Brunswick: Rutgers University Press, 2015.

"Kerry Condemns Image of Boy with Severed Head," *USA Today*, August 12, 2014, available at www.usatoday.com/story/news/world/2014/08/12/kerry-condemns-severed-head-image/13939635/

Kerry, John, "Under US Leadership, World Will Defeat ISIS," *Boston Globe*, September 25, 2014, available at www.bostonglobe.com/opinion/editorials/2014/09/25/under-leadership/a2kyeND3mQrf5ct5oRj4dK/story.html

Kobos, Sarah, "Syrian Torture Images on Display at U.N.: To Look or Look Away," *ABC News*, March 14, 2015, available at https://abcnews.go.com/International/syrian-torture-images-display/story?id=29627005

Kozol, Wendy, "Battlefield Souvenirs and the Affective Politics of Recoil," *Photography and Culture*, 5, 1, 2012, 21–36.

Kozol, Wendy, *Distant Wars Visible: The Ambivalence of Witnessing*, Minneapolis: University of Minnesota Press, 2014.

LaCapra, Dominick, "Lanzmann's 'Shoah': 'Here There Is No Why,'" *Critical Inquiry*, 23, 2, 1997, 231–269.

Larson, Frances, *Severed: A History of Heads Lost and Heads Found*, New York: Liveright, 2014.

Larson, Frances, "ISIS Beheadings: Why We're Too Horrified to Watch, Too Fascinated to Turn Away," *CNN*, January 13, 2015a, available at www .cnn.com/2015/01/13/opinion/beheadings-history/

Larson, Frances, "Why Public Beheadings Get Millions of Views," *TED Talk*, September 2015b, available at www.ted.com/talks/frances_larson_ why_public_beheadings_get_millions_of_views/transcript?language=en

Laurent, Olivier, "What the Image of Aylan Kurdi Says About the Power of Photography," *Time*, September 4, 2015, available at https://time.com/4 022765/aylan-kurdi-photo/

Layne, Christopher, "Obama's Missed Opportunity to Pivot Away From the Middle East," *Insight Turkey*, 17, 3, 2015, 11–21.

Levi-Strauss, David, *Between the Eyes: Essays on Photography and Politics*, New York: Aperture, 2003.

Linfield, Susie, *The Cruel Radiance: Photography and Political Violence*, Chicago: University of Chicago Press, 2010.

Linfield, Susie, "Syria's Torture Photos: Witness to Atrocity," *New York Review of Books*, February 9, 2019, available at www.nybooks.com/dail y/2019/02/09/syrias-torture-photos-witness-to-atrocity/

Lovejoy, Bess, *Rest in Pieces: The Curious Fates of Famous Corpses*, New York: Simon and Schuster, 2013.

Lovejoy, Bess, "Why So Much Controversy Over Tamerlan Tsarnaev's Corpse?" *The Guardian*, May 11, 2013b, available at www.theguardian .com/commentisfree/2013/may/11/boston-marathon-explosions-tamerlan-tsarnaev

Lowe, Paul, "The Forensic Turn," in Kennedy, Liam, and Caitlin Patrick, eds, *The Violence of the Image: Photography and International Conflict*, New York: IB Tauris, 2014, 211–234.

Lyford, Amy, and Carol Payne, "Photojournalism, Mass Media, and the Politics of Spectacle," *Visual Resources*, 21, 2, 2005, 119–129.

MacAskill, Ewen, "British Soldier Posed Thumbs Up With Body of Taliban Fighter in Afghanistan," *The Guardian*, May 9, 2014, available at www .theguardian.com/uk-news/2014/may/09/british-soldier-posed-thumbs-up-body-taliban-fighter-afghanistan

Mackey, Robert, "Brutal Images of Syrian Boy Drowned Off Turkey Must Be Seen, Activists Say," *The New York Times*, September 2, 2015, available at www.nytimes.com/2015/09/03/world/middleeast/brutal-images-of-syrian-boy-drowned-off-turkey-must-be-seen-activists-say.html

Maclear, Kyo, *Beclouded Visions: Hiroshima-Nagasaki and the Art of Witness*, Albany: SUNY Albany Press, 1999.

Malec, Brett, and Marianne Garvey, "Libyan Dictator Dead: Hollywood Takes to Twitter to Talk About It," *E News*, October 20, 2011, available at www

.eonline.com/news/270629/libyan-dictator-gadhafi-dead-hollywood-takes-to-twitter-to-talk-about-it

Malik, Nesrene, "If You Watch ISIS's Videos You Are Complicit in its Terrorism," *The Guardian*, February 4, 2015, available at www.the guardian.com/commentisfree/2015/feb/04/isis-videos-complict-terrorism-death-hostage-killers

Marlin-Bennett, Renee, Marieke Wilson, and Jason Walton, "Commodified Cadavers and the Political Economy of the Spectacle," *International Political Sociology*, 2, 2, 2010, 159–77.

Mbembe, Achille, "Necropolitics," *Public Culture*, 15, 1, 2003, 11–40.

McConnell, D. and B. Todd, "Admiral's Email on Photos of Osama Bin Laden's Corpse: "Destroy Them"', *CNN*, February 12, 2014, available at www.cnn.com/2014/02/11/politics/e-mail-photos-destroyed-osama-bin-laden/

McCourt, David, "Practice Theory and Relationalism as the New Constructivism," *International Studies Quarterly*, 60, 3, 2016, 475–485.

McKelvey, Tara, "Fox News Explains Why it Showed Jordanian Pilot Video," *BBC News,* February 5, 2015, available at www.bbc.com/news/world-us-canada-31013455

Mead, Nick, "The Legacy of James Foley, Panel Grapples with War Reporting," *Washington Square News*, February 27, 2020, available at https://nyunews.com/news/2020/02/27/middleeast-war-photographyja mesfoley?fbclid=IwAR1c6cqW8LMPdciXCOXjKCfT4lZwP3SlmuNn f3QUDx6dkHXTq7vwSsLNkT4

Meade, Amanda, "News Corp Australia Defends Use of James Foley Beheading Images," *The Guardian*, August 21, 2014, available at www .theguardian.com/media/2014/aug/21/news-corp-australia-defends-james -foley-beheading-images

Mieszkowski, Jan, *Watching War*, Stanford: Stanford University Press, 2012.

Miller, Steven, *War After Death: On Violence and Its Limits*, New York: Fordham University Press, 2014.

Mills, Catherine, "Linguistic Survival and Ethicality: Biopolitics, Subjectivation, and Testimony in *Remnants of Auschwitz*," in Norris, Andrew, ed, *Politics, Metaphysics and Death: Essays on Giorgio Agamben's Homo Sacer*, Durham: Duke University Press, 2005, 198–221.

Mirzoeff, Nicholas, *Watching Babylon: The War in Iraq and Global Visual Culture*, London: Routledge, 2005.

Mirzoeff, Nicholas, *How to See the World*, New York: Basic Books, 2016.

Mitchell, Victoria Coren, "Watching Execution Videos Not Only Hurts the Grieving. It Also Harms Us Dreadfully," *The Guardian*, December 13,

2014, available at www.theguardian.com/commentisfree/2014/dec/14/watc
hing-execution-videos-islamic-state-hurt-grieving-relatives-brutalises-us

Mitchell, W. J. T., *Iconology: Image, Text, Ideology*, Chicago: University of
Chicago Press, 1986.

Mitchell, W. J. T., "There are No Visual Media," *Journal of Visual Culture*,
4, 2, 2005, 257–266.

Mitchell, W. J. T., *Cloning Terror: The War of Images, 9/11 to the Present*,
Chicago: University of Chicago Press, 2011.

Mitford, Jessica, *The American Way of Death Revisited*, New York: Vintage
Books, 1998.

Moeller, Susan, *Compassion Fatigue: How the Media Sell Diseases, Famine,
War, and Death*, London: Routledge, 1999.

Moeller, Susan, Joanna Nurmis, and Saranaz Barforoush, "Images of Our
Dead Enemies: Visual Representations of bin Laden, Hussein, and
Qaddafi," in Jeffords, Susan, and Fahed al-Sumait, eds, *Covering bin
Laden: Global Media and the World's Most Wanted Man*, Chicago:
University of Illinois Press, 2015, 112–139.

Moller, Frank, "Photographic Interventions in Post-9/11 Security Policy,"
Security Dialogue, 38, 2, 2007, 179–196.

Moller, Frank, *Visual Peace: Images, Spectatorship, and the Politics of
Violence*, London, Palgrave, 2013.

Monk, Daniel Bertrand, "Who's Afraid of ISIS." Presentation and Remarks
at "Who's Afraid of ISIS" Workshop, Colgate University, September 10,
2016.

Moos, J., "Few US Front Pages Feature Dead Gadhafi, Many International
Papers Show Body," *Poynter*, October 21, 2011, available at www
.poynter.org/2011/few-us-front-pages-feature-dead-gadhafi-many-inter
national-papers-showbody/150386/

Moran, Rick, "Desecrating the Dead: An Alternate View," *American
Thinker*, January 15, 2012, available at www.americanthinker.com/blo
g/2012/01/desecrating_the_dead_an_alternate_view.html

Morini, Daryl, "Do Not Celebrate the Death of a Dictator," *E-IR*,
October 24, 2011, available at www.e-ir.info/2011/10/24/do-not-
celebrate-the-death-of-a-dictator/

Mount, Harry, "Is it Wrong to Feel Pleased at Gaddafi's Death," *The
Telegraph*, October 21, 2011.

Mueller, Carl, and Marsha Mueller, "ISIS Killed Our Daughter. They
Cannot Have the Last Word on U.S. Hostages," *Washington Post*,
November 18, 2019, available at www.washingtonpost.com/opinions/isi
s-killed-our-daughter-they-cannot-have-the-last-word-on-us-hostages/20
19/11/18/58aa9f7a-07ef-11ea-8ac0-0810ed197c7e_story.html

Muppidi, Himadeep, *The Colonial Signs of International Relations*, New York: Columbia University Press, 2012.

Newman, Lily Hay, "Did Twitter and Youtube Make the Right Call in Suppressing Images of James Foley's Beheading?" *Slate*, August 21, 2014, available at www.slate.com/blogs/future_tense/2014/08/21/james_foley_beheading_did_twitter_make_the_right_call_in_suppressing_the.html

Nichols, Michelle, "Graphic Torture Photos from Syria on Display at United Nations," *Reuters*, March 10, 2015, available at www.reuters.com/article/us-mideast-crisis-syria-un/graphic-torture-photos-from-syria-on-display-at-united-nations-idUSKBN0M628420150310

Norris, Andrew, "Giorgio Agamben and the Politics of the Living Dead," in Norris, Andrew, ed, *Politics, Metaphysics and Death: Essays on Giorgio Agamben's Homo Sacer*, Durham: Duke University Press, 2005, 1–30.

O'Hehir, Andrew, "From 9/11 To The ISIS Videos: The Darkness We Conjured Up," *Salon*, September 6, 2014, available at www.salon.com/2014/09/06/from_911_to_the_isis_videos_the_darkness_we_conjured_up/

O'Loughlin, Ben, "Images as Weapons of War: Representation, Mediation, and Interpretation," *Review of International Studies*, 37, 1, 2011, 71–91.

Ollivant, Douglas, "The Barbaric Terrorists of the Islamic State Are a Threat to the US Homeland," *The New Republic*, August 23, 2014, available at https://newrepublic.com/article/119193/isis-beheading-james-foley-open-eyes-islamic-states-terror

Osborne, Samuel, "Turkey Coup: Images Showing Soldier Beheaded by Government Supporters May Not be Genuine, it is Claimed," *The Independent*, July 16, 2016, available at www.independent.co.uk/news/world/europe/turkey-coup-latest-news-istanbul-ankara-erdogan-twitter-social-media-a7140541.html

Papailias, Penelope, "(Un)Seeing Dead Refugee Bodies: Mourning Memes, Spectropolitics, and the Haunting of Europe," *Media, Culture, and Society*, 41, 8, 2019, 1048–1068.

Parashar, Swati, "On Images, Stories, and the Need to Hear More," *E-IR*, October 8, 2015, available at www.e-ir.info/2015/10/08/on-images-stories-and-the-need-to-hear-more/

Paraszczuk, Joanna, "A Drowned Syrian Boy as ISIS Propaganda," *The Atlantic*, September 11, 2015, available at www.theatlantic.com/international/archive/2015/09/aylan-kurdi-isis-propaganda-dabiq/404911/

"Paris Attacks: Gunman Said Kouachi Given Unmarked Grave," *BBC News*, January 17, 2015, available at www.bbc.com/news/world-europe-30863985

Parkhill, Chad, "On The Memefication Of Aylan Kurdi, And The Power And Ethics Of Sharing Photos," *Junkee*, September 9, 2015, available at https://junkee.com/on-the-memefication-of-aylan-kurdi-and-the-power-and-ethics-of-sharing-photos/65078#G76XtzXoqHGGHU11.03

Perlmutter, David, "Photojournalism and Foreign Affairs," *Orbis*, 49, 1, 2005, 109–122.

Phelan, Peggy, "Atrocity and Action: The Performative Force of the Abu Ghraib Photographs," in Batchen, Geoffrey, Mick Gidley, Nancy Miller, and Jay Prosser, eds, *Picturing Atrocity: Photography in Crisis*, London: Reaktion, 2012, 51–61.

"Pics of Marines Burning Bodies Trigger U.S. Military Investigation," *TMZ*, January 15, 2014, available at www.tmz.com/2014/01/15/iraq-soldier-bodies-on-fire-marines-investigation-military-photos/

Pollock, Griselda, "Feminism/Foucault – Surveillance/Sexuality," in Bryson, Norman, Holly, Michael, and Keith Moxey, eds, *Visual Culture, Images, and Interpretation*, Hanover, NH: Wesleyan University Press, 1994.

Power, Samantha, *A Problem from Hell: America and the Age of Genocide*, New York: Basic Books, 2002.

Price, Bryan, "Targeting Top Terrorists," *International Security* 30, 4, 2012, 9–46.

Price, Richard, "A Genealogy of the Chemical Weapons Taboo," *International Organization*, 49, 1, 1995, 73–103.

Price, Richard, "International Norms and the Mines Taboo: Pulls Toward Compliance," *Canadian Foreign Policy Journal*, 5, 3, 1998, 105–123.

Pritchard, Elizabeth, "*Bilderverbot* Meets Body in Theodor W. Adorno's Inverse Theology," *Harvard Theological Review* 95, 3, 2002, 291–318.

Prosser, Jay, "Introduction," in Batchen, Geoffrey, Mick Gidley, Nancy Miller, and Jay Prosser, eds, *Picturing Atrocity: Photography in Crisis*, London: Reaktion, 2012, 7–14.

Puente, Maria, "'I Went Way Too Far': Kathy Griffin Apologizes for Trump 'Beheaded' Photos," *USA Today*, May 31, 2017, available at www.usatoday.com/story/life/tv/2017/05/30/kathy-griffin-stirs-fury-pic-holding-mock-decapitated-head-donald-trump/102321134/

Purnell, Kandida, "Power/Resistance and Dead American Soldier-Bodies," Paper Presented at International Studies Association Northeast, November 2014.

Purnell, Kandida, "Grieving, Valuing, and Viewing Differently: The Global War on Terror's American Toll," *International Political Sociology*, 12, 2018, 156–171.

Ramirez, Ainissa, "Black Images Matter: How Cameras Helped – and Sometimes Harmed – Black People," *Scientific American*, July 8, 2020, available at www.scientificamerican.com/article/black-images-matter-how-cameras-helped-mdash-and-sometimes-harmed-mdash-black-people/

Ranciere, Jacques, *The Emancipated Spectator*, London: Verso, 2011.

Rankine, Claudia, "The Condition of Black Life is One Of Mourning," *New York Times*, June 22, 2015, available at www.nytimes.com/2015/0 6/22/magazine/the-condition-of-black-life-is-one-of-mourning.html

Reilly, R. J., "Osama Bin Laden Photo Release Considered by Appeals Court," *Huffington Post*, 10 January 10, 2013a, available at www.huffingtonpost .com/2013/01/10/osama-bin-laden-photos_n_2444717.html

Reilly, R. J., "Dead Osama bin Laden Photos Don't Have To Be Released by CIA, Appeals Court Rules," *Huffington Post*, May 21, 2013b, available at www.huffingtonpost.com/2013/05/21/osama-bin-laden-photos_n_3312970.html (last accessed 6 June 2016).

Richardson, Allissa, "Why Cellphone Videos of Black People's Deaths Should be Considered Sacred, Like Lynching Photographs," *The Conversation*, May 28, 2020, available at https://theconversation.com/why-cellphone-videos-of-black-peoples-deaths-should-be-considered-sacred-like-lynching-photographs–139252

Ristovska, Sandra, "Human Rights Collectives as Visual Experts: The Case of Syrian Archive," *Visual Communication*, 18, 3, 2019, 333–351.

Ritchie, L. Carol, "Family of US Hostage Held By ISIS Hopeful She is Alive," *WBUR*, February 7, 2015, available at www.wbur.org/npr/384499297/f amily-of-u-s-hostage-held-by-isis-hopeful-she-is-alive

Ritchin, Fred, "Why Violent News Images Matter," *Time*, September 2, 2014, available at www.time.com/3705884/why-violent-news-images-matter/

Roberts, Hilary, "War Trophy Photographs: Proof or Pornography," in Batchen, Geoffrey, Mick Gidley, Nancy Miller, and Jay Prosser, eds, *Picturing Atrocity: Photography in Crisis*, London: Reaktion, 2012, 201–208.

Robinson, Piers, "CNN Effect," in Bleiker, Roland, ed, *Visual Global Politics*, London, Routledge, 2018, 62–67.

Rogers, Amanda, "Inside the Caliphal Boardroom-Battleground of Islamic State Nation Branding, Corporatized Insurgency, and the Future of Transnational Conflict," Conference Paper, "Who's Afraid of ISIS" Workshop, Colgate University, September 10, 2016.

Rose, Gillian, *Visual Methodologies: An Introduction to the Interpretation of Visual Materials*, London: Sage, 2001.

Rosenblatt, Adam, *Digging for the Disappeared: Forensic Science After Atrocity*, Palo Alto: Stanford University Press, 2015.

Ross, Andrew, *Mixed Emotions: Beyond Fear and Hatred in International Conflict*, Chicago: University of Chicago Press, 2013.

Rubin, Barry, "What Gaddafi's Death Teaches the Middle East … and Should Teach the West," *Rubin Reports*, October 20, 2011, available at www.crethiplethi.com/what-gaddafis-death-teachesthe-middle-east-and-should-teach-the-west/islamic-countries/libya-islamic-countries/2011/

Rubin, Rebecca, Ted Johnson, and Lawrence Yee, "Kathy Griffin Apologizes After Drawing Outrage for Beheading 'Trump' in Photo," *Variety*, May 30, 2017, available at https://variety.com/2017/tv/news/kathy-griffin-trump-beheading-photo–1202448058

Rushdy, Ashraf, "Exquisite Corpse," *Transition*, 9, 3, 2000, 70–77.

Sauer, Frank, *Atomic Anxiety: Deterrence, Taboo, and the Non-Use of US Nuclear Weapons*, London: Palgrave, 2015.

Schlag, Gabi, "The Afterlife of Osama bin Laden: Performative Pictures in the 'War on Terror,'" *Critical Studies on Terrorism*, 12, 1, 2019, 1–18.

Schrader, Benjamin, *Fight to Live, Live to Fight: Veteran Activism After War*, Albany: SUNY Albany Press, 2019.

Schwartz, Carly, "Majority of Americans Think Watching ISIS Beheadings is Disrespectful to The Victims," *Huffington Post*, November 21, 2014, available at www.huffingtonpost.com/2014/11/21/isis-beheading-videos_n_6194498.html

Sentilles, Sarah, "How We Should Respond to Photographs of Suffering," *The New Yorker*, August 3, 2017, available at www.newyorker.com/books/second-read/how-we-should-respond-to-photographs-of-suffering

Sentilles, Sarah, "When We See Photographs of Some Dead Bodies and Not Others," *The New York Times*, August 14, 2018, available at www.nytimes.com/2018/08/14/magazine/media-bodies-censorship.html

Shah, Nisha, "Gunning for War: Infantry Rifles and the Calibration of Lethal Force," *Critical Studies on Security*, 5, 1, 2017, 81–104.

Shah, Nisha, "Death in the Details: Finding Dead Bodies at the Canadian War Museum," *Organization*, 24, 4, 2017b, 549–569.

Shapiro, Michael, *Cinematic Geopolitics*, London: Routledge, 2008.

Shaw, Neil, "Fake Post Seems To Show Shemima Begum Beheading a Man," *Plymouth Herald*, February 21, 2019, available at www.plymouthherald.co.uk/news/plymouth-news/fake-post-claims-show-shemima–2567567

Shelton, Tracey, "The Most Disturbing Fake Videos Making the Rounds in Syria," *The World*, November 12, 2012, available at www.pri.org/stories/2012-11-12/most-disturbing-fake-videos-making-rounds-syria

Shim, David, *Visual Politics and North Korea: Seeing is Believing*, London: Routledge, 2014.

Shinko, Rosemary, "Ethics After Liberalism: Why (Autonomous) Bodies Matter," *Millennium*, 38, 3, 2010, 723–745.

Siegel, Harry, "How War Can Make Dehumanizing and Horrific Events seem Normal," The *Daily Beast*, April 18, 2012, available at www.thedailybeast .com/articles/2012/04/18/how-war-can-make-dehumanizing-and-horrific-events-seem-normal.html

Sinha, Shreeya, "Obama's Evolution on ISIS." *The New York Times*, June 9, 2015, available at www.nytimes.com/interactive/2015/06/09/world/mid dleeast/obama-isis-strategy.html

Sledge, Michael, *Soldier Dead: How We Recover, Identify, Bury, and Honor our Military Fallen*, New York: Columbia University Press, 2007.

Sliwinski, Sharon, *Human Rights in Camera*, Chicago: University of Chicago Press, 2011.

Sluka, Jeffrey, "Terrorism and Taboo: An Anthropological Perspective on Political Violence Against Civilians," *Critical Studies on Terrorism*, 1, 2, 2008, 167–183.

Smith, Helena, "Shocking Images of Drowned Syrian Boy Show Tragic Plight of Refugees," *The Guardian*, September 2, 2015, available at www .theguardian.com/world/2015/sep/02/shocking-image-of-drowned-syrian-boy-shows-tragic-plight-of-refugees

Snyder, Brianna, "Why I Can't Stop Watching Horrifying ISIS Decapitation Videos," *Wired*, February 11, 2015, available at www.wired.com/2015/ 02/on-watching-gore-and-death-online/

Solomon, Ty, "Embodiment, Emotions, and Materialism in International Relations," in Ahall, Linda, and Thomas Gregory, eds, *Emotions, Politics, and War*, London: Routledge, 2015, 58–70.

Sontag, Susan, *On Photography*, New York: Picador, 2001.

Sontag, Susan, "Looking at War," *New Yorker*, December 9, 2002, available at www.newyorker.com/magazine/2002/12/09/looking-at-war

Sontag, Susan, *Regarding the Pain of Others*, New York: Picador, 2003.

Southall, Ashley, "Military Opens Investigation into Photos of Dead Iraqi Militants," *The New York Times*, January 16, 2014, available at www .nytimes.com/2014/01/16/world/middleeast/military-opens-investigation-into-photos-of-dead-iraqi-militants.html

Spagat, Michael, Andrew Mack, Tara Cooper, Joakim Kreutz, "Estimating War Deaths: An Arena of Contestation," *Journal of Conflict Resolution*, 53, 6, 2009, 934–950.

Steele, Brent, *Alternative Accountabilities in Global Politics: The Scars of Violence*, London: Routledge, 2013.

Stein, Janice Gross, "Taboos and Regional Security Regimes," *Journal of Strategic Studies*, 26, 3, 2003, 6–18.

Stepputat, Finn, ed, *Governing the Dead: Sovereignty and the Politics of Dead Bodies*, Manchester: Manchester University Press, 2014.

Stille, Alexander, "Who Murdered Giulio Regeni?" *The Guardian*, October 4, 2016, available at www.theguardian.com/world/2016/oct/04/egypt-murder-giulio-regeni

"Syria's President Speaks: A Conversation with Bashar al-Assad," *Foreign Affairs*, March/April 2015, available at www.foreignaffairs.com/interviews/2015-01-25/syrias-president-speaks

Tait, Sue, "Autoptic Vision and the Necrophilic Imaginary in CSI," *International Journal of Cultural Studies*, 9, 1, 2006, 45–62.

Tait, Sue, "Pornographies of Violence? Internet Spectatorship on Body Horror," *Critical Studies in Media Communication*, 25, 1, 2008, 91–111.

Tannenwald, Nina, "The Nuclear Taboo: The United States and the Normative Basis of Nuclear Non-Use," *International Organization*, 53, 3, 1999, 433–468.

Taylor, Adam, "From Daniel Pearl to James Foley: The Modern Tactic of Islamist Beheadings," *The Chicago Tribune*, August 21, 2014, available at www.chicagotribune.com/news/nationworld/chi-foley-pearl-islamist-beheadings-20140821-story.html

Taylor, John, *Body Horror: Photojournalism, Catastrophe, and War*, New York: NYU Press, 1998.

Tomlinson, Simon, "22 Minutes of Sickening Savagery: Carefully Edited and Highly Choreographed Footage that ISIS Knows Will Horrify the West – and Entice Even More Jihadists to Their Cause," *Daily Mail*, February 3, 2015, available at www.dailymail.co.uk/news/article-2938299/One-sickening-acts-committed-film-Carefully-edited-highly-choreographed-footage-ISIS-knows-horrify-West-entice-jihadists-cause.html

Tomson, Chris, "In Pictures: ISIS Beheads Captured Iraqi Army Soldiers," *Al Masdar News*, January 4, 2017, available at www.almasdarnews.com/article/pictures-isis-beheads-captured-iraqi-army-soldiers-18-graphic/

Torriero, E. A., and Christine Spolar, "Pentagon Releases Grisly Photos to Prove Hussein Sons are Dead," *Baltimore Sun*, July 5, 2003, available at www.baltimoresun.com/bal-te.sons25jul25-story.html

Tuttle, Ian, "The ISIS Butchers: Beheading for the Cause." *National Review*, August 20, 2014, available at www.nationalreview.com/article/385882/isis-butchers-beheading-cause-ian-tuttle

Twomey, Christina, "Severed Hands: Authenticating Atrocity in the Congo 190–1913," in Batchen, Geoffrey, Mick Gidley, Nancy Miller, and Jay Prosser, eds, *Picturing Atrocity: Photography in Crisis*, London: Reaktion, 2012, 39–50.

Twomey, Christina, "The Incorruptible Kodak," in Kennedy, Liam, and Caitlin Patrick, eds, *The Violence of the Image: Photography and International Conflict*, New York: IB Tauris, 2014, 9–33.

Usborne, D., K. Sengupta, P. Walker, C. Milmo and R. Hall, "Gaddafi Killed in Libya," *Fraser Coast Chronicle*, October 21, 2011, available at www.frasercoastchronicle.com.au/news/gaddafi-killed-libya/1145560/

"US Military Raid on ISIS Leader was Named for Arizona's Kayla Mueller," *KTAR News*, October 28, 2019, available at https://ktar.com/story/28192 11/us-military-raid-on-isis-leader-was-named-for-arizonas-kayla-mueller/

Verdery, Katherine, *The Political Lives of Dead Bodies*, New York: Columbia University Press, 1999.

Vick, Karl, "Don't Take the Bait: The US Should Not Send Troops To Fight ISIS," *Time*, February 26, 2015, available at http://time.com/3723617/d ont-take-the-bait-the-u-s-should-not-send-troops-to-fight-isis/

"Video Included: ISIS Terrorists Burn Alive Muslim Pilot Moaz Al-Kasasbeh," *Moroccan Times*, February 3, 2015, available at http://themor occantimes.com/2015/02/13985/video-included-isis-terrorists-burn-alive-muslim-pilot-moaz-al-kasasbeh

Virilio, Paul, *War and Cinema: The Logistics of Perception*, London: Verso, 1989.

Vuori, Juha, and Rune Saugmann Andersen, "Introduction: Visual Security Studies," in Vuori, Juha, and Rune Saugmann Andersen, eds, *Visual Security Studies: Sights and Spectacles of Insecurity and War*, London: Routledge, 2018, 1–20.

Vuori, Juha, and Rune Saugmann Andersen, eds, *Visual Security Studies: Sights and Spectacles of Insecurity and War*, London: Routledge, 2018.

Walt, Stephen, "10 Ways to Tell if Your President is a Dictator," *Foreign Policy*, November 23, 2016, available at http://foreignpolicy.com/2016/11/23/ten-ways-to-tell-if-your-president-is-a-dictator/?utm_source=Sailthru&utm_me dium=email&utm_campaign=New%20Campaign&utm_term=Flashpoints

Weber, Cynthia, *International Relations Theory: A Critical Introduction*, London: Routledge, 2005.

Weisband, Edward, "On the Aporetic Borderlines of Forgiveness: Bereavement as a Political Form," *Alternatives*, 34, 4, 2009, 359–381.

Wilcox, Lauren, *Bodies of Violence: Theorizing Embodied Subjects in International Relations*, Oxford: Oxford University Press, 2014.

Williams, Michael, "Words, Images, Enemies: Securitization and International Politics," *International Studies Quarterly*, 47, 4, 2003, 511–531.

Williams, Sherri, "How Does a Steady Stream of Images of Black Death Affect Us?" *NBC News*, July 11, 2016, available at www.nbcnews.com/news/nbcblk/editorial-how-does-steady-stream-images-black-death-affect-us-n607221

Wing, Naomi, "US Troops Unloaded 'over a hundred bullets' into Osama bin Laden's Dead Body, Sources Claim," *Huffington Post*, March 13, 2014, available at www.huffingtonpost.com/2014/03/13/osama-bin-laden-death-shooting_n_4958147.html

Winkler, Carol, Kareem El Damanhoury, Aaron Dicker, and Anthony Lemieux, "Images of Death and Dyng in ISIS Media: A Comparison of English and Arabic Print Publications," *Media, War, and Conflict*, 12, 3, 2019, 248–262.

Withnall, Adam, "If These Extraordinarily Powerful Images of a Dead Syrian Child Washed Up on a Beach Don't Change Europe's Attitude to Refugees, What Will?" *The Independent*, September 2, 2015, available at www.independent.co.uk/news/world/europe/if-these-extraordinarily-powerful-images-dead-syrian-child-washed-beach-don-t-change-europe-s-atti tude-refugees-what-will-10482757.html

Wood, Amy Louise, *Lynching and Spectacle: Witnessing Racial Violence in American, 1890–1940*, Chapel Hill: UNC Press, 2009.

Young, Craig, and Duncan Light, "Corpses, Dead Body Politics, and Agency in Human Geography: Following the Corpse of Dr. Petru Groza," *Transactions of the Institute of British Geographers*, 38, 2012, 135–148.

Zech, Steven, and Zane Kelly, "Off With Their Heads: The Islamic State and Civilian Beheadings," *Journal of Terrorism Research*, 6, 2, 2015, 83–93.

Zelizer, Barbie, *About to Die: How News Images Move the Public*, Oxford: Oxford University Press, 2010.

Zevnik, Andreja, "War Porn: An image of Perversion and Desire in Modern Warfare," *International Journal of Baudrillard Studies*, 11, 2, 2014, unpaginated.

Zevnik, Andreja, "The Politics of the Face: The *Scopic Regime* and the (Un) Masking of the Political Subject," *Journal for Cultural Research*, 20, 2, 2016, 122–136.

Zizek, Slavoj, *The Sublime Object of Ideology*, London: Verso, 1989.

Zizek, Slavoj, *For They Know Not What They Do: Enjoyment as a Political Factor*, London: Verso, 2008.

Index

CAMBRIDGE STUDIES IN INTERNATIONAL
RELATIONS